THE

AFRICAN RENAISSANCE

AND THE

AFRO-ARAB SPRING

THE
AFRICAN
RENAISSANCE
AND THE
AFRO-ARAB
SPRING

A SEASON OF REBIRTH?

EDITED BY
Charles Villa-Vicencio
Erik Doxtader
and Ebrahim Moosa

Georgetown University Press / Washington, DC

"Tunisia: A Successful Revolution?" reprinted by permission of *Foreign Affairs*, (September 17, 2013). Copyright 2013 by the Council on Foreign Relations, Inc. www.ForeignAffairs.com.

Library of Congress Cataloging-in-Publication Data

African renaissance and Afro-Arab spring : a season of rebirth? / Charles Villa-Vicencio, Erik Doxtader, and Ebrahim Moosa, editors.
    pages cm
    Includes bibliographical references and index.
    ISBN 978-1-62616-199-3 (hardcover : alk. paper)—ISBN 978-1-62616-197-9 (pbk. : alk. paper)—ISBN 978-1-62616-198-6 (ebook)
    1. Africa—Politics and government—1960–   2. Arab Spring, 2010–   I. Villa-Vicencio, Charles, editor.   II. Doxtader, Erik, editor.   III. Moosa, Ebrahim, editor.
DT30.5.A36567   2015
960.3'312—dc23

2014027265

⊗ This book is printed on acid-free paper meeting the requirements of the American National Standard for Permanence in Paper for Printed Library Materials.

16 15   9 8 7 6 5 4 3 2 First printing

Printed in the United States of America

Cover design by Trudi Gershenov Design.

Contents

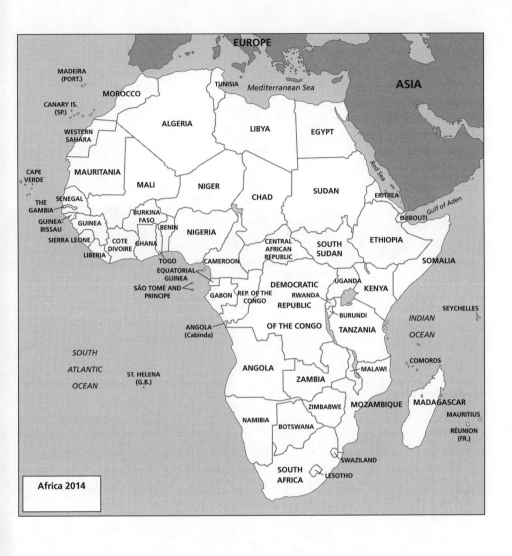

Africa 2014

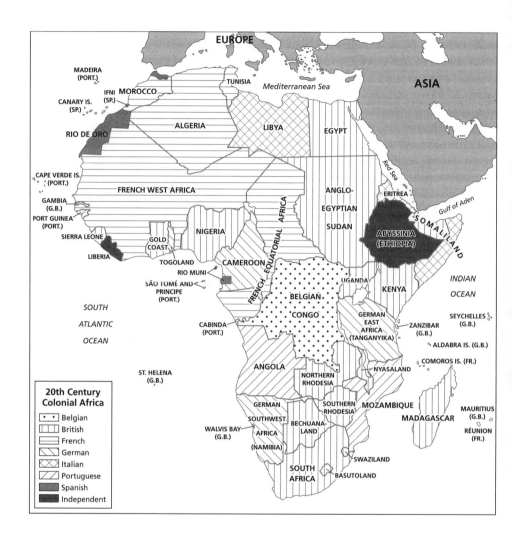

20th Century Colonial Africa

| Belgian |
| British |
| French |
| German |
| Italian |
| Portuguese |
| Spanish |
| Independent |

Foreword

The Arab Reawakening

An African Renaissance Perspective

THABO MBEKI

The year 2011 began with popular uprisings in the Arab world that started in the African Maghreb and Egypt. Described by some as an Arab Reawakening, we must answer the question whether, in reality, these uprisings do not also represent an African Reawakening.

Those of us committed to the renaissance—the rebirth of Africa—have an obligation to understand what the popular uprisings in the African Maghreb and Egypt mean in the context of that renaissance.

Simply put, do the uprisings advance or retard this African rebirth?

One of the central objectives of the African Renaissance is the creation of the necessary space for the peoples of Africa to determine their destiny. The renaissance visualizes a democratic Africa, consistent with and focused on the objective—the people shall govern! It will be a genuine renaissance only if it is the product of the conscious activity of the African masses across their various racial, ethnic, class, gender, and other social divides.

Surely we should understand the concept and practice of reawakening as an expression of the social processes according to which the masses of the people act in the political sphere as conscious and purposeful determinants of their own destiny, committed to fashion the nature of their societies through their own actions.

The African Renaissance should be a manifestation of an African Reawakening, while the reawakening should serve as the motive force for the achievement of the renaissance.

In what sense then should we promote the African Reawakening expressed in the popular uprisings in the African Maghreb as an integral part of the African democratic revolution?

The historic African struggles for liberation from imperialist and colonial domination sought to achieve both national independence and the transfer of power to the people—that is, genuine democratic rule. Accordingly, these struggles were an expression of the commitment of the African masses to achieve their own national democratic revolutions.

As Africans we are very familiar with our own history, which is littered with many instances during which the national democratic revolutions were subverted and aborted, including through military coups and the establishment of dictatorial governments through other means.

In all these instances, when the national democratic revolutions were compromised, inevitably state power was used not to advance the interests of the people as a whole but fundamentally to serve the interests of a narrow national ruling elite, which would invariably ally itself with foreign interests determined to achieve their own objectives, regardless of the fate of the African masses.

We can therefore say that the crisis of governance in Africa during years of independence, with all its consequences, developed from the subversion or abortion of the national democratic revolutions for which the African masses fought as they engaged in struggle to liberate themselves from imperialism and colonialism.

The popular uprisings in North Africa have affected particularly Tunisia, Libya, and Egypt.

What is common to the politics of these three African countries is that the ruling group in each country had been in power for more than two decades before 2011 with no possibility to change this reality through democratic elections.

Effectively, the systems of governance established in this part of the African Maghreb and Egypt constituted a negation of the objectives of the African democratic revolution and were inimical to the achievement of the renaissance of Africa to the extent that they were constructed to prevent the masses of people in this part of the African Maghreb from shaping their own futures.

Surely, ordinary common sense must communicate the message that these systems could not have survived as long as they did if they were not buttressed by pervasive repression, consciously targeted at denying the people the right freely to express their will, and therefore to determine their destiny, which is a fundamental feature of the African democratic revolution.

The tenancy of the entrenched ruling elites in these North African countries could only be guaranteed by continued repression, which, inevitably, would lead to growing discontent and therefore ever greater repression.

In these countries we are dealing with masses of people who have experience as conscious actors in the struggle to determine their own destiny. They gained this experience in the struggles for independence against imperialism and colonialism, in efforts to reconstruct their countries as independent and democratic African states, and in the struggle for the liberation of the people of Palestine. Thus, the sustained abuse of state power to demobilize them as conscious agents of change, to perpetuate exclusive rule by particular elites, and therefore to subvert the national democratic revolution assumed that these masses would come to unlearn the lesson that they are makers of history.

The popular uprisings in the African Maghreb and Egypt prove that this has failed. At the same time, the cold fact is that nobody, including the heroic masses of the African Maghreb and Egypt, knows the shape and content of the new societies which will emerge as a consequence of the historic popular uprisings that have perhaps defined the very essence of the African second decade of the twenty-first century.

Our concern is whether and in what way the popular uprisings constitute the following:

- a reassertion of the right of the African masses to determine their destiny and recover their democratic right to govern
- a resumption of the struggle for the victory of the national democratic revolution
- a rebellion against the abuse of power by ruling elites to enrich themselves at the expense of the people
- an affirmation of the determination of the African masses to ensure that the national wealth is used to end poverty and underdevelopment and to bridge the disparities in income, wealth, and opportunity
- confirmation of the determination of the masses of the African people to achieve their human dignity and the commitment to rely on their native intelligence and labor to realize their all-round development

As militants of the African Renaissance we cannot but be inspired by the fact that the masses of the people in the African Maghreb and Egypt have engaged in struggle as courageously as they have to pursue these objectives, all of which constitute the very core elements of that renaissance.

To some within the "left" and especially the "right," the end of the Cold War signified that the Age of Revolution had ended. Significantly, the right argued that history had reached its final station, suggesting that a dominant feature of the new epoch was that the historic popular upheavals characteristic of all revolutions had run their course.

For the right, in essence, this meant propagating a thesis that henceforth fundamental social change would be a top-down process and therefore there was no alternative but to depend on the ruling elites on our continent to pursue the objectives of African national democratic revolutions.

In this paradigm the masses of the people would still have the possibility to publicly express their views, including by taking to the streets. However, such popular action would serve essentially to influence the "top" to take the right decisions. This did not exclude the possibility that this top could, in its own interest, mobilize the "bottom" to take to the streets essentially as a mass army to legitimize the narrow interests of the ruling elites.

The popular uprisings in the African Maghreb and Egypt have shattered the illusion that the Age of Revolution has ended and that only the ruling elites have the capacity to reinstate into African reality the objectives of the African democratic revolution.

Strangely, contrary to what would have happened during the Cold War years and the two centuries before, the 2011 uprisings in the African Maghreb were welcomed both by the broad left and the broad right tendencies in contemporary global politics.

Does this suggest that now there is a benign global convergence between the left and the right around the inalienable and universal entitlement of the individual to democratic rule and human rights, regardless of nationality, and between Africa and the erstwhile colonial powers?

As activists of the African Renaissance, and given both our experience and African actuality, we have to ask ourselves whether, in this regard, appearance truly coincides with and represents our reality.

It would seem self-evident that, by all standards, the inspiring popular uprisings in the African Maghreb and Egypt are indeed popular. At the same time, both left and right, in Africa and the rest of the world, have understandably characterized these uprisings as revolutions. Yet, by definition, revolution means a fundamental change in the social order. Such revolutionary change results in the birth of new societies that set themselves the task to achieve—and actually pursue—objectives fundamentally different from those that characterized the old order overthrown by the revolution. The mere removal from power of heads of state and their associates does not in itself amount to revolutionary change, even as it is both substantially and symbolically important.

The reality is that both the left and the right have celebrated globally the important fact of the popular uprisings, which represent an affirmation of the right of all human beings freely to participate in the process to determine their destiny.

This constitutes a celebration of, and support for, the right of every individual to express his or her will and therefore to influence the future. It does not, however, address the vitally important issue of the end result of the exercise of this right. As activists of the African Renaissance we must therefore, even as we lend maximum support to the popular uprisings, keep our focus on the fundamental question of what kind of societies the uprisings will produce. We must, at all costs, resist the temptation to assume that these uprisings, heroic, inspiring, and welcome as they are, amount to the national democratic revolutions marking the resumption in the African Maghreb and Egypt of the processes that would lead to the victory of the African Renaissance.

It is perfectly possible that this is exactly what will happen. It is, however, critically important that we not take this possibility as a sufficient condition for the beginning of the process leading to the rebirth of Africa and that we therefore recognize the popular uprisings do not necessarily amount to the reassertion of the primacy of the African democratic revolution.

As activists of the African Renaissance, we warmly welcome the popular uprisings in Afro-Arab states in the expectation that they represent popular national democratic revolutions.

We therefore hope that as an expression of such revolutions, they will result in the following:

- the establishment of truly democratic systems of governance, even as the specific forms of government would take into account the peculiarities of each country;
- the assertion of the genuine independence of each and all African countries;
- the construction of new societies free of discrimination, including racial, ethnic, and gender inequality;
- the use of democratic power to ensure a better life for all the people, and therefore the elimination of poverty and underdevelopment;
- a sustained effort to create an egalitarian society by reducing gross inequality in wealth, income, and opportunity and to eradicate systemic corruption;
- the restoration of the dignity of all Africans by asserting their equality with all other members of the human family;
- the positioning of Africa and the African Diaspora as an equal participant in the processes that determine the future of humanity as a whole.

This surely means that the African masses actively involved in the struggle for change should know not only what they are fighting against but also what new social order they are struggling to establish. These masses should develop a level of consciousness such that they are able to reject neocolonial superintendence and act independently to determine the future of their countries and societies.

All this presents the challenge to all activists of the African Renaissance not only to express solidarity with the popular uprisings, but also to engage the risen masses to develop a common African perspective focused on joint action to achieve Africa's renaissance.

The masses engaged in mass struggle should be mobilized to see themselves as activists for the renaissance of Africa and not only as activists for the victory of the national democratic revolutions in their countries.

In this context we should recall the impulses that, during the last century, resulted in the convening of the Pan-African Congresses and the formation, before the birth of the Organization of African Unity (OAU), of the Casablanca bloc to which, to the best of our knowledge, Tunisia, Egypt, and Libya belonged.

At the base of these desires was the realization that we would not succeed as Africans to overcome the legacy of slavery, imperialism, and colonialism; to defeat poverty and underdevelopment; and to gain our rightful place in the ordering of international affairs if we did not combine in action to confront our shared challenges. Such efforts affirmed that the various struggles for independence, separate and disparate as they might have seemed, were nevertheless part of an integrated whole because all of them constituted a common struggle for the victory of the African democratic revolution and Africa's renaissance.

As an expression of this, throughout their existence both the OAU and the African Union (AU) have worked very hard to define the content of this African national democratic revolution. Thus Africa's ruling elites have, over the decades, at least in formal collective resolutions, elaborated a common agenda that essentially binds the peoples of Africa to act together to define their future. This common political, economic, social, and cultural agenda, in all its principal elements, represents a firm, credible, and realizable expression of the African democratic revolution around which all Africa should unite to achieve the fundamental aspirations of the African masses.

All popular insurrections, such as those that have engulfed the African Maghreb and Egypt, teach the masses many lessons they cannot learn from books. These lessons generate energies that would otherwise lie dormant and give the ordinary people the confidence that they can and must be their own liberators.

This is happening in the African Maghreb and Egypt. It will inevitably have an impact on the rest of Africa, serving as an example of what can be done. It is not, however, a given that the popular uprisings will result in the reassertion of the national democratic revolution in Africa and therefore an advance toward the victory of the African Renaissance.

Today, the popular uprisings hold a learning opportunity for the people. They provide the space for the African movement in favor of the African democratic revolution and the attendant African Renaissance. This movement knows well that there are many powerful external forces convinced that Africa is directly and immediately relevant to their own exclusive interests, which do not necessarily have anything to do with the welfare and uplift of the African people. These players have already switched to "super-drive mode," seeking to influence the outcomes of the popular uprisings in their favor.

The African movement for the victory of the African democratic revolution and the African Renaissance must therefore engage the risen masses in the African Maghreb and Egypt, conscious that the success of both the revolution and the renaissance can be achieved only within the context of an intense global struggle that will determine the future of Africa for a large part of this century.

At the dawn of the twentieth century, during the 1900 First Pan-African Congress, the Pan-Africanist W. E. B. Du Bois, addressing the African challenges of the day, said, "The problem of the twentieth century is the problem of the colour line."

The peoples of Africa, Asia, and Latin America, supported by far-sighted people in Europe and North America, acted together successfully to address this "problem."

At the dawn of the twenty-first century, we said that as Africans we would ensure that this, the twenty-first, would be an African century. The African movement for the victory of the African democratic revolution and the African Renaissance must act now to help ensure that the popular uprisings in the African Maghreb serve as a platform to accelerate the success of that revolution and renaissance.

These popular uprisings must succeed in their intention to renew the hopes of the African masses that their liberation from foreign rule also means their liberation from autocracy, hunger, poverty, ignorance, disease, and dehumanization.

Once more it is imperative to pose the question: Where are the African intelligentsia, whose task it is to narrate accurately what is unfolding in the African Maghreb and Egypt, as a result of which narrative the ongoing events might serve truly to advance the African national democratic revolution and therefore the African Renaissance?

Introduction

Beginning Again?

The Question of a Continent

ERIK DOXTADER, CHARLES VILLA-VICENCIO,
AND EBRAHIM MOOSA

The question of Africa is open—again. The promise of an African Renais-sance remains unfilled. The hope of the Afro-Arab Spring waxes and wanes.[1] There is too much change and there is too little—the winds of change blow with ferocity and then not at all. While professing a commitment to transformation, governments remain loath to risk change that might undermine their own power. Dissatisfaction grows but remains unheard. Dissent coalesces into movements that seem to lack direction let alone a sense of a clear endgame. Over and over, the first act of the play promises a revolution that comes to naught in the second. The urgent desire to begin again is cut short—again.

This book does not aim to answer the question of Africa—the question itself has yet to be properly and fully understood! Nor does it attempt to speak for the continent—how to move beyond such (mis)representations is surely part of the question at hand, particularly given the ways in which Africa is often referred to as if it were a single country. Rather, its wager is that the contemporary question of Africa may emerge partly in the light of the African Renaissance *and* the Afro-Arab Spring. All too often, it seems that these two phenomena—whether understood as heteroge-neous events, complex discourses, or modes of transformation—are unfolding in different worlds. The distance may prove costly, not least if the widespread desire for rebirth and the hope of popular democratic movements both speak to the question of Africa's historical definition and how it may yet define itself—for itself.

Looking from south to north and back again, the chapters that compose this book investigate the respective dynamics of renaissance and renewal. At one level, this inquiry sheds important light on the possibilities, dilemmas, and risks of radical political, economic, and cultural change in contemporary Africa and what may be expected if such change fails to unfold. At another, it opens space to ask whether and how the Afro-Arab Spring and the African Renaissance are underwritten by a shared concern for a common set of problems—that is, a collection of issues that confound the continent's politics, constrain its development, and limit its role on the world stage. Individually and together, the critical reflections that follow demonstrate that, in the name of beginning again, Africa is struggling anew—and in new ways—with how to best promote political freedom, economic equality, transitional justice, religious tolerance, and the rejuvenation of culture. The stakes of these struggles are high.

A Resonating Question of Change

It has been twenty years since Nelson Mandela stood on the steps of the Union Building in Pretoria and heralded the beginning of South Africa's nonracial democracy. An event that few predicted, South Africa's turn from apartheid was a watershed moment for the country and the continent. With it came one of the world's most progressive constitutions, a dramatic new approach to political transition, and a palpable sense that Africa had turned a decisive corner. This optimism was evident in a variety of ways. With Mandela's leadership, the underlying logic of South Africa's negotiated revolution was deployed in the name of resolving several of the continent's ongoing conflicts. To the fascination of national, continental, and international audiences, the Truth and Reconciliation Commission (TRC) appeared to turn standing norms of transitional justice on their head.

In mid-1997, just a year after the TRC began its work, Thabo Mbeki, who was then South Africa's deputy president, traveled to the United States and delivered a lengthy speech in which he declared that "the African Renaissance is upon us." The claim was both an assessment and a call for action. As Mbeki put it, "It is not given to every generation that it should be present during and participate in the act of creation. I believe that ours is privileged to occupy such a space." Supported not least by the South African "miracle," there was an opportunity to begin again:

> This generation remains African and carries with it an historic pride which compels it to seek a place for Africans equal to all the other peoples of our common universe. It knows and is resolved that, to attain that objective, it must resist all tyranny, oppose all attempts to deny liberty by resort to demagogy, repulse the temptation to describe African life as the ability to live on charity, engage the fight to secure the emancipation of the African woman, and reassert the fundamental concept that we are our own liberators from oppression, from underdevelopment and poverty, from

the perpetuation of an experience from slavery, to colonisation, to apartheid, to dependence on alms.[2]

While this vision for an African Renaissance did not initially attract the same kind of attention as Mandela's magnanimity and the TRC's efforts to come to terms with the past, Mbeki's resolve was rewarded. Through an extended campaign, one that very much defined his abruptly ended presidency, the promise of a renaissance is now a central thread in African political discourse. It frames policy debates over national, continental, and global economic growth and redistribution, shapes the form and content of Pan-Africanism, invigorates thought about the nature and power of African culture, and challenges Africa's leaders not only to represent but also to honor the will of those they claim to serve. Today, the African Renaissance is an idea that matters.

The ultimate importance of Mbeki's vision may be its implicit warning—miracles are not enough. Transitions do not ensure democracy. The retreat of colonial power does not assure material equality. Africa's independence does not guarantee its standing in the world. A generation on, there is increasing evidence to suggest that this warning has not been taken to heart, by either supporters or critics of the renaissance. Discontent is growing. The gap between expectation and reality is increasing. The relationship between accountability and power is far from stable. The rift between haves and have-nots is deepening.[3] The line between the slow process of reconciliation and undue waiting is increasingly blurry. A country and continent is still waiting for its rebirth. And while fundamental transformation does not and cannot happen overnight, the promise of transition and transformation can only go unkept for so long. At some point, discontent erupts into something more.

More than four decades before South Africa's transition, in July 1952, a Free Officers' revolution, spearheaded by Gamal Abdel Nasser in the wake of Arab nationalism, promised an end to monarchical authoritarianism and colonial hegemony. Sub-Saharan African leaders were inspired by this movement. Mandela himself identified with the Algerian War of Independence (1954–1962) against French colonialism and traveled there during the revolutionary phase of his career. Yet, Egypt, the most influential Arab country in North Africa and the Midde East, gradually slipped into a military dictatorship, as did Algeria. It took the Iranian revolution of 1979, under the leadership of Ayatollah Khomeini, to kindle the aspirations of Muslim-majority nations—from Mauritania to the Maldives Islands—for freedom from political tyranny and autocratic rule. However, Iran's revolutionary zeal could not transform the country into a model Islamic democracy, nor could it curb Iran's enthusiasm for exporting Shiite theocracy. And in the wake of the catastrophic and debilitating war with Iraq, Iran gradually became an authoritarian theocracy, albeit more democratic than any of its neighbors.

Iran's repression of the Green Movement, following the disputed 2009–2010 elections that returned President Mahmoud Ahmadinejad to office, was a harbinger of what was to follow a year later in the Arabic-speaking world. On January 14, 2011, mass uprisings ousted the Tunisian dictator, Zine el-Abidine Ben Ali. In Egypt, Hosni Mubarak was removed from power on February 11, 2011, and on October 20, 2011, Libyan leader Muammar Qaddafi was captured and killed. In the aftermath of these events, three dynamics have done much to frame the terms and define the momentum of the Afro-Arab Spring. First, Tunisia continued on a wobbly path of transition to democracy. Second, Syria remains in the grip of a fratricidal civil war with no end in sight, with its instability bleeding into neighboring Iraq. Feeling disenfranchised by the ruling Shiites, Iraq's Sunni population seems to have fallen under the spell of an al-Qaeda-affiliated insurgency called the Islamic State of Iraq and Syria (ISIS). Whether Iraq will be partitioned remains to be seen. But there is every sign of serious instability in Iraq in the foreseeable future with proxy wars between Sunni and Shia being sponsored by Iraq's neighbors. And third, Egypt, the beacon and hope for rebirth in the Arabic-speaking world, undertook a path to democracy with the election of Mohamed Morsi in June 2012, a path that was shortened when he was deposed by Abdel Fattah el-Sisi following a wave of popular protest. In May 2014 el-Sisi, then field marshal, was elected to power in a lackluster show of democracy—47 percent of voters turned out for a contest in which el-Sisi won with 97 percent of the vote.

Eruption has very much defined popular interpretations of the uprisings that have profoundly and variously altered the landscapes of Tunisia, Egypt, Libya, and other countries of the Sahara, the Sahel, and further in the Central African Republic (CAR), Mali, Nigeria and Sudan. Save for Tunisia, the Afro-Arab Spring did not simply or quietly emerge. As Garth le Pere puts it: "In the broader Afro/Arab region the waves of protests and social upheavals that drew their impulse from and were emboldened by the North African experience were driven by similar structural factors. Most crucial among these were changing demographic dynamics and realities, the failure of authoritarian paternalist regimes, and popular demands for greater political participation and representation."[4]

What hangs in the balance is the question of power—its location, distribution, and capacity to gather the forces of democratization, faith, and culture and render them into coherent and ethical forms of governance. The question is large, complex, and fraught. Hopes for a season of regeneration have given way to stifling heat. Spring has become a crucible. While millions of people gathered in so many squares around the world to express their frustrations and hopes, there may well have been a shortage of vision and a dearth of practitioners who could translate mass power into sustainable reform. Without an ethical sense of renaissance, premised on human decency and political agility, visionary wisdom, compassion, and pragmatism, the movement seems unlikely to generate fundamental change.

What runs between the Cape and Cairo? This question has been asked before—with disastrous results. Today, it is tempting to view the African Renaissance and the Afro-Arab Spring as counterparts, if not two pieces that somehow speak to the whole. From such a perspective, events in the north and south are moments in which Africa has defied its history in the name of making history and creating an unprecedented opportunity for political transformation and cultural-social renewal. Similarly, the events between 1994 and 2014—the span between the birth of democracy in South Africa and the installation of the military through the ballot box in Egypt—can be read as mirror images: the risk of the renaissance's failure can be seen in the tumult of spring just as the impulses of a new season can easily and swiftly wither if they are not guided by an ethics and architecture for renewal.

Yet, for all their intuitive appeal, these assessments may be premature. Humility and decency require that we hope for better outcomes, but we should not be blinded by reality. It is perhaps too soon to make definitive claims about whether these events are readily comparable, let alone related. For one, the popular movements that have defined the Arab Spring have not relied on the discourse that underwrites the campaign for an African Renaissance. The uprising brought the fall of several leaders who embraced the call for a renaissance at the same time that many of those who have led the Afro-Arab Spring, with notable exceptions in Tunisia, have largely ignored Thabo Mbeki's principled call that a renaissance must "resist all tyranny, oppose all attempts to deny liberty by resort to demagogy," and foster self-reliance. At a larger level, the impulse of the Afro-Arab Spring is not singular. Countries and regions have approached it variously, contingent on particular political, cultural, social, and regional milieus such that there is no obvious way to wrap the call for renewal into the fold of rebirth. The difficulty is underscored by the widespread presumption, readily evident in the media, that one event is largely a product of West Asia while the other is a properly African initiative.

All of this reflects the difficulty of speaking to the question of Africa and identifying the forces that may or may not be reshaping its landscape. At one level the difficulty has much to do with how external powers long dominated the continent without ever recognizing it. Africa was left to float. Neither here nor there, it existed in a nonactual (or exotic) way. It did not actually matter, which meant that its exploitation came with no burden of accountability. At another level, however, the question of Africa has more than a little to do with a certain ambivalence that surrounds the idea of "Africa" for many of those who nevertheless identify as African. The Arabic-speaking world, despite immense oil riches in some parts, remains largely at the mercy of external powers, especially the United States, Europe, and now increasingly Russia and China in a unipolar world. A century ago the revolutionary Jamal al-Din al-Afghani, who with his cohort of scholar activists popularized Islamic reform, warned that internal despotism and external imperialism were the lethal enemies of the Islamic world and the developing world.

The South African author Zakes Mda suggests that the idea of an "African identity" and the quest for "African unity" are recent phenomena. Arabs at the turn of the Common Era used the word *Afriquia* for what is today the Arabic and Berber-speaking parts of the African continent. The Romans, in turn, captured Carthage in 146 CE and soon extended their dominance from parts of modern Libya to Mauritania. They referred to the region as their African proconsular province. Berber-speaking nomadic people in North Africa and the Maghreb, across the Sahara and into the Sahel—were every bit as African as Bantu-speaking people in sub-Saharan Africa. Mda makes the point that until about a hundred years ago the inhabitants of the continent did not generally refer to themselves as Africans. They recognized and celebrated various identities that were based on ethnicity, clan, family, gender, language, and class while recognizing a common humanity that bound the different groups together, which allowed a particular group to be absorbed into another group, either in peace building or through war. They called themselves *Abantu*, *Khoikhoi*, and other names that designate and validate the humanity of the different groups. As such, Mda suggests the notion of being African is "an identity-in-the-making."[5] Africa includes a plurality of identities that make for a common humanity although this propensity, like so many other cultural values, is often forgotten. It could, nevertheless, be a significant anthropological contribution that Africa makes to the global debate on coexistence and identity.[6]

In a certain sense, the expectation for stable African unity is a colonial imposition. Yet, at institutional and local levels, the professed appeal of Pan-Africanism is frequently obscured by endless ideological debates over how best to create unity while at the same being trumped by economic nationalism that sometimes boils over into overt xenophobia or territorial wars. If such divisions reflect the fact that the African continent's diverse politics, cultures, and languages afford no ready way for its fifty-four countries to interact, they also demonstrate the continuing struggle to dismantle the line that has long separated northern and southern Africa. As famously inscribed by Hegel, this line was all but unbreachable: "Africa proper" existed only "to the land south of the Sahara desert," a land and people that lacked "any integral ingredient of culture" and "no history in the true sense of the word."[7] Today, in the wake of the colonialism that Hegel helped legitimize, this line is an unofficial but altogether real referent for disputes over where to find the continent's real power and how to explain the various forces that are presently reshaping Africa.

Yet the line that divides Africa through a desert is as artificial as the line that separates it from West Asia or East of Suez. Populations in Yemen, parts of today's Saudi Arabia, and other countries of the Arabian Gulf not only share a vast ocean border with the Horn of Africa and the African east coast as far as Mozambique, but they also share an Afro-Arab ethnicity dating back beyond a millennium. Africa and West Asia together make up more than half of the world's Muslim population, sharing a common yet internally diverse religious and cultural heritage. Africa makes up at least 45 precent of the estimated 1.2 billion Muslims globally. And some 32 percent of Christianity's estimated 2.18 billion adherents reside in Africa, in all their ecumenical, racial, and linguistic diversity. In addition, some 13 million Christians reside in Arabic-speaking North Africa and the Middle East. Apart from Israel, a significant portion of the world's Jewish community lives in South Africa with dwindling populations in North Africa. At the same time indigenous African religious traditions survive independently and in the diaspora, where they remain in lived conversation with forms of Islam and Christianity. In other words, the complex cultural and faith tapestry of Africa constitutes a phenomenal experiment in the intertwined destinies of various sections of humankind in what scholars from Toynbee to the American historian Marshall Hodgson identified as part of the Afro-Eurasian *oikoumene*, an ensemble of civilizations that gives this continguous landmass a unique history. The rich potential of this cultural and civilizational diversity has yet to be fully understood by either advocates of an African renaissance or Arab reformers. A crucial question is whether both Islam and Christianity can play a vital role in the reconstruction of society in the same measure to which they both gave prophetic voice to grievances and dissatisfaction.

The assumption that what happens on the continent must necessarily have continental implications is simplistic and flouted by both history and facts on the ground. In the same breath, real-time events demonstrate that northern and southern Africa cannot be cordoned off and reduced to different worlds. One thing is certain: The African Renaissance and the Afro-Arab Spring reverberate. Large-scale migration from North African and sub-Saharan regions toward southern Africa and across the Mediterranean has already altered the landscapes of both regions by increasing the threads of an unanticipated but hopefully life-giving cosmopolitanism. The impact of the Afro-Arab Spring is evident in the Ansar al-Sharia, remnants of Colonel Muammar Qaddafi's African mercenaries who caused widespread political upheaval in Mali. In Northern Nigeria the group Boko Haram has invited international condemnation for its widespread terror and destruction, and the civil war in Somalia has yet to abate. The relative courses of the Arab Spring and the aspirations for an African Renaissance are felt across countries, regions, the continent, and the world.

With yet uncertain outcomes, the Afro-Arab Spring and African Renaissance are felt at personal, political, cultural, and economic levels. And, thus, what reverberates resonates. For all their potential differences and similarities, the two movements evoke one another. They sound calls for fundamental change that do not so much echo one another as coalesce into a deep and unsettling vibration. This vibration runs through bodies, communities, and institutions. It runs across borders. It runs backward and forward, to and fro, an oscillating movement that may shatter concentration or form the basis of rhythm. The ambiguity is a question of equilibrium—past, present, and future.

What resonates from the Cape to Cairo is a set of interlocking questions. Some of these questions have yet to be fully formulated. Many have yet to be taken up in a detailed way. All of them are increasingly urgent. How are the African Renaissance and Afro-Arab Spring both underwritten by a concern for how oppressed and alienated people regain human dignity? What are the structural, political, and cultural obstacles to modes of radical transformation that account for historical injustice without rebalkanizing society? Do these obstacles suggest ways in which the unfinished project of renaissance can inform the work of an open-ended spring? How do the popular and unstable democratic movements in North Africa bear on the promise of a continental rebirth that appeared to first take hold in the south? How are these two events reshaping the meaning of Africa? Around what problems do they coalesce and intersect? What do the African Renaissance and the Afro-Arab Spring reveal about Africa's pasts? What do they portend for its futures?

Revolutionary Dilemmas

Africa stands at a moment when it can move in any number of directions, some for better and some for worse. But, of course! Why should it be otherwise? For century upon century, Africa's "ambiguity" has been figured as a problem and then used as a pretense to exploit the continent's "contingent" resources, colonize its "wayward" people, and impose plans for its "proper" development. It is worth saying in the clearest possible terms: Some visions of African stability have amounted to little more than criminal intent; some forms of its unity have promised stability at the cost of devastating division; some calls for its development have been wholly disingenuous attempts to paralyze its creativity. The question of Africa cannot be answered until it is honestly posed—as a question.

Is Africa restless? It is, although this diagnosis comes with no small amount of baggage. The much vaunted end of history was never much more than an opening for so-called realists to predict and peddle a "clash of civilizations," a barely politically correct rendition of that old chestnut: The natives are restless and must be calmed—by whatever means necessary and for everyone's good. At some level, this is still the message. Too often it seems that the drone strikes stop only long enough for Western leaders to complete whistle-stop tours dedicated to preaching the gospel of sincere assistance on the condition of temperance.[8] True restlessness is a function of being told to stay in one's place.

Across Africa, the weight of the past continues to unsettle even as fewer and fewer are willing to accept that history can be blamed for all the problems at hand. While the Western human rights industry could not quite grasp it, there was something quite proper and perhaps even good about Robert Mugabe's 2002 proclamation: "So Blair, keep your England and let me keep my Zimbabwe." The difficulty, however, was that Mugabe's position negligently begged the questions of how liberation struggles can be remade into sustainable and just forms of government and the conditions under which heroic leaders of independence movements must be held responsible for trampling on the freedoms of those they claim to represent. The double bind is difficult to cut. Too often, hair-trigger critics naively presuppose that transitions nullify the force of history and the leaders of new governments have always had access to power. And, just as often, new leaders create unrealistic expectations in order to rationalize their unbridled appropriation of sovereign power.

Ali Mazrui suggests that the impact of Western colonialism on Africa was and is essentially "shallow rather than deep, transitional rather than long-lasting."[9] He argues that although it was never fully internalized by Africans, the colonial form of control through a supreme governor, assisted by carefully chosen magistrates and native chiefs, was nevertheless adopted by postindependence leaders. His analysis holds true for Middle Eastern rulers too. Western colonialism, Mazrui argues, has given rise to a brand of African leaders who have seized the material benefits of Western forms of capitalism through militarization and privatization at the same time that they neglect transparent and accountable governance, democratic values, and human rights.

In one sense, the past is never past—inherited structures and norms haunt each generation in ways that can never be fully anticipated and that leave it underequipped to deal fully with new challenges. Responding to the industrial revolution that swept across England and Europe in the latter decades of the eighteenth century, Karl Marx warned that "the tradition of all the dead generations weighs like a nightmare on the brain of the living."[10] In another sense, however, the past is a choice, a decision about what to remember and what to forget. Every generation confronts this opening, to the terror of elders who are all too quick to wring their hands about the dangers and immorality of the new ways. As many of those who institutionalized Marx's thought well demonstrated, the authoritarian's first play is to justify the virtuous revolution through an unquestionable and monolithic appeal to historical necessity.

With respect to Africa, it is thus useful to recall Breyten Breytenbach's call to discern and understand the values that independence and liberation have brought to the continent.[11] He asks: To whom does contemporary Africa really belong? Are Africans living in borrowed clothes? Is there a particularly African way of understanding and administering power? Is this essentially negative or potentially positive? How do colonialism, global realities, contemporary African politics, and talk of an African Renaissance impact each other? Is there a specifically African notion of peace and coexistence? To what extent do contemporary African responses to conflict carry the marks of African traditional mechanisms for survival, development, and peaceful coexistence? And do African notions of peace offer positive incentives in the global quest for peace?

These are live questions. As Shamil Jeppie demonstrates in the chapter that opens this book, radical transformation is a slow, contested, and unpredictable process. Looking across the events that have defined the Afro-Arab Spring and the armed liberation struggles that have changed the sub-Saharan landscape, Jeppie discusses ways in which history both conditions and constrains the impulse for revolution. This may link northern and southern Africa at the same time that it creates questions about the appropriate means and ends of change.

Radical transformation is a slow and contested process. Political change in the wake of entrenched patterns of authoritarian rule frequently includes cycles of insurrection, reforms, implosions, tactics and countertactics, recalcitrance and repression. Countries clearly differ in the way they have dealt with the residue of colonialism, postcolonial reform, and the institution of democratic governance. Thus, as Don Foster observes in his chapter, there is little to be gained by collapsing the collective images of an Arab Spring and an African Renaissance. And yet, as Foster shows, the frustrating false starts that all too frequently haunt African political and economic transformation reveal a shared set of questions and dilemmas, many of which take the form of structural and attitudinal obstacles to transition.

Thinking (Beyond) Transition

If it is to generate any meaningful answers, the question of Africa cannot reduce the continent to a single condition. It cannot presuppose a one-size-fits-all solution or lead to a teleology of development. The evident and widespread desire to begin again appears in the midst of diverse, dizzying, and often contradictory forms of change. Some African states are failing outright. Some are struggling to build peace, while their neighbors are funding the conflict at the same time that they are wrestling with their own question of how to sustain opposition to leaders who have either overstayed their welcome or undermined democracy's promise. Still others are in various states of transition—there are constitutions to be written, economies to be rebuilt, and deep divisions to be healed. And some are doing quite well, even as relative stability brings doubts about whether early twenty-first-century foreign investment amounts to a Faustian bargain and whether global trade is another name for a stacked deck.

It is no exaggeration to say that the South African transition remains something of a beacon. In 1994 it seemed to many that the pieces were being put together in a way that made a coherent picture. On the edge of outright and likely endless civil war, the leaders of the struggle and government took a step back from the brink and began the protracted work of developing a vocabulary for negotiations. Trust was built—in fits and starts. A concrete plan to end apartheid emerged slowly. Power was devolved and reconstructed in an interim constitution that opened the door to democratic elections and paved the way for a process of reconciliation that included conditional amnesty for perpetrators, a victim-centered attempt to come to terms with the past, and the possibility of reparation. Altogether, it was an innovative, appealing, and seemingly tidy package.

In his account of South Africa's settlement, Charles Villa-Vicencio wonders whether it was perhaps too tidy. On his reading, many involved in the settlement overlooked the fundamental limits of the South African transition in order to reach a settlement that benefited some to the neglect of others. For their part, critics of the settlement did not always care to look at both sides of the coin or offer anything more than a fantasy about how the end of apartheid might have unfolded otherwise. Looking in between with a sense of historical detail frequently missing from discussions of South Africa, Villa-Vicencio suggests South Africa's settlement is less a model than a cogent perspective for asking questions about the scope, mechanics, and ends of political and economic transitions in deeply divided countries across Africa. It is precisely this problem of division and repair that focuses Helen Scanlon's chapter and its concern for the costs that attend the increasingly mandatory truth-telling processes that are thought to promote healing and speed transformation. Focusing on South Africa's TRC, Scanlon details the gendered nature of deep division and points to the ways in which widespread norms of transitional justice in Africa do not assure "gender-inclusive" reconciliation.

While the last word on the South African transition has yet to be written, one of its decisive lessons is that the end of a transition—a moment which is itself difficult to locate—is the beginning of arduous labor. Democratic constitutions are works in progress, all the more so when they delineate socioeconomic rights that do not concede the finitude of available resources. Set into economies in which rapid transformation may well be another word for collapse, the resulting tension produces justifiable frustration and increasingly angry charges of corruption, where the latter not infrequently rests on the naive belief that a constitution can speak to and redress all contingencies—past, present, and future. This does not deny that those who oversee new governing institutions frequently succumb to actual corruption, a crime that takes many forms and comes with the added symbolic weight of underscoring the divide between powerful and powerless, rich and poor, represented and excluded. This weight does have a tipping point, even as the appeal of such a fulcrum too often serves as a way to energize and rationalize a populism that simply replaces one kind of corruption with another. More than one thing hangs in the balance. And the balance is not ready-made.

The Arab Spring reaches across the physical and psychological reality of the Suez Canal that divides the Arabian Peninsula and North Africa. Across this expanse, it has demonstrated the extent to which people are prepared to go in pursuit of fundamental reform. The self-immolation of Mohamed Bouazizi in Sidi Bouzid, the occupation of Tahrir Square in Cairo, and the events culminating in the killing of Muammar Qaddafi in Sirte are in one sense new struggles but in another sense a culmination of earlier struggles in these countries and elsewhere. In this respect, the eruptions were not random. They drew specifically on history, not least as they looked back to the ancient Islamic empires and the imposition of the infamous Sykes-Picot Agreement that divided Arab states in the Middle East between the French and the English at the conclusion of World War I.[12]

That delegations from Tunisia, Egypt, and Libya each visited South Africa after the removal of the respective country's long-time authoritarian leader— President Zine el-Abidine Ben Ali in Tunisia, Hosni Mubarak in Egypt, and Muammar Qaddafi in Libya—is significant. Its limitations aside, the South African political compromise was seen as having possible *procedural* implications for transitional justice developments in these countries. Against this backdrop Ibrahim Sharqieh's chapter turns to the Tunisian case and reflects on the "laudable progress" that has been made in Tunisia's framework for transitional justice. In contrast to Libya, the country's constituent assembly has not insisted on purging all elements of the previous regime, a decision that has enhanced the possibilities of political dialogue. With respect to Libya, Asif Majid's chapter considers the historical and contemporary tensions that have appeared since the end of the Qaddafi regime. Noting the high level of political-cultural division, the inability of Libya's fragile central government to disarm warlords and militias, and low levels of political inclusion, Majid finds that the current Libyan state is characterized by a power vacuum that both complicates the path of transition and inhibits reconciliation. Emphasizing concerns that reach to the heart of *substantial* political transition, the assessments offered by Sharqieh and Majid suggest that one lesson of the Afro-Arab Spring for postapartheid South Africa is that poor and alienated communities cannot be excluded from the benefits of a political settlement. This is a lesson that has not gone unheeded in South Africa, where critics of government policy warn of South Africa's pending "Tunisia Day" of resistance and point to the lesson of post-Qaddafi Libya: Nation building in deeply divided societies needs to include minority and regionally estranged communities.[13]

Fault Lines—North and South

The complex dynamics and dilemmas of Africa's transitions shed light on Thabo Mbeki's decision to promote and pursue an African Renaissance at a moment when the South African miracle was front and center. At a point when the country, the continent, and the world were paying far more attention to the possibilities of reconciliation and the work of the TRC, Mbeki spent some of South Africa's political capital to promote a vision for the continent that led critics to ask whether he was doing so to divert attention away from the economic failings of the South African settlement. That said, from Mbeki's perspective, South Africa's transition could set the stage for an African Renaissance—the next logical and necessary step in consolidating South Africa's turn away from its apartheid past—and promote the possibility of democratic transition in other African countries.

When authoritarian regimes in the Arab world and in Africa are faced with the possibility of losing power and access to material wealth, they have proven themselves adept at crushing pro-democratic movements in the name of promoting both political stability and democracy. The "deep state" in Egyptian politics has worked this option with efficiency. In his chapter Ebrahim Rasool argues that, in his endeavor to lead the Muslim Brotherhood and secularists into political coexistence, President Mohamed Morsi fell victim to the extremists in the Muslim Brotherhood as well as to the manipulative forces of the deep state. This opened the way for General Abdel Fattah al-Sisi, the Egyptian chief of the army, to lead the coup d'état that overthrew Morsi's democratically elected government and to ban the Muslim Brotherhood, yet to be heralded as the defender of democracy by a coalition of business, military, and political leaders.

The developments that have led to the current Egyptian impasse have roots that reach deep into a history of dissent.[14] Against overt and subtle forms of Orientalism, the larger Arab Spring demonstrates that citizens are neither passive nor backward in responding to caliphs and political leaders in Muslim-majority countries[15] Consider just a few moments of uprising, revolt, and revolution: the Iranian revolution in 1979; the overthrow of the military-led government of President Gaafar Numeiri in Sudan in 1985 by students, workers, and professionals; the Islamic occupation of poor urban quarters in Cairo in 1992; the Palestinian intifadas of 1987 and 2000; uprisings in Yemen in protest against the invasion of Iraq by the United States in 2003; the Lebanese Cedar Revolution in 2005, which led to the withdrawal of Syrian troops from Lebanon; the Egyptian April 6 Movement that in 2008 mobilized Egyptians to show solidarity with textile workers on strike in El-Mahalla El-Kubra; and prodemocracy rallies in Yemen and Iran, as well as campaigns of civil resistance in Bahrain, Jordan, Saudi Arabia, and other Gulf States.

With something of this history in mind, the overthrow of Hosni Mubarak in Egypt, along with the popular demonstrations that swept across the Arab world in 2011, was read by many analysts and leaders in the West as a sign of emerging peace and democracy in the Middle East. The prediction was premature, not least as the endgame of the Arab Spring has yet to unfold. Thus, the evident interplay of historical, economic, political, religious, and cultural factors that constitute the shifting bedrock of the uprisings in the Arab Spring has spurred a growing literature dedicated to explaining the dynamics of the uprisings and the persistence of authoritarianism. This work shows some of the ways in which the Arab Spring is shaped and complicated by deep-seated frustration with material and nonmaterial deprivation, new forms of communication, meddling by external geopolitical groups, and the need to forge coalitions across entrenched divisions. Tunisia has found common ground in the creation of a constitution, Libya has to date failed to find political consensus for constitutional government, and Egypt has crushed what was a brave democratic endeavor. The futures of countries of the Maghreb, the Sahel, and further south balance on a knife edge. The demise of Afro-Arab authoritarianism hangs in the balance. The struggle for democracy and human rights is not done. Arguably, it has entered a new and more intense phase.

The realities of cultural, religious, and tribal divisions, fueled by demands for resources, are tearing at the seams of several African states. This is evident in South Sudan and the Central African Republic. Looking to Nigeria, scholars of Islam and organizations across the continent have condemned the atrocities of Boko Haram as a blatant misuse of Islamic teachings in the name of political extremism.[16] At the same time it is important to recognize that the situation has roots in the estrangement of Muslims in the north that can be traced back to the amalgamation of the northern and southern British protectorates to form the consolidated Colony of Nigeria in 1914 and the independent state of Nigeria in 1960. The merger resulted in the alienation of the mainly Muslim Hausa and Fulani ethnic groups in the north from the Yoruba and Igbo groups in the south, who are mainly Christians or adherents of African traditional religion. It also entrenched political and economic power largely in the south, a consolidation that was aggravated by the imposition of Western education as a vehicle for evangelism in the north. Tensions have also reemerged between the government of Mali and Tuareg Islamic separatists in the northern part of the country. Prime Minister Moussa Mara has stated that his government is "at war" with the separatists and called for international support to crush the uprising.[17]

Intense conflict and violence inside oppressive states develop in different directions. The state can fall apart as in Somalia, Lebanon, Yugoslavia, and Syria. Alternatively, conflict may hold an opportunity for historically entrenched enemies to collectively address the problems that have brought a nation to the brink of collapse. Despite the failure of the postapartheid state to grasp the opportunities with the political creativity needed, the historic South African settlement provided an example of what can be achieved, at least procedurally, in a deeply divided society. It provided a space within which the country was given the opportunity to begin again.

Each country and region has its own unique challenges. The Arab Spring cannot be reduced to a religious-secular conflict. Middle East and North African countries are nevertheless significantly shaped by the influence of Islamic political theology. In his chapter Ebrahim Moosa provides a detailed analysis of the political theology underlying the Arab Spring, primarily as it played out in Egypt. Moosa points out that the absence of a political theology consonant with democracy and the nation-state has created a theological Babel tower in Muslim politics. He identifies the roots of this battle in the twentieth century and explains the tragedy of theological politics in Egypt when Morsi was deposed and the military reinstalled. It remains to be seen whether a theological paradigm shift in Islam could underwrite democratic inclusivity in Muslim state building. His main argument is that calls for a nonauthoritarian political theology made a century ago have gone totally unheeded by religious and political elites.

In the chapter that follows, Abdulkader Tayob takes up the tension between religion and secularism in light of the fact that "the relationship between religion, nation, and state is far from settled in postapartheid South Africa." Concerned partly with the promise and limits of South Africa's tradition, Tayob's reflection sheds important light on the question of how societies can open spaces to stage the interplay between constitutional order and faith-based pluralism.

Katherine Marshall, in turn, provides a discerning analysis of the "complex gender dynamics in North Africa" and how questions of gender have been included in and excluded from the dynamics of the Arab Spring. Looking at the nexus of cultural-religious practice and human rights, Marshall's chapter contends that while "gender equality, at least on the surface and in formal policy statements and constitutions, has long been officially accepted as a norm across the region," current reforms have yet to transform "the deeply patriarchal nature of Arab politics and society."

A Change of Season?

Between 1963 and 2002, there were some two hundred attempted and actual coups d'état in Africa. Many resulted in a significant number of deaths. Very few advanced the cause of democracy. And, for the most part, these events went unchecked. Founded on a principle of "non-interference in the internal affairs of [member] states," the Organization of African Unity had neither the inclination nor the leverage to oppose military forces intent on overthrowing standing though sometimes corrupt governments. This presumption began to change in 2002 with the formation of the African Union (AU) and its expressed commitment to actively oppose "unconstitutional change of government" in member states.

Focused on development, democratization, economic growth, and peace and security across the continent, the AU was grounded in a concern to promote good governance and collective security through such mechanisms as the AU Peace and Security Council, the New Partnership for Africa's Development (NEPAD), and the African Peer Review Mechanism (APRM). It has also committed to an African criminal court, a body that will operate parallel to the International Criminal Court (ICC). With these mechanisms, the AU has taken concrete steps to advance democratization and development. It has, for instance, used NEPAD and the APRM to shape economic policy and encourage political accountability. It has also variously suspended the AU memberships of Mauritania, Guinea, Niger, Madagascar, Côte d'Ivoire, and Mali for what it saw as the unjustified removal of democratically elected governments.[18]

The African Union remains a work in progress, a promise of continental stability and development that is hampered by political, economic, and institutional constraints, including inconsistent buy-in from member states, deep historical division and economic scarcity, conflicting demands from international monetary institutions, an organizational structure that provokes infighting, inadequate financial resources, and a limited capacity to take retributive action against non-compliant states or to resist the intervention of global powers. In this light Chris Landsberg's carefully argued chapter considers the gap between the AU's promise and its power in relation to the ongoing struggle to define and enable a new Pan-Africanism. As Landsberg notes, the difficulties are not simply with the AU itself: "The early hopes of the Arab Spring and the African Renaissance simply cannot be realized without AU promises being implemented by member states, across Africa, from north to south." In a basic sense the possibility of Pan-Africanism may hinge on the emergence of a unity in difference, the capacity and willingness of individual countries to make concrete contributions to the "formation of common institutions and the promotion of cosmopolitan values."

How will Africa begin again? How might the parts come together to compose the whole? How might the whole gather and support the parts? Central to the debate over the future of the African Union, these questions reach to the very heart of the African Renaissance. As the call for a renaissance holds out the question of Africa, Erik Doxtader's chapter considers the potentially productive dilemmas that attend an African appeal to the European concept of a renaissance and then contends that an African rebirth may depend on more than policymaking. In the name of making Africa anew, Doxtader suggests that the long-standing idea of an African renaissance is rooted in the discovery of a shared concern for language and the invention of a vocabulary with a constitutive power, a power of self-definition held in common by all of those who would profess "I am an African."

Spring is a fragile season. It can be delayed by a hard winter and preempted by a fiery summer. There is little easy about opening and then sustaining a moment of regeneration. And yet, for all the contingency of spring, for all the ways in which its promise may not arrive at the expected moment, its anticipation and appearance are nevertheless felt. A turn unfolds, even as its terms and implications are not yet entirely visible. There is a turn in the making. In the movements of the African Renaissance and the Afro-Arab Spring, the question of Africa is open. Individually and together, the essays that follow afford an opening into this space, a chance to think and reflect on what remains to be seen and what might unfold otherwise—for Africa.

Notes

1. Here, "Afro-Arab Spring" is used to highlight our concern for the African continent. In the chapters that follow the more inclusive "Arab Spring" is frequently employed to portray the broader nexus between African, Middle Eastern, and Gulf State Arab countries.

2. Thabo Mbeki, "Address by Executive Deputy President Thabo Mbeki, to Corporate Council on Africa's 'Attracting Capital to Africa' Summit," April 19, 1997, www.sahistory.org .za/archive/address-executive-deputy-president-thabo-mbeki-corporate-council-africas-attract ing-capital-.

3. Kim Wale, *Confronting Exclusion: Time for Radical Reconciliation—South African Reconciliation Barometer Survey: 2013 Report* (Cape Town: Institute for Justice and Reconciliation, 2014).

4. Garth le Pere, "A Revolution Betrayed?," *The Thinker* 50 (2013): 9.

5. At a symposium on identity organized by the Institute for Justice and Reconciliation, Cape Town, October 2003. See Charles Villa-Vicencio, *Walk with Us and Listen: Political Reconciliation in Africa* (Washington, DC: Georgetown University Press, 2009), 116.

6. To this, one can grasp the way in which colonization saw an influx of Europeans into Africa—with some settlers (in time) becoming natives. See Mahmood Mamdani, "Beyond Settler and Native as Political Identities: Overcoming the Political Legacy of Colonialism," *Comparative Studies in Society and History*, 42, no. 4 (2001): 651–64.

7. G. W. F Hegel, *Lectures on the Philosophy of World History*, trans. H. B. Nisbet (Cambridge: Cambridge University Press, 1980), 173, 190.

8. Hillary Rodham Clinton, "The United States—South Africa Partnership: Going Global," remarks at the University of Western Cape, Cape Town, South Africa, August 8, 2012, www.state.gov/secretary/20092013clinton/rm/2012/08/196184.htm.

9. Ali A. Mazrui, *The Africans: A Triple Heritage* (Boston: Little, Brown, 1986), 14.

10. Karl Marx, *The Eighteenth Brumaire of Louis Bonaparte* (London: International, 1994); also available at www.slp.org/pdf/marx/eighteenth_brum.pdf.

11. Breyten Breytenbach, "Imagine Africa," paper delivered at the Vitalizing African Cultural Assets Conference, Gorée Island, March 5–7, 2007.

12. Eric Chaney, "Democratic Change in the Arab World, Past and Present," *Brookings Papers on Economic Activity*, Spring 2012, www.stanford.edu/dept/islamic_studies/cgi-bin/web /wp-content/uploads/2012/03/chaney.pdf.

13. Moeletsi Mbeki, "South Africa: Only a Matter of Time before the Bomb Explodes," *Leader*, February, 12, 2011, www.leader.co.za/article.aspx?s = 23&f = 1&a = 2571.

14. Alain Badiou, *The Rebirth of History: Times of Riots and Uprisings* (London: Verso, 2012); Asef Bayet, *Making Islam Democratic: Social Movements and the Post-Islamist Turn* (Palo Alto: Stanford University Press, 2007).

15. Yacoob Abba Omar, "The Uprisings," *The Thinker* 59 (2014): 40–44.

16. Sami Aboudi, "Saudi Arabia's Top Cleric Says Nigeria's Boko Haram Smears Islam," Reuters, May 9, 2014, www.reuters.com/article/2014/05/09/us-nigeria-girls-saudi-idUSBREA 480MU20140509.http://barnabasfund.org/US/News/News-analysis/Top-Islamic-clerics-con demn-Boko-Haram-kidnappings-girls-converted.html?method = PRINT.

17. "Mali 'at War' with Tuareg Rebels," Al Jazeera English, May 19, 2014, www.aljazeera .com/news/africa/2014/05/mali-at-war-with-tuareg-rebels-201451815152681548.html.

18. Membership was restored only after the necessary constitutional reforms were implemented. At present, the AU memberships of the CAR, Egypt, and Guinea-Bissau remain under suspension.

1

From Cairo to the Cape

The Dilemmas of Revolution

SHAMIL JEPPIE

T
he historic events in North Africa since December 2010 have affected in multiple ways the countries sharing common borders across the immense Sahara Desert and even countries further to the south. Mali in the west and the Republic of Sudan in the east are among the countries of the Saraha and Sahel that have not been directly affected by sustained uprisings or revolutionary stirrings but were and are influenced by the Arab Spring. The coup d'état in Mali in late March 2012 was led by middle-ranking officers furious with the government's inability to deal with an armed insurgency by the Tuaregs in the northern parts of the country. The Tuareg insurgents eventually declared independence for the country's entire northeastern region known as the Azawad. The insurgents were apparently emboldened by well-equipped and trained Tuareg fighters who had fled Libya after the uprising, the North Atlantic Treaty Organization (NATO) bombing of that country, and the eventual killing of Colonel Qaddafi in October 2011. Malian soldiers in distant northern towns such as Kidal, Timbuktu, and Gao simply fled from their posts when the rebels entered these towns. The coup d'état, the subsequent withdrawal of the military, the installation of a caretaker president (who was then attacked in his office), and the occupation of key northern towns by different factions of the rebels—including a militant Wahhabi group called Ansar al-Din—led to a wholly unstable situation in Mali. This is the most outstanding case of the unintended consequences and external impact of the so-called Arab Spring on the continent. In January 2013, the French landed in Mali to recover Malian territory taken by the rebels.[1]

The Arab Spring was watched with great interest throughout the continent. Rulers and ruled alike kept an eye on the dramatic developments in Tunis and in Maydan al-Tahrir (Tahrir Square) in Cairo. Other rulers feared that similarly

1

threatening events could unseat them, while various sections of the citizenry were keenly interested in adapting some of the lessons from the protests to the situations in their own countries.

Thus, in Zimbabwe there was a de facto ban on people communicating about the events in Egypt, and some persons who had watched footage of protests in Cairo were arrested.[2] In Senegal there were large and persistent popular protests beginning in June 2011 against the presidential reelection campaign of Abdoulaye Wade. The eighty-year-old had secured a high court judgment allowing him to run for a third term. He was eventually beaten in the runoff by his former protégé, Macky Sall.[3]

The Arabic-speaking ruling elite in northern Sudan remained unaffected until June 2012 although there were attempts during 2011 to stage protest meetings. The Sudanese were preoccupied with other significant developments: the breakup of the Sudan and birth of South Sudan in July 2011 and, soon thereafter, a border war between the two states and ongoing instability along the border. In late June 2012, however, increasing numbers of protesters took regularly to the streets to protest the government austerity measures and the rising cost of living. The Bashir government cracked down hard on these protests and, in an attempt to restore its faltering legitimacy, invoked Sharia and promulgated what it said was a fully Islamic constitution. Sporadic protests have continued through 2013.[4]

The Arab Spring thus influenced society and politics far beyond those countries where Arabic is the dominant language. Writing from the southern end of the continent, I want to first offer a reading of the events of the northern parts of the continent and place them in larger and deeper historical context. I hope to introduce some considerations regarding the understanding of these events as revolutions that I believe are not often enough raised, probably because the events are still in the making; thus, the actors are too deeply involved in keeping the process of protest and revolt alive, and commentators are mostly concerned about keeping abreast of them. Second, I shall try to make the case for a comparative reading of these developments with a specific period and experience in the history of southern Africa (ca. 1975–ca. 1994), an exciting but also very violent period that saw the last of the settler-colonial regimes of the region surrender power to majority parties in democratic elections.

Intifadah and *Thawra* Begin in Africa

An extensive political science literature is devoted to authoritarianism in the Arab world, reflecting both a reality and a disciplinary perspective—perhaps bias—that is concerned only with the state. Thus, until the Arab Spring, what literature there was on social movements in those regions was almost wholly concerned with Islamist organizations. Yet there is a pattern of mobilization, protest, and periodic resurgence of movements against the authoritarian state. In March 1985 an uprising spread through Khartoum, capital of the Republic of Sudan, while the country's president, Ja'afar Numayri, was on a trip to the United States; the revolt led to his removal from power and exile. Only a few weeks after the popular uprising against his rule, his party apparatus, security services, and supporters had to make way for an interim military authority. By April 1986 a new civilian government was in power. This was a major achievement for the Sudanese, who had lived with the authoritarian and capricious regime of Numayri since 1969. His rule began in the name of socialism with support from the well-organized Sudanese Communist Party; it ended after his turn to sharia punishment, his implementation of the so-called September laws with support from the well-organized Sudanese Muslim Brothers, and his move to ally himself with the West. The popular *intifadah* against the Numayri regime is one of many heroic uprisings among the Sudanese. The Sudanese uprising is also a reminder of the long-standing capability of peoples in the region to rise up against repressive and unpopular governments.[5]

Two years later, in December 1987, and thousands of kilometers to the northeast of Khartoum, Palestinian youth, who had known only Israeli military occupation since 1967, began an uprising that would continue for years. It would lead to the Oslo Accords, another round of uprisings (the second *intifadah* of 2000), and the introduction of new forms of repression. But the 1987 uprising introduced the term *intifadah* into the vocabulary of the region and the world. After this time many people across the world saw *intifadah* as a specifically Palestinian phenomenon. People celebrated the *intifadah* in other parts of the Middle East, looking for spaces in which to contest the oppressive situations in which they found themselves.[6]

Skirmishes and radical contestation occurred across the region. *Intifadah* came to define rebellion and uprisings against the state. It generally was used in cases where the power imbalance was huge and the issues very clear rather than when protests became more sustained uprisings or military insurrections.[7]

Through the 1980s, the 1990s, and into the new millennium, the states of North Africa and the surrounding region confronted their opponents using militaristic tactics and capacities. This response began after the assassination of Anwar al-Sadat, who was killed during a military parade in October 1981 by army officers linked to the Islamic Group and Islamic Jihad.[8] With this assassination came a major state crackdown by the military, with armed resistance and also outright terrorism spreading across Egypt. After the withdrawal of Soviet troops from Afghanistan in 1988 and 1989, many Arab fighters who had left Egypt to fight in Afghanistan returned to Egypt in pursuit of what was being promoted as permanent revolution to achieve liberation from oppressive rule. Nobody used the term *intifadah* to describe these activities, instead using the word *irhab*, or terrorism. The state used this threat of *irhab* to muzzle opposition and crack down on any potential *intifadahs*. The state even managed to win over organized sections of the secular left in the fight against this terror, which was being carried out in the name of religion. Thus the last *intifadah* in Egypt was the so-called bread riots of January 1977 that shook the Sadat government. Resistance to the state remained mostly dispersed, sporadic, and unorganized.

In North Africa in the 1990s Algeria was far more dangerous than Egypt. The latter endured a low-intensity war between the state and Islamist groupings but nothing compared to what was going on in Algeria. The large-scale armed conflict between the Algerian military and Islamist militants quickly became a civil war in the 1990s. The cause of the conflict was the cancellation of a second round of elections in which the opposition Islamic Salvation Front (FIS) was bound to win based on their massive victories during the first round. The FIS presented a major challenge to the ruling party, and there was a strong possibility that it could win the elections of 1991. Consequently, the elections were canceled, which resulted in leading members either fleeing the country or taking up arms. Between 1992 and 1998 a civil war plagued the entire country. Tens of thousands were killed, mostly at the hands of groups such as the Armed Islamic Group (GIA) and the state's paramilitary forces. The Algerian state has always spoken of its fight against *irhab*. Tens of thousands of Algerians died in the brutal civil war. With memories of the repression and civil war of the 1990s still fresh, the attempt at *intifadah* in Algeria while there was an Arab Spring in the region was half-hearted.[9]

What has happened in the region since December 2010 is described among the actors there as a revolution (*thawra*). This is especially the case in Egypt. It is not necessary to narrate here the chronology of events since the immolation in Tunis of the hawker Mohamed Bouazizi, the fleeing of Ben Ali, and the impact of these events on other states.

In Tunisia the overthrow of the ruler took about one month. Within about a year the country had a new government. Tunisia is among the smallest of the countries of the region—in geographical extent and in population size. The elite, which had ruled the country since its independence in 1956, grew increasingly out of touch with the country's people and their culture, language, and economic struggles. The state and the elite were oriented to the West, and France in particular. The fear of *irhab* was used by the state to stifle opposition and dissent. However, the uprising against the Ben Ali dictatorship was nonviolent and, in fact, largely limited to seeing the removal of the man, his wife, and the elite around him. To what extent it was a *thawra* is another matter, which we shall explore in a moment.

Egyptians with any political education have had profound affection for the term *thawra*. In popular speech and media, *intifadah* is far too limited and timid to describe major events in modern Egyptian history. Even a coup d'état is described as a *thawra*: The modern Egyptian revolutions are the 'Urabi Revolution in 1882, the Nationalist Revolution in 1919, a 1952 coup d'état to end about one and a half centuries of monarchy, and finally the events of 2011 and of mid-2013. In Egypt the use of the term "revolution" is sometimes more specific, and a revolution is seen not so much as a process covering a period of a year or a few years but as an event that happened on a particular month and day. So we have the "Revolution of January 25," which refers to the date Mubarak left office for the resort town of Sharm al-Sheikh. The Egyptian novelist Sonallah Ibrahim is rare among Egyptian intellectuals in having consistently spoken of these events as an *intifadah* and not a *thawra*.[10]

So far I have paid some attention to a few Arabic words. This brings me to the role of communication in the recent events. Language specialists inside the region have bemoaned the decline in standards of Arabic usage across the region. Some foreign specialists have noted the major dialectical differences across the Arabic-speaking world and have found the differences are in fact growing. In other words, there is a steady breakup of the Arabic linguistic community—the basis of Arab nation building and nationalism. However, the speed at which news of events spread through Al Jazeera and other regionwide media points to a lively persistence of the linguistic ties that bind the region. The dramatic events in Tunis were immediately taken up in Cairo, then in Tripoli and Manama and Sana'a and Damascus. There is thus a basis for invoking the signifier "Arab" for the events in the region. Some of the slogans are the same, demands expressed in simple terms such as "The people want the fall of the system" or "Dignity" or "Go (Leave)." It appears then that the elements of an Arabic identity that transcend the fragile nation-states (products of twentieth-century imperial power) remain attractive and powerful. The new communication media—mobile phone, e-mail, Facebook, and Twitter—were undoubtedly important, but their significance tends to be overestimated. They were tools, and in their absence other instruments of communication would have been found to spread the information. Equally important was the existence of a symbolic space—Tahrir Square, Liberation Square—where citizens could convene in opposition to oppressive rule.

A deep resentment of the regimes had led to sustained and frequent acts of resistance throughout Egypt for at least three or four years before the events of 2011. Egypt was actually on the brink of revolution or a major rebellion for some time. Many critical intellectuals and activists were aware of what was happening in the small towns in the Nile Delta and the industrial towns outside Cairo, but they were also aware of the vast state security apparatus ready to apply ruthless repression in the face of any protests. The April 6 movement emerged as a group of young people mobilizing support for the labor movement and in particular for a minimum wage. The young men and women—from middle-class families of Muslim and Coptic faiths—were unprepared for the events of 2011 in which they had played a catalytic role.[11]

What were the conditions in Egypt on the eve of the *intifadah* of 2011? Dissatisfaction with the Mubarak regime had been growing over the previous decade.

Using the cover of engaging in a "war on terror," the regime was able to tighten the screws on opposition even further. Mubarak presented Egypt to the West as a bulwark against extremist terrorism, safe for investment, and presented himself as a moderate leader keen on democracy. Thus Obama chose Cairo as the place where he would address the Muslim world on relations between the West and Islam. As long as the regime kept the peace with Israel, aid (largely for the military) of US$3 billion per annum would be forthcoming from the United States. Mubarak in fact bent over backward in promoting good relations with Israel—far beyond what any previous Egyptian ruler had done, and possibly as far as the Jordanians. Thus the imprisonment of Palestinians in Gaza was also the work of Egyptian security and military forces.

Mubarak and the obedient men around him grew ever more distant from their populace, the country, the region, the continent. His party always won elections by huge margins, opponents were imprisoned and disappeared, and the security apparatus and military were in control of large parts of the economy and the operations of government. Living standards and income were in decline, yet the small elite around Mubarak and the National Democratic Party (NDP) continued to enrich themselves. Forty percent of Egyptians lived on between one and two US dollars per day. Rates of unemployment and underemployment were very high. There was no minimum-wage legislation. The official trade union federation was filled with NDP members and completely opposed to worker interests. The education system was in total disarray with most children still functionally illiterate on completion of primary school. While higher education expanded rapidly under Mubarak with Cairo having about one million students at its three state universities, university graduates often went without jobs for many years after graduation. The lucky ones went to work in the Gulf. Corruption was a way of life. Mubarak committed himself to undoing whatever remained of the popular measures to redistribute wealth first introduced in the wake of the 1952 revolution, led by Gamal Nasser, that brought the rule of King Farouk to an end.

Mubarak was effectively attempting to reintroduce a form of monarchical government with himself as the founder of a new dynasty. Meanwhile his son Gamal was being groomed to take over from him. This hereditary transfer of power was a pattern for other Arab states without monarchies, such as Libya and Syria. (The history of monarchy in the Middle East is, in fact, a recent development, with the dynasties of Jordan and Saudi Arabia both being twentieth-century inventions. Only Morocco has a dynasty with temporal depth in the Arab world; Morocco's Alawite dynasty dates back to 1665. When Arab Spring movements emerged in Morocco, the existence of the monarchy itself was not questioned. There were demands for a constitutional monarchy that resulted in the adoption of a new constitution and a democratically elected government under King Mohammed VI.)

Egypt is the largest state in the region. It is in many ways and in many matters a leader in the Arab world. But the country where the Arab Spring started, Tunisia, was also run by a small elite removed from the masses, had a ruler far too long in office, and contained an educated sector but few employment opportunities. These, among other factors, resulted in the rebellion following Mohamed Bouazizi's self-immolation in Sidi Bouzid.

Libya and Syria had social policies in place that sought to address the social and economic problems of the majority. Gross inequalities were indeed addressed there, and social indicators for health, mortality, and education (including for women) were positive. Libya had the best indicators in Africa. However, in both countries the regimes were determined to hold onto power and eliminate opposition, which made them hugely unpopular. Both used radical and populist rhetoric as a way to increase their popularity; this worked better for certain audiences abroad than it did internally. But Qaddafi was not overthrown in a revolution: Without underplaying the role of the rebels, the NATO campaign against Qaddafi's regime brought him down. The struggle for power is far from over in Libya.[12] For geopolitical reasons Syria is given different treatment. The regime has been able to hold onto power in the face of a deeply divided opposition. Significant disagreements among Syrians are likely to continue for months, if not years, to come.

The level of militarized conflict seen in Syria and Libya did not, however, occur in Egypt, where opposition to the Mubarak regime was driven by a genuine, if internally very divided, mass movement with a range of political organizations giving leadership to the uprising.[13] Egypt's oldest, and indeed the region's oldest and largest, Islamic movement, the Muslim Brotherhood, entered Tahrir Square rather haltingly but through its well-developed networks was able to emerge as the strongest party in the country's democratic election. It was at one point also widely believed that the Brotherhood in Syria would be the beneficiaries of any regime change, should it occur.

In Egypt the military has acted as or pretended to be an arbiter or middleman. The military will seek to maintain this position, with too much to lose in any other arrangement. Egypt's 1952 revolution was the work of officers. The Ikhwan's associates in the Sudanese military led the coup of 1989 that overthrew the civilian government elected after the *intifadah* of 1985.[14]

That Mubarak's last prime minister was allowed to run in the presidential election at all is curious. A revolution that allows a figure from the ancien regime to contest the election is indicative of the power of that regime. That the candidate, Ahmad Shafiq, could win enough votes to contest the runoff reflects the strength of support for some kind of return to the status quo ante. The remnants of Mubarak's now-dissolved party and the old regime's bureaucracies also provided support for Shafiq's campaign. But it also reflects the nature and leadership of the revolutionary or oppositional forces, their divergence and plurality.

This perhaps speaks of the way the events of the eighteen months unfolded. There was a wellspring of popular unrest and dissent, which was very largely unorganized. The organized political forces of radical bent were rather distant from this environment. The repressive state had been successful in co-opting some elements of the Left in the name of the war on terror and against radical Islam. Even the Ikhwan was unprepared for the launching of the momentous events of January 2011. There was thus an organic quality to the emergence of the *intifadah* that became a revolution. Perhaps Egyptians can rightly use that term for the genuine human changes that occurred during 2011. Grand structures did not change and may not change for some time yet. However, there was a tremendous energy and dignity in the abilities to speak up, to speak back, to move around and move freely, to take possession of public spaces and walk tall. This was not the work of radical Islam or terror but of an organic, impulsive movement. It was a movement against the arrogance of Mubarak and his like; it still remains to be seen whether it will be movement forward.

To the extent that the movement was an organic response to oppression, it was a revolution—though perhaps more like the events of 1848 than *thawra* in any classical sense (French, Russian, Iranian). However, even in the revolutions of 1848, which overthrew the conservative orders of vast parts of Europe, victories were limited until further changes were instituted in the 1850s. As Arno Mayer has put it, Egyptians in 2011 saw "persistence of the old regime."[15]

Only in hindsight shall we be able to say to what extent 2011 was a revolution and what was achieved. But a whole range of human activities and ideas is being changed and influenced within Egypt, within other states, and across the region. Old-fashioned nationalism and pan-Arabism may not be revived, but here is the basis for regaining sovereignty, and in a much fuller sense.

Since the launch of the uprisings in Tunisia in December 2010, the term *thawra* has been used to describe these events. Are they really revolutions? Does the removal of a ruler, his cabinet, and the businessmen close to him constitute a revolution? Most of the remaining structure of the states—and their supporters and supporting institutions—that have experienced these revolutions in recent years remained and remain in place. One thinks of the media in Tunisia and the judiciary in Egypt. One thinks of the place of the military in all the states that hold onto their privileges; the generals in Egypt have effectively declared that they will remain above any civilian authority or oversight. In effect, Egypt is experiencing a conservative coup d'état in revolutionary conditions.

Yet, we have to admit that there have been major changes and shifts in power relations, in the way in which ordinary people have taken their individual and collective agency to new heights. Fear has been transcended. Public spaces have been repossessed as common spaces in which to gather and from which to speak back to repressive states.[16]

On the whole, the Afro-Arab region is undergoing a transformation. We do not know where this transformation is really leading, but the status quo has been shaken at its core and is changing. On the one hand, there are mass movements for change and for continuing a path of revolution, but, on the other hand, there are strong initiatives to halt the process.

An Arab 1848 Moment

Thinking of contemporary events in comparative historical terms opens many possibilities for seeing the present in clearer, even more objective, light; however, it can be misleading to insist that events of the present or recent past can be squeezed into a paradigm from another time or place. There is suggestive potential, though, in surveying the events in North Africa and the Middle East between 2011 and the end of 2013 through the lens of the dense events in Europe in the period from late 1847 through the end of 1848; these were the so-called revolutions of 1848 that deeply impacted deeply subsequent European history.[17] The historic formative events of that period lasted about a year and also had a knock-on effect spreading from country to country, from France to Germany to Italy to various parts of the Austro-Hungarian Empire. These events were meant in some ways to complete the work that had begun with the French Revolution about sixty years earlier. Millions of European workers and peasants for the first time came to act politically in their respective societies. Serfdom was ended, and the landed nobility's power was weakened as the power of the state increased. Constitutionalism, civil rights, social and workers' rights, and nationalism were all raised as significant issues during that year. Although there were many gains, by the end of the sustained revolts of 1848 there were only some limited political reforms. The most conservative politicians, such as the powerful Austrian statesman Metternich, fled, but the dominant classes held onto power. I will not use this comparison on this occasion, although it is a possible comparable historical process to think through. Instead, I want to use an example from one part of Africa to think about another part of the continent and the Middle East. We could compare the unfolding events in North Africa and the Middle East with those that took place in the period between 1975 and 1980 in southern Africa.

Insights from Revolution in Southern Africa

By the early 1970s, most of the North African states were already celebrating a decade of independence from colonial rule; meanwhile, at the other end of the continent the struggle against colonialism was still in progress. In 1970 white settler rule in southern Africa looked like it would be in place for another century. The closest comparable case of settler-colonialism in North Africa was Algeria under the French (1830s to 1962). The Algerian struggle against the French was of considerable significance to southern African liberation movements. Indeed, Nelson Mandela traveled secretly to an Algerian guerrilla training camp in Morocco, where he met Ahmad Ben Bella and received elementary military training right at the close of the war against France in 1962.

In the 1970s the liberation movements were making progress in their armed struggles against colonial rule; the anticolonial movements had only turned to armed struggle in the 1960s. This was the case in South Africa and South West Africa (SWA), which had been ruled by South Africa since the end of World War I; it was the same in Angola and Mozambique, two of the region's Portuguese colonies, and in Rhodesia, a British colony where the white settler population had unilaterally declared independence in 1965.

Following a wave of decolonization in the late 1950s and 1960s, armed struggles sought liberation from white minority and colonial rule in Angola, Mozambique, Rhodesia, and South Africa and a number of other states in the region earned their independence: Tanzania (1961), Zambia (1964), Malawi (1964), Botswana (1966), and the small enclave kingdoms of Lesotho (1966) and Swaziland (1968). It is not necessary to go into the details of what kind of colonial arrangements they were subjected to by the British (colony, protectorate, and so on) or the complicated constitutional arrangements in the years immediately before the transfer of power. British colonial agreements at the formal level can give the impression that there was power sharing between the representatives of London and the indigenous authorities. In the post–World War II period, when it appeared that decolonization would be inevitable, the British engaged with political movements to prepare the colonies gradually for independence. Britain in many ways was successful in managing the decolonization process to suit its political and economic interests.[18] By the mid-1960s all its former colonies were independent.

One effect of independence was that the new presidents and dominant parties (usually the former liberation movements) in these now-sovereign states could make their own decisions, such as whom to host on their soil and whom to recognize politically. Independent Zambia, under Kenneth Kaunda, and Tanzania, under Julius Nyerere, would thus come to play an important role in offering bases to resistance movements such as the African National Congress (ANC) of South Africa and the Frente de Libertação de Moçambique (FRELIMO) fighting the Portuguese in Mozambique. Indeed, FRELIMO was founded in Tanzania in 1962.

The alteration of the region's colonial landscape was not, however, achieved through any unique or coordinated action on the side of the liberation movements. They were motivated by a common purpose and supported each other whenever necessary, but their unity of purpose did not propel them to a new level of struggle that would lead to independence. Dramatic political change in Portugal in the early 1970s was of crucial significance. This was entirely unpredictable. The long dictatorship in Portugal—Estado Novo, which began in 1933—was overthrown in the so-called carnation revolution in 1974. This is not, however, the place to elaborate on the complex forces that brought about this change, which resulted in the rapid dissolution of Portugal's African empire.

The liberation movements in the two southern African Portuguese colonies, Angola and Mozambique, had fought a brutal guerrilla war through the mid- to late 1960s, and they finally achieved independence a year after the overthrow of the dictatorship in Lisbon. The year 1975, which saw independence for the Portuguese colonies, was a turning point for the region. If the dictatorship in Portugal had not been overthrown, then the liberation movements in the colonies would have had a much longer, bloodier fight. Portugal was the last European colonial power and the poorest to have colonies in Africa. The whole of southern Africa would change with the break in the last and weakest link in the colonial system.

This was the era of the Cold War, and national liberation movements were viewed in the West, most strongly in the United States, as part of a global communist project. Cuban military support for liberation movements, including military deployment in Angola, and the Soviet Union's support of these movements were seen as evidence of a communist alliance that expressed the true nature of the nationalist movements.[19] Everything had to be done to prevent genuine national liberation. Angola had a number of competing liberation movements— Movimento Popular de Libertação de Angola (MPLA), Frente Nacional de Libertação de Angola (FNLA), União Nacional pela Independência Total de Angola (UNITA)—and the United States used this competition to destabilize the country at the time of independence. Its purpose was to frustrate the chances of the communist bloc gaining an ally in southern Africa. In Angola the United States and later South Africa would join forces with UNITA in the southeastern part of the country. In Mozambique FRELIMO would shortly face similar destabilization from a group called Resistencia Nacional Mocambicana (RENAMO), which was supported by the Rhodesian and South African governments. But the liberation of Angola and Mozambique had profound implications for the struggle against the apartheid regime in South Africa.[20]

In South Africa the historic victories against Portuguese colonialism were viewed with fear by the white minority but celebrated by the black population. Black students held rallies in various South African cities to celebrate the liberation of Angola and Mozambique. But the real emergence of youth onto the political landscape in South Africa happened with the uprising across the country that began in June 1976 in the sprawling townships known as Soweto. From here protests spread, and students organized and fought police and security forces. If 1975 was the *external* turning point for the region that created a space for the armed wing of the liberation struggle in South Africa, then the events that started in Soweto in June 1976 represent the *internal* turning point. Since the massacre at Sharpeville and the subsequent banning of the major political movements such as the ANC in 1961, protest inside South Africa had been minimal. The state repressed its opponents more rigorously in the 1960s than it ever had before. The South African liberation movements had started their armed struggle in the early 1960s but to little effect; with the liberation of Angola and Mozambique they were able to establish military camps closer to home. After Soweto, thousands of youth left the country to join the armed struggle.[21]

In 1979 and 1980 the white minority in Rhodesia finally gave in to the forces of liberation led by the Zimbabwean African National Union (ZANU) and the Zimbabwean African People's Union (ZAPU), and an independent Zimbabwe was born. Only SWA and South Africa remained in white minority hands. The South West African People's Organization (SWAPO) had conducted a guerrilla war against the South African Defense Force (SADF) from Angola since the 1960s. In pursuit of the SWAPO guerrillas the SADF entered Angola in 1975 in an undeclared "border war" that brought thousands of young white conscripts to fight. The SADF had been engaged in skirmishes across the border since the mid-1960s, but the mid-1970s saw a larger military engagement, which escalated over the following decade. This locked South Africa into an undeclared war on foreign territory where it supported a faction among the Angolans in an attempt to forestall independence in SWA and contain Angola's communist regime. But eventually, in 1989, SWA won its independence and was reborn as Namibia.

Following the liberation of the Portuguese colonies (1975), the Soweto uprising (1976), and the liberation of Zimbabwe (1980), the South African state gradually concluded that there had to be some reform of the apartheid system. While the racists remained committed to the apartheid system, they looked for ways to reform aspects of it. Sections of the capitalist class also realized the need to "adapt or die" if capitalism were to survive. They pursued a campaign of counterinsurgency and military superiority against the newly liberated frontline states. They fought a long border war against Angola and supported movements to overthrow the governments in Angola and Mozambique.

Internally, the state modified some apartheid laws and began complicated programs to convince the oppressed population that the system was improving. This strategy, of course, did not work. During the 1980s the resistance to apartheid became even more extensive, and increased pressure was exerted on the white minority by the international community through boycott and divestment campaigns.

Freedom for the frontline states, together with the Soweto uprising, defined the period from 1975 to 1980. The revolutions in Angola and Mozambique and the events of Soweto did not bring the apartheid state down but played a major role in its demise. The capitalist class knew that, from then on, there was no going back to the system of racial capitalism that had been in place for decades. By 1988 the state was talking to Nelson Mandela in prison about his release, as well as about permitting political movements such as the ANC and eventually starting negotiations.[22] The period of negotiations was filled with tension and violence as the talks started and ended and restarted and broke down amid distrust and various attempts to frustrate the process, until finally a date for the country's first democratic elections was set and the writing of the country's constitution began. The story of the events that led to the first democratic elections in 1994 is now well-known. The new constitution was only completed and ratified by the new democratic national assembly two years later in 1996.

Comparisons on a Continent

The two regions of Africa we have looked at here are not only at two opposite ends of the continent, they have very different histories and patterns of political and economic development. From Morocco to Egypt there is a centuries-long tradition of Islam (overwhelmingly Sunni) and Arabic culture, with substantial numbers of people between Morocco and Algeria who speak Berber dialects. French colonial penetration began in Egypt in 1798 and in Algeria in 1830. It would dominate the entirety of North Africa except for Tripoli, which was conquered by Italy in 1911, and Egypt, a country with substantial French cultural influence, British rule, and a monarchy with Ottoman origins. Independence came through armed insurrection in Algeria (1962), through a military takeover in Egypt (1952), and through negotiation elsewhere.

At the other end of the continent, southern Africa experienced Dutch, British, and Portuguese colonial rule, starting in the Cape in 1652 and elsewhere through the course of the nineteenth century. Southern Africa was culturally and linguistically more diverse than North Africa. The discovery of diamonds and gold from the 1860s onward deeply affected the patterns of colonial domination and the later politics of resistance. The existence of an extractive economy and the large number of rural dwellers who were forced to provide cheap labor in the mines was very different from the situation in North Africa.[23]

Decolonization in North Africa took place from the early 1950s to 1962; in South Africa it reached its climax with the first democratic elections in 1994—more than thirty years after the French left Algeria. The North African states, on the whole, showed practical and symbolic solidarity with the struggles for independence in southern Africa. Egypt, under Nasser, hosted many liberation movements. Algeria aided these movements materially, and Algiers was a major supporter of liberation movements in southern Africa. Other North African states did not establish diplomatic relations with South Africa until after the end of apartheid.

However, by the turn of the century all the Arab states had ruling elites who had lost the legitimacy that came with the independence struggles. Cronyism, corruption, persistent economic problems, and a lack of genuine democratic governance spawned the movements and popular dissent that led to the so-called Arab Spring. The Palestinian issue remains unresolved with Arab states giving only rhetorical support to the cause of Palestinian liberation. This still remains a crucial factor in the politics of the region, just as apartheid in South Africa remained central to the politics of the larger southern Africa region after other countries were freed of minority rule.

The Arab Spring began in December 2010 in Tunisia, a country where change was least expected. It spread to Egypt, Libya, and throughout North Africa—except Algeria, where it may still come—and was taken up in Syria but then turned into a deeply sectarian, foreign-dominated conflict. In the first half of 2013, despite the elections in Tunisia, Egypt, and Libya, subsequent events in these countries indicate that the future of the Arab Spring remains uncertain. The military took center stage in July 2013 in Egypt, unseated the country's first democratically elected president, massacred hundreds of protesters, banned the Muslim Brotherhood, and imprisoned thousands of people.

There are considered in this essay a concatenation of events in southern Africa as a basis for comparative African reflection. Detienne has recently argued, "Comparables cannot be constructed without experimentation."[24] The plea of this essay is for comparative thinking that transcends the Sahara Desert and looks across the borders of nation-states for a basis for African renewal.

Notes

1. For useful overviews of the events described in this paragraph see Thurston and Lebovich, *Handbook on Mali's 2012–2013 Crisis*; Lindberg, *War in Mali*; Wooten, "Mali, March 2012."

2. CNN International, "Zimbabweans Found Guilty of Watching Arab Spring Videos."

3. BBC News Africa, "Senegal 'Set for Abdoulaye Wade–Macky Sall Run-Off.'"

4. This Wikipedia article gives some idea of protests in Sudan: "Protests in Sudan (2011–Present)," http://en.wikipedia.org/wiki/Protests_in_Sudan_(2011–present).

5. But in 1989 there was a coup d'état led by Omar El-Bashir, who remains in power. Salih, "The Sudan, 1985–9: The Fading Democracy."

6. See excellent coverage of the Palestine *intifadah* in the *Journal of Palestine Studies* from 1988 onward.

7. During the mid- to late 1980s in South Africa, as uprisings spread through the country, activists occasionally used the word *intifadah* to describe those events. The word had been learned from the international media coverage of the events in Palestine and by activists who had strong sympathies for the Palestinian struggle.

8. Kepel, *Prophet and the Pharaoh*, 191–222.

9. Martinez, *The Algeria Civil War, 1990–1998*; Roberts, *Battlefield of Algeria*.

10. Lindsey, "Et Tu Sonallah?"

11. El-Mahdi and Marfleet, *Egypt: The Moment of Change*.

12. Roberts, "Who Said Gaddafi Had to Go?"

13. Bamyeh, "Anarchist Method, Liberal Intention, Authoritarian Lesson."

14. Roberts, "Who Said Gaddafi Had to Go?"

15. Meyer, *Persistence of the Old Regime*.

16. Bamyeh, "Anarchist Method," 1–15.

17. Rapport, *1848: Year of Revolution*; Sperber, *European Revolutions, 1848–1851*; Donald and Rees, *Reinterpreting Revolution in Twentieth-Century Europe*.

18. Darwin, *Britain and Decolonization*.

19 Gleijeses, *Conflicting Missions*.

20. Baines and Vale, *Beyond the Border War*; Saunders and Sapire, *Liberation Struggles in Southern Africa*.

21. Lodge, *Black Politics in South Africa since 1945*.

22. Mandela, *Long Walk to Freedom*, 352.

23. See Amin, "Underdevelopment and Dependence in Black Africa."

24. Detienne, *Comparing the Incomparable*, xiv.

Bibliography

Amin, Samir. "Underdevelopment and Dependence in Black Africa-Origins and Contemporary Forms." *Journal of Modern African Studies* 10, no. 4 (December 1972): 503–24. www .jstor.org/stable/160011.

Baines, Gary, and Peter Vale, eds. *Beyond the Border War: New Perspectives on Southern Africa's Late-Cold War Conflicts*. Pretoria: Unisa, 2008.

Bamyeh, Mohamed A. "Anarchist Method, Liberal Intention, Authoritarian Lesson: The Arab Spring between Three Enlightenments." *Constellations* 20, no. 2 (June 2013): 1–15.

BBC News Africa. "Senegal 'Set for Abdoulaye Wade–Macky Sall Run-Off.'" February 27, 2012. www.bbc.co.uk/news/world-africa-17176798.

CNN International. "Zimbabweans Found Guilty of Watching Arab Spring Videos." March 19, 2012. http://edition.cnn.com/2012/03/19/world/africa/zimbabwe-video-arrests/.

Darwin, John. *Britain and Decolonization*. Basingstoke: Macmillan, 1988.

Detienne, Marcel. *Comparing the Incomparable*. Translated by Janet Lloyd. Stanford: Stanford University Press, 2008.

Donald, Moira, and Tim Rees, eds. *Reinterpreting Revolution in Twentieth-Century Europe*. Basingstoke: Macmillan, 2001.

El-Mahdi, Raba, and Philip Marfleet. *Egypt: The Moment of Change*. London: Zed, 2009.

Gleijeses, Piero. *Conflicting Missions*. Chapel Hill: University of North Carolina Press, 2002.

Kepel, Gilles. *The Prophet and the Pharaoh*. London: Al Saqi, 1985.

Lindberg, Emy. *War in Mali: Background Study and Annotated Bibliography, July 2012–March 2013*. Occasional Paper, Nordiska Afriainstitutet, June 2013.

Lindsey, Ursula. "Et Tu Sonallah?" *The Arabist* (blog), August 25, 2013. http://arabist.net /blog/2013/8/25/et-tu-sonallah.

Lodge, Tom. *Black Politics in South Africa since 1945*. London: Longman, 1983.

Mandela, Nelson. *Long Walk to Freedom*. Randburg: Macdonald Purnell, 1994.

Martinez, Luis. *The Algeria Civil War, 1990–1998*. New York: Columbia University Press, 2000.

Meyer, Arno. *The Persistence of the Old Regime*. New York: Pantheon, 1981.

Rapport, Mike. *1848: Year of Revolution*. London: Abacus, 2009.

Roberts, Hugh. *The Battlefield of Algeria, 1988–2002*. New York: Verso, 2003.

————. "Who Said Qaddafi Had to Go?" *London Review of Books* 33, no. 22 (November, 17 2011). www.lrb.co.uk/v33/n22/hugh-roberts/who-said-Qaddafi-had-to-go.

Salih, Oman. "The Sudan, 1985–9: The Fading Democracy." *Journal of Modern African Studies* 28, no. 2 (June 1990): 199–224.

Saunders, Christopher, and Hilary Sapire. *Liberation Struggles in Southern Africa: New Local, Regional, and Global Perspectives*. Cape Town: UCT Press, 2012.

Skocpol, Theda. *States and Social Revolutions: A Comparative Analysis of France, Russia, and China*. New York: Cambridge University Press, 1979.

Sperber, Jonathan. *The European Revolutions, 1848–1851*. New York: Cambridge University Press, 1994.

Thurston, Alexander, and Andrew Lebovich. *A Handbook on Mali's 2012–2013 Crisis*. Northwestern University Program of African Studies, Isita Working Paper Series No. 13–001, September 2013.

Williams, David. *On the Border: The White South African Military Experience, 1965–1990*. Cape Town: Tafelberg, 2008.

Wooten, Stephen. "Mali, March 2012." Field Sites—Hot Spots. *Cultural Anthropology Online*, June 2013. www.culanth.org/fieldsights/308-mali-march-2012.

2

Gathering the Pieces

The Structural, Social, and Psychological Elements of African Renewal

DON FOSTER

E valuations of Africa are dominated by doomsayers. Optimists are in a minority and the majority of global analysts give little serious attention to Africa. Even those with compassion and concern for the roughly nine hundred million people and fifty-four nation-states composing Africa have negative expectations for the future of the continent. These include renowned scholars such as Martin Meredith, who concludes his excellent history of the fifty years of African independence by arguing thus: "In reality, fifty years after the beginning of the independence era, Africa's prospects are bleaker than ever before."[1] Pierre Englebert, an equally well-published analyst of the African state, observes: "Despite its good intentions, granting sovereignty to Africa's post-colonies has been poisonous to Africans."[2]

Then there are the views of commentators who balance hope and realism in assessing the fortunes of Africa. They include scholars such as Steven Radelet and Robert Rotberg as well as political figures such as Kofi Annan, former secretary-general of the United Nations (UN), and Nkosazana Dlamini-Zuma, current chairperson of the African Union (AU). In delivering the Desmond Tutu lecture, Kofi Annan observed: "Africa is a continent with tremendous resources, but none more than the talent of its young people. . . . [T]hey care deeply about our world, and are actively engaged in fostering positive changes. With courage and vision Africa can ensure a stable, prosperous and equitable society."[3]

"Walk with us and listen," as Villa-Vicencio reminds us in the title of his book on reconciliation.[4] It is a plea for understanding and solidarity rather than the usual imposition of solutions from the outside. A less usual approach, one suggested by Fathali Moghaddam, is to examine the psychological factors that inhibit or facilitate the development of democracy on the continent.[5]

The ordinary people of Africa deserve much better than the lot dealt by colonial conquest, the Cold War, structural adjustment programs, and neoliberalism, along with authoritarian and dictatorial leadership. There is little doubt that the events dubbed the Arab Spring and ideas related to an African Renaissance, have, if nothing else, given many people hope of a real turning point rather than another false dawn.

Systematic Challenges

Despite the undeniable upswing and signs of the long-awaited "rebirth," there are also enormous challenges, difficulties, and problems. The list of problems in various parts of the continent is lengthy and real: climate change, issues related to geography (landlocked countries and droughts), degraded infrastructure, poor education, disease, wars and continuing strife, crime, insecurity, poverty, and rampant corruption.

In the Mothers' Index produced by Save the Children, African countries fill the bottom 12 places of 176 listed countries.[6] Among the lowest 26 countries, 22 are African. The highest ranked African country is Tunisia at 56, with Libya at 57 and then South Africa, the third highest in Africa, at 77. Child mortality rates in Africa are the highest in the world—among the highest are Angola (158 deaths per thousand live births), Central African Republic (164), Chad (169), Democratic Republic of the Congo (168), and Sierra Leone (185)—while Finland, Sweden, and Norway record three deaths per thousand live births. Schooling is limited: nearly one in two African girls drops out of school, and only about 4 percent make it to university. Many African states have few women in national government and low participation of women in public life.

Suffice it to say, Africa has long been the victim of imperialism, authoritarianism, kleptocracy, and dictatorship. This makes the demands for democracy and accountable governance vitally important.

The Arab Spring

Demonstrations and demands for change in 2011 spread, with differing degrees of intensity, through Algeria, Lebanon, Jordan, Mauritania, Sudan, Oman, Yemen, Libya, Morocco, Western Sahara, Saudi Arabia, and the United Arab Emirates.

There were differences in the uprisings, but they had three things in common. Firstly, all were in support of democracy and against authoritarian and dictatorial rule. Secondly, protesters were—in the main—educated, young, and broadly middle class, but often unemployed and impoverished. Both men and women participated, but in some cases where regime change occurred, women were excluded from the interim governments that were put in place. Formal political parties and groupings were often ignored and bypassed in the political uprisings in the Arab Spring countries, largely because of a lack of trust in these structures. Thirdly, and perhaps most importantly for understanding the dynamics of these social movements, all were mediated by social media networks. Mobile phones, Twitter, the Internet, YouTube, videos, WikiLeaks, and Facebook groups were all brought into play by a younger group of smart women and men who feel at ease in everyday life with these new communication technologies. Videos of state brutality spread rapidly through networks. The television network Al Jazeera played a major role, "communicating in Arabic that the unthinkable was happening," with the impact of the social media well captured in the title of Manuel Castells's book: *Networks of Outrage and Hope.*[7]

Two years on, some of the energy and a lot of the optimism have drained from the potential of the Arab Spring. Syria is locked in a deadly civil war, outside interventions have failed, and the death toll mounts alarmingly. Tunisia is engaged in protracted negotiations between the coalition Islamic government and the secular opposition groups. Libya is struggling to contain rival rebel groups and militias. In Morocco reforms have been modest. In Egypt the situation has gone backward after the July 3, 2013, coup d'état by the military that removed democratically elected Mohamed Morsi from power.

The African Renaissance

Like the Arab Spring, the concept of an African Renaissance is a source of optimism, despite the setbacks it has experienced. In a similar vein, it has been dented but not quite crushed. The notion of an African Renaissance is not entirely new, having been given first airing in the wake of the independence of a string of African states in the 1960s. More recently it was prompted by President Nelson Mandela soon after the euphoria of democratic elections in South Africa in April 1994 and at an Organization of African Unity (OAU) summit in June 1994. Thabo Mbeki drove the idea forward in an endeavor to reverse the negative stereotype of Africa and Africans. His words provide a clear and bold picture of the intended Renaissance: "The new African world which the African renaissance seeks to build is one of democracy, peace and stability, sustainable development and a better life for the people, nonracism and nonsexism, equality among the nations, and a just and democratic system of international governance. None of this will come about of its own. In as much as we liberated ourselves from colonialism through struggle, so will it be that the African renaissance will be victorious only as a result of a protracted struggle that we ourselves must wage."[8]

Mbeki boldly called on Africans to be "ready and willing to be rebels against tyranny, instability, corruption and backwardness," and he further called for the "cancellation of Africa's foreign debt, and an improvement in terms of international trade."[9]

Developments in Africa

There have been a number of false dawns, and ordinary African people have borne the brunt of these disappointments. But a solid body of evidence now points to positive milestones for Africa on a range of topics including governance, economics, and human development. However, a number of challenges still remain, including a shallow skills base, communication limitations, demographic growth, and a lack of modern infrastructure—as well as climate change that not only ravages the geography of African states in the Sahel, the Horn of Africa, and elsewhere but also results in massive political destabilization.[10] The following sections briefly examine the state of development in Africa.

Governance

The Ibrahim Index of African Governance is a useful tool for assessing the performance of fifty-four states across Africa (for unknown reasons both Sudan and South Sudan are not included).[11] The 2013 report gives an overall score per country, derived from ninety-four indicators in four main categories: "Safety and Rule of Law," "Participation and Human Rights," "Sustainable Economic Opportunity," and "Human Development." It also tracks changes in performance from 2000 to 2012. The picture is one of progress, with forty-six of fifty-two countries showing improved scores during this period. The only decline is in the category of "Safety and Rule of Law," where the overall average score has dropped since 2000.

Reflecting on the index, Robert Rotberg reminds us that governance involves more than holding of elections. Effective governance includes service delivery as the basis for improvements in the lives of citizens, and states high on the index have also moved away from dictatorial rule (Table 2.1).

Economics

Economic growth has increased sharply over the past decade. This is perhaps the most striking sign of improvement in Africa's fortunes. The International Monetary Fund (IMF) has evaluated the past ten to fifteen years as being the best ever for sub-Saharan Africa. The last two or three years have seen overall growth rates, fueled by a commodities boom, at roughly 5 percent per annum, which is akin to the takeoff rates in Asia some thirty years ago. Nigeria, which has a population of about 170 million people, showed a growth rate in gross domestic product (GDP) averaging 6.8 percent between 2005 and 2013. Rwanda expected to see economic

TABLE 2.1
Best and Worst Performers: Index of African Governance, 2013

Top 12 States	Score (maximum) 100	Bottom 12 States	Score (maximum 100)
1. Mauritius	82.9	• 41. Nigeria	43.4
2. Botswana	77.6	42. Guinea	43.2
3. Cape Verde	76.7	43. Congo	43.0
4. Seychelles	75.0	44. Côte d'Ivoire	40.9
5. South Africa	71.3	45. Equatorial Guinea	40.9
6. Namibia	69.5	46. Guinea-Bissau	37.1
7. Ghana	66.8	47. Zimbabwe	35.4
8. Tunisia	66.0	48. Chad	33.0
9. Lesotho	61.9	49. Central African Republic	32.7
10. Senegal	61.0	50. Eritrea	31.9
11. São Tomé	59.9	51. Democratic Republic of Congo	31.3
12. Zambia	59.6	52. Somalia	8.0

growth of 7.5 percent in 2013 and hoped for more than 8 percent in 2014, helped by "strong exports and the restoration of aid."

Despite the terrorist attack in Nairobi on September 21, 2013, the Kenyan growth target for 2013 remained unchanged at between 5.5 and 6 percent. Growth of this sort ought to enable improvements in both infrastructure and human development; some of the growth results from trade within Africa, providing an added benefit.

Imports from other parts of Africa into South Africa, almost negligible in the early 1990s, increased by nearly 30 percent between 1994 and 2012. While recognizing that many African countries have a small economic base, many economists are optimistic that, correctly managed, current trends could be the beginning of an economic renaissance on the continent. The IMF, in forecasts for the next few years, suggests that nearly half of all the African states will achieve growth rates above 3.5 percent. At the top of this IMF list are Mozambique and the DRC at over 8 percent; the Ivory Coast, Ethiopia, and Rwanda at over 7 percent; and a whole string of countries including Tanzania, Uganda, Ghana, Malawi, and Kenya at more than 6 percent. The North African states of Egypt, Algeria, and Morocco also reflect a growth rate above 3.5 percent. The standout downward trend is in South Africa, whose growth rate is currently below 3 percent and is forecast to remain at much the same level for the foreseeable future.[12]

Communications

As the Arab Spring demonstrated, new communication technologies can have a substantial impact on social change. The weaker the state, the greater the need for citizens to access, use, and control information. The use of mobile phones across Africa has grown at an extraordinary rate. In 1999 less than 10 percent of people in Africa (mainly those living in South Africa and Senegal) were users of mobile phones, but by 2012 this had increased to roughly 66 percent of the population of the continent, with over 500 million users. The potential for development is considerable. At this stage, however, the use of the Internet via computers is more limited, with only roughly 5 percent of people in sub-Saharan Africa having viable access to computers.

Demographics

Population growth in Africa is likely to have a major impact on development. Unless economic growth exceeds population growth, situations across Africa will decline further. There are population estimates that suggest the continent will be home to 10 billion people by the end of the century. Africa is urbanizing at a rapid rate, cities are expanding, and an estimated 60 percent of Africans will live in cities by 2050, posing questions as to whether the continent will meet the educational and employment challenges that will result from this growth. Some estimates anticipate a Nigerian population of 750 million people by 2050, which would make Nigeria's population one of the largest in the world. Other estimates indicate the projected population growth in several African countries:

Mozambique: from 23 million at present to 77 million
Zimbabwe: from 10 million to 21 million
Zambia: from 13 million to 140 million
Democratic Republic of the Congo: from 66 million to 212 million
Malawi: from 15 million to 129 million

According to these estimates, South Africa's birth rate will not grow significantly, although the influx of people from other African countries is likely to continue at an alarming rate.

Infrastructure

Population growth requires infrastructure development: water and sanitation, food security, energy, arteries of communication, commerce, schools, and clinics and hospitals. Approximately 70 percent of people in sub-Saharan Africa have no access to proper sanitation, 40 percent lack good sources of potable water, and about half of Africa is often deprived of water as a result of droughts. All these issues heighten the vulnerability of people in this region to disease. On the energy front, only about half of the people in sub-Saharan Africa have consistent connections to electricity. Only in the past few years has Africa begun to invest in large-scale energy-generating capacity. On the positive side, there have been discoveries of natural gas off the coast of Africa as well as new discoveries of oil and coal. Recent years have also seen large dam-building and hydro projects as part of a new resolve to address energy limitations.

Enter the Chinese, who provide further reason for renewed belief in African economic growth. Rotberg refers to a "happy synergy" between Africa and China.[13] If Africa's basic infrastructure and development is to catch up with other parts of the word, it will be thanks to Chinese investment, skills, technology, and labor, as China needs energy resources and other commodities that Africa has. This is pushing up the prices of natural resources. Three-quarters of all Chinese investment in Africa is for the construction of infrastructure and roads, rail, harbors, dams, bridges, buildings, and hydro schemes—with more than a million Chinese people working in Africa. Indeed, more Chinese have been working in Africa in the past decade than the number of Europeans who have worked in Africa over the past four hundred years. Clearly this includes a downside, with China needing to hire more African people in its workforce. Africa will need to manage this process with diplomatic, political, and economic care. The standard Western cynicism concerning Chinese involvement in Africa is, however, giving way to a measure of realism that recognizes China is helping to address Africa's infrastructural needs.

The upside of economic growth in Africa is an emerging middle class—a status that acts as a catalyst in drawing Africans into the commercial life of their respective countries. Importantly, they become more politically engaged, demanding better service delivery and beginning to hold political leaders to standards of responsible governance and transparency. Furthermore, they are exposed to the global media. Over 60 percent of Africans have access to cell phones, and the majority of urban dwellers are able to view television networks that include Al Jazeera and SABC Africa, as well as CNN, BBC, and Sky News. Africans are beginning to feel part of the global village, they are aware of prodemocracy movements around the world, and they are able to give their children, including more girls, access to education. As a result of protests and demands made by citizens who are aware of their rights and are beginning to claim them, gender-based violence is increasingly being exposed and addressed.

Psychological Dimension of Social Change

Freud was one of the first to put a psychological spoke in the political wheel in a 1933 essay on the "question of a *Weltanschauung*."[14] Indignant about the Russian experiment of communism and critical of the Marxist overemphasis on economic factors, Freud exclaimed: "It is altogether incomprehensible how psychological factors can be overlooked." Skeptical of communist claims of social transition, he suggested that "a transformation of human nature such as this is highly improbable," concluding that social change cannot succeed without harnessing deep-seated psychological aspects of existence. He noted that "a sweeping alteration of the social order has little prospect of success until new discoveries have increased our control over the forces of nature and so made easier the satisfaction of our needs."[15] Africa, like so many countries recovering from exploitation and trauma, is faced with inevitable and persistent psychological impediments.

Eighty years have passed since Freud wrote his *New Introductory Lecture*. This baton has now passed to Fathali Moghaddam.[16] Reminding us that dictatorship, not democracy, is the norm of history, Moghaddam has identified some key social psychological factors that inhibit democratic tendencies and carry within themselves the capacity to plunge countries back into dictatorship.[17] These factors include the following:

- *Perceived threats to society or to a particular group*, arising from politico-economic uncertainty and instability. The new ruling elite demand obedience and conformity. Minority and vulnerable groups, in turn, resist. As a result, those who stand to benefit from the new order support authoritarian rule and do not tolerate dissent. Moghaddam argues that such threats are exacerbated by accelerating globalization, which results in contact between new groups of people who have had little prior contact.[18] The newcomers are different, not fitting into the preconceived culture demanded by the elite. The results of such contact range from xenophobia in South Africa in recent years to a Norwegian extremist shooting more than 70 people and citing the imagined threat of an "Islamic invasion" as justification for what he did.
- *Situational factors that promote dictatorship* as the best solution to overcome current social problems. Important groups with influence and resources, such as portions of the business sector, the military, and/or religious groups, promote dictatorship. The "key feature of these groups/institutions is that they enforce continuity of styles of meaning-making and behaviours that support dictatorship."[19]
- *The psychological process of categorization and its consequences*, such as exaggeration of between-group differences (for example, stereotyping and discrimination) and in-group favoritism. Categorization results in processes of ethnocentrism that separates in-groups from out-groups. Dictatorships shape citizens to be intolerant of difference in general and of out-groups in particular. This is spurred on by authoritarian tactics and categorical thinking, which gives rise to the "*we* are right; *they* are wrong" syndrome.[20]
- *Potential dictator figures.* By using psychological and material resources to benefit certain groups to the exclusion of others, emerging dictators promise

the "birth," "revival," or "resurrection" of a new social order. Leadership elites clearly vary in their ability to exploit and activate these psychological factors; Africa has produced an abundance of dictators adept at such behavior. Moghaddam writes of the operation of these factors as the "springboard model of dictatorship." This model gives priority to contextual and situational processes in contrast to traditional reductionist approaches that are individualist and focus on personality and intrapersonal traits.

Moghaddam's model warns us of the need for vigilance within the context of social change. Considering societies in transition, such as Egypt and South Africa, Moghaddam invokes the old adage "the more things change, the more they stay the same." This is the "paradox of revolution." Leaders change and political parties change, but corruption, inequality, poverty, and hardship for the masses remain much as before—which is the case in Egypt, South Africa, and elsewhere on the continent. In the process of change the gap between the elite and poor escalates and mistrust increases.

Setting out a wider model of social transition, Moghaddam distinguishes between three types of rule.[21] A *first-order system* exists when both formal law and other informal norms of society endorse group-based inequalities and injustices. A prime example is apartheid South Africa. A *second-order system* exists where constitutional and legal platforms suggest the possibility of democratic change and in so doing heighten expectations, while the informal values and norms of everyday life continue to support sexism, racism, and ethnocentrism. This is a situation prevalent in contemporary South Africa. The ideal form of transition is a *third-order system* in which formal legal structures and informal norms support justice, fairness, tolerance, and nondiscrimination. This, Moghaddam argues, "is an ideal not achieved by any major society." Decidedly, there are no instances of this level of rule in Africa.

Change within a system is clearly easier to achieve than change between systems, such as a shift from a first-order to a second-order system. Leaders might change while institutions continue to reflect the old order. Between-system change requires a high degree of psychological dexterity to enable institutional and attitudinal change. This involves crosscutting categorization, acceptance of ambiguity and uncertainty, and the toleration of difference. It entails a change in human relations such as gender equality, acceptance of out-groups, equal voice for minority groups, and shared living spaces. Between-system change necessitates new forms of social consciousness (and conscience) in order to enable and maintain the new system. Many revolutions, such as those involved in the Arab Spring and in African independence in the 1960s, are important steps in a renewal process. They appeared to be far-reaching at the time of their occurrence, when regime change followed. Often, however, they failed to produce a change in systems. Moghaddam's scheme enables us to think more critically about turning points in Africa and also points to psychological barriers that must be overcome in the struggle for more open and democratic societies.

Leadership

Leadership is vitally important in securing democratic transition and genuine development in Africa. In his recent important summation of the challenges and opportunities in sub-Saharan Africa, Rotberg concludes that "Africa needs a new breed of leaders to prosper."[22]

The dominant African perception of leadership is that of an individual with dominant personality traits—effectively a "big chief." This perception is rooted in the "great man" syndrome involving a charismatic savior figure or superman image. The leader is set apart as one with special skills, often regarded as innate, not unlike the standard model of a genius. For the past seventy years or so empirical psychologists have sought to identify the elusive qualities of charismatic leadership, but that search has ended in failure because they failed to realize that good leadership is fundamentally a group process. Good leaders and group members are bound together in complex relations with deep psychological dimensions.

This identity model of leadership is developed, among others, by Haslam, Reicher, and Platow, who build on the social identity theory of Henri Tajfel.[23] It sees leadership as a group process in which leadership positions are conferred by followers who are engaged in governance as active citizens. Effective leaders thus emerge when there is an appropriate fit between the social identities of both leader and members. The identity model of leadership can be summarized in terms of four effective leadership guidelines:

- *Leaders need to be in-group prototypes*, people who exemplify what their followers can become by appealing to their positive inner values.
- *Leaders need to be in-group champions*, serving the immediate needs of their followers without making enemies of the broader community.
- *Leaders need to be entrepreneurs of identity*, providing different groups in the broader community with a realization of whom and what they can become.
- *Leaders need to create a future identity*, enabling groups to embrace others in creating a new and broader community.

To this end, Haslam, Reicher, and Platow identify three principles of categorization in leadership:[24]

- *"Category boundaries define the size of the mobilization."* If one is attempting to move a nation, then appeals to sectarian, class, or ethnic boundaries alone are inadequate and ineffectual. Leaders need to appeal to the immediate and long-term values of their followers while persuading them to coexist with those who have hitherto not been part of their communities.

- *"Category content defines the direction of mobilization."* How norms and values of a group are defined shapes the kind of actions that are viewed as appropriate. For instance, if the aims and values of a group are prodemocratic, then it would be seen as inappropriate to attack and harm opposition party members.
- *"Category prototypes define who can influence the mobilization."* To move the group, leaders need to be the embodiment of group identity. They also need to identify entrepreneurs among their followers who can assist in the process of group mobilization.

This theoretical discussion is directly relevant to Africa. Firstly, it begins to show why African leaders who cling to narrow sectarian interests have failed to become good national leaders. Secondly, it suggests that good group processes are required to support good leadership. Thirdly, it underlines the importance of Nelson Mandela–type leaders as quintessential models of effective leadership. This is *not* primarily because of the many individual traits that are attributed to Mandela: charisma, charm, presence, skills, compassion, steadfastness, capacity for forgiveness, and so on. He had all these attributes, but the model reminds us that his leadership prowess was derived from his prototypical active membership in a group—the African National Congress (ANC)—and from the values, norms, aims, and goals of the ANC. Remarkably, when Mandela sought to represent these values, he did not do so in an exclusive way, and when he became president of the newly democratic South Africa, he shifted the boundaries of ANC values to include former enemies and others in the quest for a wider sense of national belonging. He changed national goals to embrace democratic institutions and directions. In so doing he infused a global constituency with new hopes and values on the basis of reconciliation and rapprochement. He was an effective leader because he was in tune with the group, changing the group boundaries and prototypes as circumstances shifted. As such, Mandela is the prime exemplar of this theory of leadership and a model for African leadership.

Haslam, Reicher, and Platow draw a clear distinction between the *psychology* of leadership that focuses on inclusivity and shared goals and the *politics* of leadership. They remind us of the difference between *effective* leadership (fascist leaders were, in a distorted way, "effective") and *good* leadership, which creates laudable outcomes. In closing they describe three types of political systems:

- In the fully democratic system, a leader facilitates the debate about whom and what a people can become. The model is of the leader as *guide*.
- In the hierarchical system, the interaction between leader and followers is truncated and asymmetrical, and the leader imposes his values. The model is of the leader as *master*.

- In a dictatorial system, the leader is the sole embodiment of the state. The leader alone is the active decision maker, and the followers are inert. The model is of the leader as *deity* (Mobutu Sese Seko, Hitler, and others).

The potency of the individualistic and heroic model of leadership, as portrayed by Mobutu and others, is often seen to be most appealing when societies fail to meet the challenges of the day and countries are tending toward collapse. In this situation the demand for a heroic savior is most tempting. The tragedy is that this often opens the way for a return to authoritarian and dictatorial systems. This is the case not least in the rise of General Sisi in Egypt, as well as in South Africa's political clamor to find a new "Mandela-type" leader in light of the country's failure to realize all that democracy promised in 1994.

Conclusion

Whither African leadership? There need to be African solutions for African problems and respect for the national sovereignty of African countries. This does not exclude regional and global critique in support of an African commitment to a better life for all the people on the continent. Chapters on the African Renaissance and the African Union in this volume develop this process further.

Does Africa have the capacity to move toward a brighter future? *Yes.* Entrenched dictatorial rule is being challenged in countries across the continent; there are improvements in governance, gains in democracy, better infrastructure, enhanced economic growth, more comprehensive and effective treatment of AIDS, women in some places of leadership, a notable increase in primary education, an emerging middle class, and a youth population that is pressing for change. Is Africa en route to addressing all the challenges it faces? *No.* As long as Africa's strongmen stubbornly cling to power or clamor to seize power, the danger is that authoritarian and dictatorial rule will destroy the hope for renewal in Africa, both North and South. The impediment to political and economic success in Africa is threatened by imposters who hold onto power at the cost of their people. This inspires the kind of uprisings seen in Arab Spring countries and elsewhere in Africa and opens the door to a new phase of malevolent authoritarian rule as oppressive forces attain power in these countries.

The claim of this chapter is that, apart from physical, economic, and governance challenges, there are also deep psychological realties that impede positive development, largely as a result of poor leadership that threatens to turn the clock back on the possibilities of political renewal. Moghaddam is correct: History rarely travels in one direction. Positive gains can unravel, suggesting that it is frighteningly easy for countries to return to dictatorial and authoritarian rule. The eyes of analysts are focused on Tunisia, Egypt, and Libya in North Africa. However,

South Africa and its closest neighbors also face new challenges in the struggle for democracy and renewal as the new elite cling to their newly acquired power. These challenges require urgent attention by both Africa and the rest of the global community.

Notes

1. Meredith, *State of Africa,* 681.
2. Engelbert, *Africa: Unity, Sovereignty and Sorrow,* 261.
3. Annan, "Strong Cohesive Societies."
4. Villa-Vicencio, *Walk with Us and Listen.*
5. Moghaddam, "Springboard to Dictatorship and the Arab Spring," 169–82.
6. Save the Children, "Surviving the First Day: State of the World's Mothers."
7. Castells, *Networks of Outrage and Hope,* 59.
8. Mbeki, "Prologue," xvii.
9. Ibid.
10. Tadesse, *Impact of Climate Change in Africa.* See also Population Action International, "Population, Climate Change, and Sustainable Development in Africa."
11. Mo Ibrahim Foundation, *Ibrahim Index of African Governance 2013.*
12. See also Rose and Teppermann, "Shape of Things to Come."
13. Ibid., 151.
14. Freud, *New Introductory Lectures in Psychoanalysis,* 215–18.
15. Ibid.
16. Moghaddam, *Psychology of Dictatorship.*
17. Moghaddam, "Springboard to Dictatorship and the Arab Spring," 169–82.
18. Moghaddam, *Psychology of Dictatorship,* 204–5.
19. Moghaddam, "Springboard to Dictatorship and the Arab Spring," 176.
20. Ibid.
21. Moghaddam, *Psychology of Dictatorship,* 90–91.
22. Rotberg, *Africa Emerges,* 215.
23. Haslam, Reicher, and Platow, *New Psychology of Leadership,* 68–72; Tajfel, *Human Groups and Social Categories.*
24. Haslam, Reicher, and Platow, *New Psychology of Leadership,* 68–72.

Bibliography

Annan, Kofi. "Strong Cohesive Societies." Third Annual Desmond International Peace Lecture, University of the Western Cape, October 7, 2013.

Castells, Manuel. *Networks of Outrage and Hope: Social Movements in the Internet Age.* Boston: John Wiley, 2012.

Engelbert, Pierre. *Africa: Unity, Sovereignty and Sorrow.* Boulder, CO: Lynne Rienner, 2009.

Freud, Sigmund. *New Introductory Lectures in Psychoanalysis.* 1933. Reprint, Harmondsworth, UK: Penguin, 1973.

Haslam, Alexander, Stephen D. Reicher, and Michael J. Platow. *The New Psychology of Leadership.* New York: Psychology Press, 2011.

Mbeki, Thabo. "Prologue." In *African Renaissance*, edited by Malegapuru William Makgoba. Cape Town: Mafube/Tafelberg, 1999.

Meredith, Martin. *The State of Africa*. London: Free Press, 2004.

Mo Ibrahim Foundation. *Ibrahim Index of African Governance 2013*. www.moibrahimfoundation .org/downloads/2013/2013-IIAG-summary-report.pdf.

Moghaddam, Fathali. *The Psychology of Dictatorship*. Washington, DC: American Psychological Association, 2013.

———. "The Springboard to Dictatorship and the Arab Spring." *SAIS Review* 32, no. 2 (2012): 169–82.

Population Action International, "Population, Climate Change, and Sustainable Development in Africa." *Policy and Issue Brief*, June 2012. http://populationaction.org/wp-content/uploads /2012/06/PAI-AFIDEP.pdf.

Rose, Gideon, and Jonathan Teppermann. "The Shape of Things to Come." *Foreign Affairs*, January/February 2014. www.foreignaffairs.com/articles/140333/gideon-rose-and-jonathan -tepperman/the-shape-of-things-to-come.

Rotberg, Robert I. *Africa Emerges: Consummate Challenges, Abundant Opportunities*. Cambridge: Polity, 2013.

Save the Children. "Surviving the First Day: State of the World's Mothers." 2013. http://www .savethechildren.org/atf/cf/%7B9def2ebe-10ae-432c-9bd0-df91d2eba74a%7D/SOWM-FULL -REPORT_2013.PDF.

Tadesse, Debay. *The Impact of Climate Change in Africa*. Institute for Security Studies, ISS Paper 220, November 2010. www.issafrica.org/uploads/Paper220.pdf.

Tajfel, Henri. *Human Groups and Social Categories*. Cambridge: Cambridge University Press, 1981.

Villa-Vicencio, Charles. *Walk with Us and Listen: Political Reconciliation in Africa*. Amsterdam: KIT, 2009.

3

Understanding a Flawed Miracle

The History, Dynamics, and Continental Implications of South Africa's Transition

CHARLES VILLA-VICENCIO

Asked what enabled South Africans to reach a relatively peaceful settlement that led to the country's first democratic elections in 1994, Archbishop Tutu famously said: "It's a miracle." The settlement also gave rise to the (re)birth of the African Renaissance that took root in African politics and to the birth of the African Union in 2002.

Democratic elections were held in South Africa in 1994 based on the Interim Constitution and a set of constitutional principles; a final constitution was drafted by a postelection constituent assembly, approved by the Constitutional Court, and signed into effect by President Mandela in 1996. The "miracle" is that representatives of a cross section of South African society, torn apart by generations of conflict, exhausted by debilitating armed conflict since 1960, and locked in hard-fought negotiations since 1990, agreed to a political settlement within which South Africans were able to explore the possibility of peaceful coexistence. Not all enemies get that right. Some prefer death.

The settlement most controversially included a conditional amnesty law that continues to be questioned by anti-apartheid campaigners who worked for many years to see the perpetrators of apartheid face criminal charges. International human rights organizations joined the fray in vocal opposition to the amnesty provision. The newly elected democratic government, however, stood firm against critics in their political constituency at home and members of the anti-apartheid community abroad. Dullah Omar, the minister of justice at the time, responded to the criticism, stating: "We are building a future for South Africans [and where] there is conflict between what the international community is saying and what is in the interests of the people of South Africa then I think that we will have to live with that kind of conflict."[1] The transition was an attempt to keep a balance between moral and legal principles on the one hand and peaceful coexistence on the other.

Born in compromise, the future of South Africa is today again at a tipping point. The 1994 settlement provided an opportunity for enemies to make peace. The question is whether the failure to provide a framework for the transformation of institutional economic inequality constitutes a fault line that undermines national reconstruction and the possibility of an enduring peace.

In 2009 the country recorded a Gini coefficient above 63, which, according to *Foreign Policy*, "makes it the third most unequal place on earth."[2] It has one of the biggest gaps between the rich and the poor in the world, bigger than that in Brazil or India. The top 10 percent of the country earns more than 50 percent of household income, and the poorest 20 percent earns less than 1.5 percent. This, together with corruption, government nondelivery, and nationwide protests, accounts for the country's deepest crisis since its democratic transition in 1994. To this we return later in the chapter. Consideration is given in what follows to the South African model of peace building, a retrospective assessment of this settlement, and the possible use of this model for redressing conflict in other parts of the African continent.

A Model of Peace Building

The South African model of political transition and peace building has caught the imagination of exponents of transitional justice and peace building, political analysts, and political conflict management practitioners around the world. It is frequently projected as an example to be adapted if not emulated in conflictual societies around the world. In so doing it is also evoked and interpreted to serve a range of different theoretical academic and political agendas—many of which fail to reflect the complex conditions within which South Africans made peace. An attempt is made in what follows to provide insight into a peace building endeavor within a situation that many saw as intractable. An understanding of these circumstances requires a consideration of the history of social divisions in South Africa, the political context within which the negotiated settlement took place, and the nature of the historic political compromise of the 1990s that emerged from a deal that was struck between the economic and political elites.

A History of Divisions

With a few notable exceptions, resistance to white racism and land deprivation by South Africa's black population was limited to peaceful protests until the African

National Congress (ANC) and Pan Africanist Congress (PAC) were banned in the wake of the Sharpeville massacre in 1960. With all channels for political opposition eliminated, the liberation movements resorted to armed resistance. The ANC launched Umkhonto we Sizwe (Spear of the Nation, MK) and the PAC established Poqo as military wings. The South African Communist Party (SACP), with which the ANC had established a working relationship, had already been banned in 1953.

Ideological differences within the liberation and resistance movements militated against unified opposition to apartheid. This, among other things, led to the establishment of the Black Consciousness Movement under the leadership of Steve Biko in the mid-1960s. Black resistance to apartheid intensified, resulting in the 1973 worker strikes in Durban and the 1976 Soweto student rebellion. The Azanian People's Organisation (AZAPO) was established in 1978, the Congress of South African Students (COSAS) in 1979, the National Union of Mineworkers (NUM) in 1982, the United Democratic Front (UDF) in 1983, the Congress of South African Trade Unions (COSATU) in 1985, and the Mass Democratic Movement (MDM) in 1988.

Importantly, the ANC was in the meantime establishing itself in exile with offices in London, Lusaka, and around the world. It expanded its support inside the country, built solidarity in Africa through the Organisation of African Unity (OAU), and coordinated international opposition to apartheid. Global opposition led to the declaration of apartheid as a crime against humanity by the General Assembly of the United Nations (UN) that came into force in 1976. This, in turn, led to an international arms boycott and investment sanctions against South Africa, which contributed to the collapse of the apartheid regime.

In South Africa forty thousand people were detained in the 1980s. An increasing number of people died in detention, and more and more people joined the armed struggle in exile. Significantly, though, at the same time as the escalation of the violent clashes between the government and the liberation movements, clandestine meetings were being held between government leaders and the ANC. Structured meetings followed, top government officials met with Nelson Mandela, and in December 1988 Mandela was moved from Robben Island to Pollsmoor Prison on the mainland and subsequently to a cottage in the Victor Verster Prison near Paarl, with open telephone lines to consult with ANC colleagues in exile and in South Africa. In March 1989 Mandela wrote to President P. W. Botha, proposing that they meet to discuss the possibility of a negotiated settlement.

The two leaders met in July 1989, and a month after that the ANC committed itself in the Harare Declaration to the possibility of negotiations. A short while later Botha suffered a stroke and was replaced by F. W. de Klerk as party leader of the National Party. De Klerk was subsequently inaugurated as president of the country in September 1989.

Negotiations and Elections

On February 2, 1990, F. W. de Klerk unexpectedly unbanned the political movements and announced that Nelson Mandela would be released from prison after twenty-seven years of incarceration.

At this time the Cold War was also coming to an end. Mikhail Gorbachev informed ANC president Oliver Tambo that the organization should no longer expect material support from the Soviet Bloc. Namibia was on the brink of independence, and the Cubans had agreed to withdraw their forces from Angola. In addition, the Reagan administration in the United States and Margaret Thatcher's government in Britain were placing pressure on the apartheid government to reach a settlement with the country's black majority. Within South Africa the MDM and the UDF called on South Africans "to make the country ungovernable."

When Mandela first met de Klerk in December 1989, shortly before Mandela's release from prison, he saw de Klerk as "a man with whom he could do business," although tensions later developed between them as negotiations unfolded. The heat of disagreement never, however, allowed either to deviate from the end they sought to achieve. This required leadership at all levels of society, in addition to that of Mandela and de Klerk, which eventually led to formal negotiations through the Convention for a Democratic South Africa (CODESA) in which all political groupings in South Africa participated.

Based on the principle of sufficient consensus—designed to ensure that recalcitrant groups could not stall progress—the decision-making power for political transition was vested in the outgoing government and the ANC as the principal negotiators, with the first plenary session of CODESA held on December 20, 1991. The ANC used its popular support and political momentum to influence negotiations, and the government recognized the need to relinquish its chokehold on political power. The ANC saw that with the economic wealth in the hands of white-owned businesses and control of the military and police in the hands of the white government, it would need to shift away from the policies and goals espoused in its prenegotiation days if it were to reach a settlement.

Huge threats to negotiations, however, still lay ahead. Government-sponsored Third Force violence spread across the country. Sixteen black people were killed in Sebokeng, and a further forty people were massacred in Boipatong, which led to the ANC breaking off negotiations with the government. Contacts were, however, maintained, and on September 26, 1992, a record of understanding was reached in the terms of which it was agreed that an election be held on the basis of an interim constitution.

A further disruption to negotiations, without doubt the most explosive of all, came on April 10, 1993, with the assassination of Chris Hani, who was arguably the most popular of the returning exiles, leader of the SACP, and chief of staff of

Umkhonto we Sizwe. This was followed on June 25 by a high-profile armed invasion of the CODESA negotiation venue by the Afrikaner Weerstandsbeweging (AWB). Again, negotiations survived. The Interim Constitution was ratified on December 22, 1993, and the country's first democratic elections were scheduled for April 27, 1994, with constitutional principles allowing for any party that secured 5 percent or more of the vote to have a representative in a Government of National Unity (GNU). The all-white Conservative Party was persuaded by Mandela to participate in the elections, and the PAC reluctantly agreed to take part. The Inkatha Freedom Party agreed to enter the process a mere seven days before the country went to the polls, but AZAPO boycotted the elections.

Elections were held from April 27 to April 29, 1994; Mandela was inaugurated as president on May 10, 1994; and preparations were put in place for the drafting of the constitution. Parliament later passed the Promotion of National Unity and Reconciliation Act, No. 34 of 1995, also known as the Truth and Reconciliation Commission (TRC) Act, with an overwhelming majority.[3] The act included a conditional amnesty for those responsible for human rights abuses between 1960 and 1994.[4] Responding to a legal challenge to the TRC Act brought to the recently established Constitutional Court by AZAPO and others, the late chief justice Ismail Mahomed spoke of the need for both victims and perpetrators to cross the historic bridge from the past to the future, not "with heavy dragged steps delaying and impeding a rapid and enthusiastic transition to the new society at the end of the bridge."[5]

The South African settlement, celebrated around the world as an example of what can be achieved through peaceful negotiations, came at a high cost. The negotiations were difficult. The process came close to collapse on several occasions. The human cost to the country was huge: fourteen thousand people were killed between 1990 and 1993, and more than four thousand were killed in the thirty-two months following the 1994 democratic elections. The threat of more violence and political collapse contributed to a sense of political realism on all sides of a conflict that could so easily have escalated into disaster for the entire country. The imperfect miracle is that the negotiations succeeded.

Political Compromise

Central to the South African settlement was the 1996 Constitution, which reflected the constitutional principles agreed to in 1994, designed "to promote equality . . . and to protect or advance persons or categories of persons disadvantaged by unfair discrimination."[6] It was signed into law by President Mandela in February 1997.

The ANC had in the meantime won 62.65 percent of the vote in the 1994 elections. With this victory came an obligation to govern a country fraught with racism and inequality. It was obliged to work within the GNU to address the expectations of the poor while seeking to reassure all South Africans of their future safety and economic well-being. In seeking to establish itself in its new role, the ANC was motivated by political expediency and its historic commitment to nonracial and nonsexist inclusivity. Its major challenges included the obligation to address the huge economic gap between black South Africans, the majority of whom voted the ANC into power, and wealthy whites. Whites were, in turn, joined by many coloureds and South Africans of Indian extraction who were anxious that their cultural and religious values be protected. The economic challenge was huge. Clearly, a new beginning, as reflected in the recently negotiated economic and minority clauses in the constitution, would not emerge from existing circumstances. Structural transformation that reached to the heart of the nation building process was required. The ANC was concerned that any attempt to protect property rights could undermine the redistribution of wealth. At the same time, they realized that any threat to nationalize parts of the economy would undermine investor confidence. Seeking to address the need both to correct existing inequalities and to grow the economy, the writers of the constitution included a set of socioeconomic clauses designed to empower the underclasses through the right to basic education, access to housing, health care services, food, water, and land. The constitution imposed on the state an obligation to take reasonable legislative and other measures within the confines of a functioning state to realize these rights. This has resulted in a number of Constitutional Court decisions to ensure such a balance is maintained.[7]

The government, importantly, insisted that the socioeconomic principles of the constitution must be supported in the broader economic policy. The ANC, through the Macroeconomic Research Group (MERG), explored a strong interventionist role for the state in economic policy but soon turned to the Reconstruction and Development Programme (RDP), which was later further adjusted in the Growth, Employment and Redistribution (GEAR) policy, designed to liberalize the financial and trade sectors. This policy contributed to the growth of a small black business elite, largely as a result of politically brokered transfers of corporate ownership. The Black Economic Empowerment (BEE) program, criticized for advancing a black elite without sufficient attention being given to the basic needs of the poor, has been reshaped to become the Broad-Based Black Economic Empowerment (BBBEE) program.[8] Government policies continue to be criticized for having deviated from the original focus on poverty relief, job creation, and development.[9]

Another major challenge facing South Africa was the issue of minority rights. This was always going to be an issue in the wake of apartheid, which had focused on racial and cultural differences. The former government eventually dropped its demands for the constitutional protection of minorities in favor of individual rights and the protection of language, culture, and religion. Section 9 of the constitution also makes provision for a human rights commission, a gender equality commission, a public prosecutor, an auditor-general, an independent electoral mommission, an independent authority to regulate broadcasting, and a commission for the promotion and protection of the rights of cultural, religious, and linguistic communities.

The question is whether these initiatives, together with the entrenched right to freedom of speech, freedom of association, and freedom of the press, have succeeded in establishing the kind of open society they were designed to create.

Transition in Retrospect

There are two standard perceptions of the South African settlement; one suggests it was a realistic settlement under the political circumstances and the other proposes that it opened the door to a delayed revolution. Effectively it was a combination of both. The final word, however, is that the 1994 settlement is today under greater threat than it has been since it was first signed.

A Realistic Settlement

The South African settlement was never going to be perfect. Neither side was prepared to surrender to the demands of the other. The settlement did, however, provide a relatively peaceful transition from a white minority government to the beginnings of democratic rule and a negotiated constitution that is held up as an example of what can be achieved in a deeply divided society. The process involved several peace building essentials today recognized as benchmarks for negotiation theory. These include the following:

- *Leadership.* The South African breakthrough in negotiations came as a result of the moral leadership of Nelson Mandela and the pragmatic leadership of President F. W. de Klerk, who convinced whites to accept the proposed settlement. The negotiations, inter alia, led to a settlement that sought to address concerns of minority groups.
- *Ethics and praxis.* The coalescence of ethical imperatives and political realism tempered by realistic decision making allowed for both immediate and future developments that were written into the constitution.
- *Secret and transparent talks.* Secret talks got under way while violence was at its height, with transparent and formal negotiations coming later.
- *Limitation of military action.* Having stretched their fighting capacity to the brink of collapse, both sides turned to the negotiation table. Not all antagonists show this level of pragmatism. Some prefer ashes to survival. Those leading a military campaign need a discerning eye and an analytical mind to negotiate peace.

- *The role of the international community.* After providing decades of de facto support to the apartheid regime, the West eventually forced South Africa's white regime to submit to democratic settlement—but only after major campaigns against apartheid, driven by the ANC and others. The collapse of the Soviet Bloc, in turn, meant that it could no longer offer support to the ANC. The terms of the settlement were, however, negotiated and owned by South Africans who resisted the demands of some international human rights organizations and declined offers of mediation by the United States.[10]
- *Civil society and the media.* Despite facing the threat of closure by the government, civil society and the media monitored and challenged the positions adopted by the government and the liberation movements. This enabled the public to evaluate the behavior of both and to understand the peace settlement when it came.
- *The struggle for the hearts and minds of a nation.* Relentless and courageous critique of the regime led to decreased control over the mindset of white South Africans by government propaganda that had been reinforced by sections of the church and related cultural organizations. The ANC, in turn, presented itself to the country as a viable alternative government. This enabled South Africans to begin to see beyond ideologically imposed perceptions of each other.
- *No reasonable alternative.* Neither side was immune from human rights violations. Both sides acknowledged the country was looking into the abyss; both sides understood the excesses of struggle without condoning them. Ultimately they accepted that a failure to overcome the obstacles to peace would result in an incalculable undermining of their own integrity and their capacity to share in the creation of a peaceful coexistence.

The South African settlement came as a result of an evolving multifaceted strategy, not fully anticipated by either side at any given point in the struggle, that persuaded enemies within South Africa that they needed one another in order to make peace. The anticipated cost of failure was such that neither side could afford not to be part of the settlement. The challenge, twenty years after the country's first democratic election, is to honor the lessons learned in the negotiation process and to develop policy and institutions that turn a negotiated constitution into practice. We know what to do; the challenge is to implement it.

A Revolution Delayed

Govan Mbeki, veteran ANC leader and father of former president Thabo Mbeki, spoke in 1994 of the need to balance "having and belonging" in the nation building process. "For political renewal to endure, the economy needs to be restructured in such a way that the poor and socially excluded begin to share in the benefits of the nation's wealth," he insisted. "People—all people, black and white—also need to feel they are part of a new nation. Those who do not feel welcome or at home . . . will not work for the common good. They can also cause considerable trouble."[11] South Africa has to date failed to grasp the historic opportunity that came in the 1990s, a chance for the country to embrace the promise of a broad and inclusive sense of "having and belonging" that minimized the racial and class differences that had brought the country to the brink of collapse. Despite the changes that have been introduced over the past twenty years, the country faces structural and racial divisions between rich and poor. While a growing black middle class has emerged, most of the poor are black—reflecting a situation similar to that which prevailed in the pre-1994 years. If South Africans are to regain the hope that typified the country at the time of its first democratic elections, legal and institutional interventions, organizational reform, and economic change will be essential. For this to happen, the fractious country needs an urgent injection of moral courage, national dialogue, and exemplary political leadership to transcend the deep structural, racial, and economic divisions that threaten to undermine its transition.

Mandela provided remarkable leadership that promoted inclusion across the political spectrum. His successor, Thabo Mbeki, was required to address economic reconstruction in a more direct manner. Yet this, too, necessitated compromises and trade-offs. "It's a very delicate thing," he observed, "to handle the relationship between these two elements [transformation and reconciliation]. It's not a mathematical thing; it's an art. . . . If you handle the transformation in a way that doesn't change a good part of the status quo, those who are disadvantaged will rebel, and then goodbye reconciliation."

The transformation side of the settlement has been slow. South Africa's liberation-cum-ruling party is plagued by internal decay and corruption, and it has a tendency to dismiss its critics as ultraleftists or counterrevolutionaries. The ANC's shift from social revolution to the promotion and protection of an economic order that benefits whites as well as an emergent and existing black elite has resulted in what is essentially a broadening of an apartheid-era economic policy. This has emerged as a major point of contention in South African politics. Sampie Terreblanche, in his monumental *A History of Inequality in South Africa*, insists that current economic policy is the result of an orchestrated campaign at the time of the country's political negotiations, led by the country's mineral and energy complexes, major corporations, and financial institutions under the influence of white business and international players.[12] Max du Preez states bluntly that the ANC's economic cluster was simply "outgunned" by economists who favored the corporate sector. His essential criticism of the ANC is not that it succumbed to the corporate assault but that it has failed to make use of the "manoeuvring room" subsequently acquired as government to improve the lot of the poor.[13]

Speculation continues concerning the details that persuaded the ANC elite not to honor their commitment to the socioeconomic principles that gave hope to the victims of apartheid who elected them to power.[14] Fearing a major collapse of the economy and political instability in 1994, at the same time they were being promised huge foreign investments and a commitment by the private sector to rebuild society, the ANC abandoned its earlier promises of large-scale nationalization, opting for an economic model of fiscal austerity and redistribution through economic growth that was bolstered by Black Economic Empowerment (BEE) initiatives, government tender procurements, affirmative action, and skills development programs.

The Marxist-Leninist language of the ANC's earlier years was modified soon after the organization was unbanned.[15] ANC leaders returned to the country to take top positions in the country's transitional structures and later in government as well as business. They were determined to provide discipline and direction within the government and among their followers. In so doing they formed the nucleus of a political vanguard that sought to manage and manipulate a political constituency that included hard-line Marxist revolutionaries, anti-Marxist nationalists, emerging black entrepreneurs, and angry young people who had gone into exile to fight for their freedom. The bulk of the ANC's support, however, came from people who simply wanted their most basic material needs to be met and who lacked what the political vanguard saw as class awareness and revolutionary solidarity.

Business, at the same time, accepted the inevitability of political change and looked to the ANC as the ruling party to control the process. The ANC, in turn, needed the support of business to grow the economy, and some of the ANC's leaders and staunchest devotees were drawn into the dominant economy through BEE initiatives. The outcome was a veiled or implicit accord between the two sides that was never fully scripted. Given an uncharted path, both sides accepted that the country's future economy could only emerge in the ensuing years.

A deal was thus struck between economic and political elites, one designed to ensure that the economic fundamentals that benefited both the old wealthy and the emerging new wealthy class remained intact. This opened the way for old and new beneficiaries to enjoy instant gratification and for the poor to become increasingly disenchanted with postapartheid economic policies, despite post-1994 infrastructural benefits and policy reforms. The financial gap between the poor and the ruling elite has increased. The poor have become poorer while the acquisitiveness of sections of the wealthy class is fueled by corruption, cronyism, and political favoritism. This has resulted in growing cynicism among those excluded from the newfound largesse of the 1994 settlement.

Political and business leaders respond by talking of the need for a mixed economy and growth through development amid indications that the country's historic settlement is under threat. The demand for economic change has resulted in ever-deepening divisions between the ANC and the trade unions. The country's largest trade union, the National Union of Metalworkers of South Africa (NUMSA), has declared its intention to withdraw support from the ANC and has called for the resignation of President Jacob Zuma.

Despite obvious deep discord in the ANC, it won the May 2014 elections, albeit with a slightly reduced national vote of 62.2 percent. It conceded 10 percent of its majority to opposition parties in the provincial election in Gauteng, which is the financial capital of the country, and the Economic Freedom Fighters (EFF) that broke away from the ANC nine months earlier gained 6.4 percent of the national vote. The challenge facing the country at present is how to move beyond the celebration of the 1994 settlement that required compromises implemented under the prudent and wise leadership of Nelson Mandela. It is time to build on the essential principles of this settlement as enshrined in the constitution by addressing the economic and institutional problems that threaten the maintenance of peace and democracy in the country.

There is a growing consensus in South Africa, among both the poor and a growing section of the middle and upper classes, that the failure to promote the socioeconomic demands of the poor with sufficient vigor has resulted in a structural fault line that threatens the long-term prospects of democratic consolidation. Since 1994 power has increasingly shifted into the hands of an economic and political elite committed to self-enrichment and accumulation through the control of public resources. This motivates critics to ask whether the current ruling elite, both within and beyond the ANC, are the obstacle to deeper change.[16]

The Continental Implications of the South African Settlement

Nothing is more important to the future of African countries than finding a platform for sustainable peace between different communities separated by a history that pits strong against weak, rich against poor, and sectarian group against sectarian group. This requires Africa's diverse peoples to rise above identity-related ideologies grounded in religion, ethnicity, and tribal affiliation and to pursue a form of nation building that celebrates difference within the borders of a common state.

Mazrui addresses this challenge by writing of "three definitions of Africa," which he describes as "white-dominated Africa south of the Tropic of Capricorn, Arab-dominated Africa north of the Tropic of Cancer, and Black Africa between the two tropics." He goes further to suggest the need for a "fourth definition of Africa" that recognizes the inclusivity and common citizenship of all Africans. White domination has today ended in areas south of the Tropic of Capricorn, and the demarcation of Arab and black Africa is less clear than it was in earlier times.[17]

To employ Mahmood Mamdani's words, some settlers have become natives.[18] Mamdani elsewhere contends that the African conflict is largely a consequence of an inadequate notion of the state (inherited from a European-Westphalian tradition), one with roots in colonial law and currency even in postindependence African countries.[19] In brief, he argues that state construction that results in political domination by a particular group with cultural specificities, to the exclusion and denigration of other groups within inherited national boundaries, is a "crime" and a recipe for violence. The essence of his argument is that settlers were inclusively regarded as a race, governed by *civil law* that invested them with certain inviolable rights. Natives, on the other hand, were divided by colonialists into distinct ethnicities (or tribes). Each ethnic group was governed according to what was perceived to be its particular *customary law*, executed by native chiefs under a single native authority controlled by the settler community.

The characterizing mark of the fight against colonialism was the struggle of African nationalists to acquire the same rights as those whites who constituted the colonial elite. The entrenched structure of colonialism and the intensity of this struggle were nevertheless such that mainstream African nationalists largely perpetuated colonial structures that separated tribal communities. The outcome was a dual perpetuation of colonialism, involving both a narrow form of nationalism and a competitive form of ethnic or tribal rivalry still witnessed in parts of Africa today. The problem of Africa, suggests Mamdani, is that nation building has been plagued by the "politicisation of culture, religion and indigeneity," which excludes those seen to be different. "You can turn the world upside down, but still fail to change it. To change the world, you need to break out of the world view . . . not just of the settler but also of the native."[20] That requires not only serious economic and cultural change but also constitutional and legal initiatives to ensure the birth of a nation at peace with itself.

This African reality makes the South African model for political transition and the institution of the TRC process an attractive option for some African states. Robert Rotberg divides sub-Saharan Africa into three groups.[21] This classification arguably hides several destabilizing factors while providing a useful basis for comparative African analysis. He places Botswana, South Africa, Namibia, Ghana, Lesotho, Tanzania, Zambia, and Benin, plus the island states of Mauritius, Seychelles, and São Tomé Príncipe, as Africa's best; Somalia, Sudan, South Sudan, the Democratic Republic of the Congo, and the Central African Republic as among the worst; and countries such as Senegal, Kenya, Rwanda, Liberia, and Nigeria as the middle-ranking group of African states. Those states named in the top and middle-ranking groups have all, with different degrees of success, committed themselves to democratic rule and the necessary structural changes to enhance human development by reaching across political, ethnic, and class divisions.

These African developments occurred in different contexts from that of South Africa and without the institution of TRC-type mechanisms. South Africa, however, has not managed to redress all the challenges that brought it to the brink of conflagration in 1994. This raises questions about why the South African TRC failed adequately to redress the past and whether different truth commissions in Sierra Leone, Liberia, and Kenya have contributed to the improved political situation in those countries. It is at the same time important not to make the TRC the whipping boy of the South African transition. The terms and structures of the South African TRC were created through the compromises agreed to in the CODESA settlement; it was subject to the Promotion of National Unity and Reconciliation Act and passed into law by a near-unanimous decision in a parliament under strong ANC control. Blame aside, the South African transition and the TRC have been subjected to three major criticisms that other African leaders need to consider in relation to transitional justice structures they may wish to institute in their own countries:

The nature of the TRC mandate. The TRC Act required the commission to provide "as complete a picture as possible" of the gross violations of human rights committed between 1960 and 1994, which the act narrowly defined as "killing, abduction, torture, or severe ill treatment."[22] The act, for example, excluded the effects of the 1913 Land Act, which deprived black people of 87 percent of the land, as well as of the Bantu Education Act, Group Areas Act, and job reservation laws, all of which impoverished and dehumanized black South Africans.

Nevertheless, the victim hearings of the commission, together with extensive media coverage of these hearings, meant that no fair-minded person could deny the broader consequences of apartheid for black South Africans. The commission further reaffirmed the UN declaration of apartheid as a crime against humanity and recommended a one-off wealth tax that was rejected by government, who insisted that the gap between black and white South Africans was being addressed through its economic policy.

Reparations. The TRC recommended a package of reparations that included a six-year pension for those it found to be victims of gross violations of human rights. It took the state five years to respond, and then it agreed to make a one-time payment of R30,000 to these victims, which was approximately six times less than that recommended by the TRC. The TRC also made a number of structural and communal recommendations. Almost two decades after the end of statutory apartheid, most of these recommendations have still not been implemented. What is clear is that neither CODESA nor the TRC effectively engaged in the structural socioeconomic debate.

Amnesty. Amnesty from prosecution was effectively offered as a quid pro quo for truth telling and reparations. A survey conducted in 2001 (three years after the formal closure of the TRC) showed that 65 percent of black South Africans accepted that amnesty was a price that needed to be paid in order to secure a peaceful transition to democracy.

The state has shown no sense of urgency in responding to the alleged three hundred major perpetrators who were denied amnesty or who failed to apply for amnesty and were referred to the Department of Justice for possible prosecution. When President Thabo Mbeki endeavored to grant pardons for crimes committed during the apartheid era to these and other alleged perpetrators, organizations of civil society referred the matter to the High Court, which ruled that perpetrators be required to publicly disclose the nature of the crimes they had committed in "an open and transparent way . . . in the spirit of the TRC."[23] This process has since stalled. The government has not consulted with victims, nor have the alleged perpetrators made the public acknowledgment of their crimes as ordered by the court. This militates against the quest for closure on past gross violations of human rights, which was the intent of the TRC act.

Suffice it to say, the country's current postapartheid government needs to be held responsible for many of the failures of governance in contemporary South Africa, while recognizing that its capacity to institute the required economic and human rights transformation continues to be restricted by the terms of the 1994 settlement.

Priority needs to be given to what Mamdani calls "survivor's justice," which requires former enemies to learn to live together by exploring ways of creating something new through a democratic process that redresses the economic injustices, racism, and other crimes of the past.[24] In the words of Wole Soyinka, in implementing the TRC the nation failed to reach beyond a "hazy zone of remorse" to "a social formula that would minister to the wrongs of dispossession on the one hand and chasten those who deviate from humane communal order on the other . . . as a criterion for the future conduct of society."[25]

For South Africa, the lesson of recent developments in North Africa's Arab Spring countries is that poor and marginalized people ultimately rise in rebellion. Countries of the Afro-Arab north can, in turn, learn from the relative transparency and inclusivity of South Africa's earlier transitional process, which gave South Africans political breathing space in which to tackle the realities that had brought the country to the brink of collapse.

The ending of formal apartheid was a crucial step forward, although residual forms of racism persist, extending from personal bias to institutional discrimination, and material privilege continues beyond the abolition of apartheid. This persuades an increasing number of South Africans that the 1994 transition did not reach deep enough. It failed to entrench the moral, economic, and political incentives necessary to move the nation forward with sufficient fortitude.

The ruling party is today hidebound by special interests, a host of incompetent middle managers in municipal, provincial, and national government, and deeply entrenched corruption. The high-profile EFF, led by Julius Malema, grabs the political headlines, and other opposition parties struggle to gain serious traction. The president and others in his inner circle live in scandalous extravagance while continuing to evoke the Mandela legacy as a ruse to distract from their own moral failure.

Pessimism grows, and sectors of society resist working within the rule of law. Chauvinist men and women constituting an emerging class of millionaire tycoons resist government regulation of the economy, while trade unions shut down mines and industry with paralyzing strikes. Organizations of the unemployed occupy the cities, bring traffic to a standstill, and destroy government infrastructure. Analysts warn of a ticking time bomb. Maybe it will be a series of smaller land mines and grass fires. Suffice it to say, South Africa is a restless nation that clamors for further change.

The good news is that there is political space in South Africa for dissidents, opponents of government, and the poor to make their voices heard—but at a price. Old habits die hard, with the mindset of the former regime periodically seeping into the present government and its security officials who demand acquiescence and obedience, albeit in different ways to different masters. Other nations in the world, not least on the African continent, have allowed their hard-won democratic victories against their colonial masters and dictators to fall victim to oppressive laws and practices, often with tacit acceptance by those citizens who benefit from government policy. South Africa dare not go there if its earlier gains are to become the basis for building a more equitable nation and contributing to democratic change on the continent.

Notes

1. Doxtader, *With Faith in the Works of Words*, 261.

2. Albertus and Menaldo, "South Africa, Unequal by Design"; World Bank, "GINI Index."

3. Green Gazette, Gazette Notices, "Promotion of National Unity and Reconciliation Act No. 34 of 1995."

4. The period covered the time between the banning of the liberation movements and the inauguration of President Mandela as the first democratically elected South African president.

5. Mahomed, D. P., Azanian People's Organization v. President of the Republic of South Africa, 1996 (8) BCLR 1015 (CC).

6. Section 9 (2) of the Constitution. See also Stacey, "We the People: The Relationship between the South African Constitution and the ANC's Transformation Policies."

7. Judgments in this regard included a situation in 1997 when the Constitutional Court upheld the decision by health authorities who refused to admit a terminally ill patient, Thiagraj Soobramoney, to Addington Hospital because his condition was judged by the health authorities to be too advanced to justify his being placed on a priority list for treatment. In 2000, on the basis of the rights of the child as stipulated in the Constitution, the Cape High Court upheld the rights of Mrs. Irene Grootboom and 899 other applicants, including 510 children, who were

evicted from an informal settlement. Taken on appeal, the Constitutional Court found there to be no violation of the rights of the child, ruling that it is the primary obligation of the parents and families to care for their children. It nevertheless found the eviction to be unreasonable to the extent that "no provision was made for relief to the categories of people in desperate need," and it required the government to provide alternative relief to the people concerned. Other judgments regarding constitutional rights include the judgment brought by the Treatment Action Campaign in 2002, which required the government to make antiretroviral drugs available to pregnant South African women.

8. Soko, "Economic Transformation."

9. MacDonald and Pape, *Cost Recovery and the Crisis of Service Delivery in South Africa*; Habib and Padayachee, "Economic Policy and Power Relations in South Africa's Transition to Democracy"; Rantete, *African National Congress and the Negotiated Settlement in South Africa*.

10. Lyman, *Partner to History*, 57–76.

11. Cape Town, April 2000. See Villa-Vicencio, *Walk with Us and Listen*, 95–96.

12. Terreblanche, *History of Inequality in South Africa, 1652–2002*.

13. Du Preez, *A Rumour of Spring*, 81.

14. See the National Planning Commission's Diagnostic Report, 2011; Habib, *South Africa's Suspended Revolution*; Calland, *Zuma Years*.

15. See Johnson, "Liberal or Liberation Framework?"

16. Albertus and Menaldo, "South Africa, Unequal by Design."

17. Mazrui, *Africans: The Triple Heritage*.

18. Mamdani, "When Does a Settler Become a Native?"

19. Mamdani, "Beyond Settler and Native as Political Identities."

20. Mamdani, "Making Sense of Political Violence in Postcolonial Africa."

21. Rotberg, *Africa Emerges*. See also Rotberg, "How Africa Can Move Forward." He bases his analysis significantly on the Mo Ibrahim Foundation's *2013 Ibrahim Index of African Governance*.

22. See the TRC Act.

23. High Court of South Africa, North Gauteng High Court, Pretoria, Case No. 15320/9, April 28, 2009.

24. Mamdani, *When Victims Become Killers*, 273.

25. Soyinka, *The Burden of Memory, the Muse of Forgiveness*, 81.

Bibliography

Albertus, Mike, and Victor Menaldo. "South Africa, Unequal by Design." *Foreign Policy*, January 3, 2014. www.foreignpolicy.com/articles/2014/01/03/south_africa_unequal_by_design.

Calland, Richard. *The Zuma Years: South Africa's Changing Face of Power*. Cape Town: Zebra, 2013.

Doxtader, Erik. *With Faith in the Works of Words: The Beginnings of Reconciliation in South Africa, 1985–1995*. Cape Town: David Philip, 2008.

Du Preez, Max. *A Rumour of Spring: South Africa after 20 Years of Democracy*. Cape Town: Zebra, 2013.

Gastrow, Peter. *Bargaining for Peace: South Africa and the National Peace Accord*. Washington, DC: United States Institute of Peace Press, 1995.

Green Gazette. "Promotion of National Unity and Reconciliation Act No. 34 of 1995." *Gazette Notices*. www.greengazette.co.za/acts/promotion-of-national-unity-and-reconciliation-act _1995-034.

Habib, Adam. *South Africa's Suspended Revolution: Hopes and Prospects*. Johannesburg: Wits University Press, 2013.

Habib, Adam, and Vishu Padayachee. "Economic Policy and Power Relations in South Africa's Transition to Democracy." *World Development* 28, no. 2 (2002): 245–63.

High Court of South Africa. North Gauteng High Court, Pretoria, Case No. 15320/9, April 28, 2009.

Johnson, Krista. "Liberal or Liberation Framework? The Contradictions of ANC Rule in South Africa." *Journal of Contemporary African Studies* 21, no. 2 (May 2003): 321–40.

Lyman, Princeton. *Partner to History: The U.S. Role in South Africa's Transition to Democracy*. Washington, DC: United States Institute of Peace Press, 2012.

MacDonald, David A., and John Pape, eds. *Cost Recovery and the Crisis of Service Delivery in South Africa*. London: Zed, 2002.

Mahomed, D. P. Azanian People's Organization v. President of the Republic of South Africa, 1996 (8) BCLR 1015 (CC).

Mamdani, Mahmood. "Beyond Settler and Native as Political Identities: Overcoming the Political Legacy of Colonialism." *Comparative Studies in Society and History* 43 (October 2001): 651–64. www.jstor.org/stable/2696665.

———. "Making Sense of Political Violence in Postcolonial Africa." *Identity, Culture and Politics* 3, no. 2 (2002): 16.

———. "When Does a Settler Become a Native? Reflections on the Colonial Roots of Citizenship in Equatorial and South Africa." Inaugural lecture as A. C. Jordan Professor of African Studies, University of Cape Town, May 13, 1998.

———. *When Victims Become Killers: Colonialism, Nativism, and the Genocide in Rwanda*. Cape Town: David Philip, 2001.

Marais, Hein. *South Africa Pushed to the Limits*. Cape Town: UCT Press, 2011.

Mazrui, Ali, *The Africans: The Triple Heritage*. New York: Little Brown, 1986.

Mbeki, Moeletsi. "Entrepreneur and Public Intellectual." In *Conversations in Transition: Leading South African Voices*, edited by Charles Villa-Vicencio and Mills Soko. Cape Town: David Philip, 2012.

Melber, Henning, ed. *Limits to Liberation in Southern Africa: The Unfinished Business of Democratic Consolidation*. Cape Town: HSRC Press, 2003.

Mo Ibrahim Foundation. *Ibrahim Index of African Governance 2013*. www.moibrahimfoundation .org/downloads/2013/2013-IIAG-summary-report.pdf.

National Planning Commission. Diagnostic Report, June 2011. www.pmg.org.za/files/docs /110913npcdiagnostic2011_0.pdf?.

Rantete, Johannes. *The African National Congress and the Negotiated Settlement in South Africa*. Pretoria: Van Schaik, 1998.

Rasool, Ebrahim. "Ambassador and Believer." In *Conversations in Transition: Leading South Africa Voices*, edited by Charles Villa-Vicencio and Mills Soko. Cape Town: David Philip, 2012.

Rotberg, Robert I. *Africa Emerges: Consummate Challenges, Abundant Opportunities*. Cambridge: Polity, 2013.

———. "How Africa Can Move Forward." *Cape Times*, January 27, 2014.

Soko, Mills. "Economic Transformation." In *Turning Points in Transition: The Story of South Africa's Road to Peace*, compiled for the Institute for Justice and Reconciliation, 144–75. Cape

Town: Institute for Justice and Reconciliation, 2011. www.ijr.org.za/publications/pdfs /Turning%20Points%20in%20Transition.pdf.

South African Democracy Education Trust. *The Road to Democracy in South Africa.* Volume 5, *African Solidarity.* Pretoria: Unisa, 2013.

Soyinka, Wole. *The Burden of Memory, the Muse of Forgiveness.* Oxford: Oxford University Press, 2000.

Stacey, Richard. "We the People: The Relationship between the South African Constitution and the ANC's Transformation Policies." *Politikon* 30 (November 2003): 133–48.

Terreblanche, Sampie. *A History of Inequality in South Africa, 1652–2002.* Pietermaritzburg: University of Kwa-Zulu Natal Press, 2002.

Villa-Vicencio, Charles. *Walk with Us and Listen: Political Reconciliation in Africa.* Washington, DC: Georgetown University Press, 2009.

World Bank, Development Research Group. "GINI Index." http://data.worldbank.org/indica tor/SI.POV.GINI.

4

Irreconcilable Truths?

Gender-Based Violence and the Struggle to Build an Inclusive History

HELEN SCANLON

The death of South Africa's former president Nelson Mandela in December 2013 renewed global reflections on his role in the "miraculous" transformation of South Africa from violent white rule to a democratic and—at least superficially—peaceful society. International and local actors alike spoke of South Africa's transformation into the rainbow nation, one that, like Mandela, refused to be imprisoned by its history. However, in the two decades since South Africa's first free and fair elections, a widening chasm has emerged between the promises of transformation and the realities of ongoing widespread poverty and inequalities.

Indeed, South Africa's beleaguered transformation is particularly apparent in terms of the prevalent level of gender-based violence, often cited as the highest in the world. This was perhaps most starkly revealed on February 14, 2013, when national sporting hero and Paralympian Oscar Pistorius shot dead his girlfriend, Reeva Steenkamp. His fame as well as his race resulted in unprecedented media attention to the scourge of gender-based violence in the country. In contrast, only a week earlier Anene Booysen, a seventeen-year-old girl who died following a gang rape, received far less media attention. As Mandela himself noted in April 1995, "Freedom would be meaningless without security in the home and in the streets."[1]

Given the Arab Spring and the significant discussions about transitions in North Africa, it is an opportune moment to reflect on the reality of transformation in South Africa and in particular the much-lauded South African Truth and Reconciliation Commission (TRC), which took place during President Mandela's term in office. As one analyst has observed, "political stability has built-in gendered costs and benefits," though South Africa has not yet reached political stability and thus awaits its effects. South Africa is currently one of the world's most unequal societies with a Gini coefficient above 63 in 2011.[2] While the South African TRC's achievements cannot and should not be dismissed, its failure to investigate the structural impact of apartheid may have in some ways allowed acceptance of the ongoing violence—in particular, gender-based violence—in the country. As Meintjes and others contend, South Africa is a society living in the "aftermath" where "the political violence against women committed in the past has direct and indirect links to current levels of sexual violence."[3] Figures related to sexual violence are contested as a result of widespread underreporting, but according to a Medical Research Council (MRC) report more than half of the women in the province of Gauteng have experienced some form of violence in their lifetime, and 75.5 percent of men admitted to perpetrating some form of violence against women at one point in their lives.[4]

Significant questions have arisen following South Africa's transition, including whether underlying social inequalities can be rectified simply through the creation of a new political and legal dispensations. These concerns raise far deeper questions about the field of transitional justice and its preoccupation with civil and political rights as the key route to ensure transformation and, ultimately, reconciliation. As a result, it is important to ask whether South Africa in fact remains imprisoned by its history and what is needed for a gender-inclusive reconciliation. This chapter explores the complexity of the South African transition with particular emphasis on the role of the TRC. It will start by framing discussions about transitional justice and will then examine the thorny issue of gender transformation in postapartheid South Africa. It concludes with a consideration of the legacy of South Africa's gendered past at this moment of critical reflection created by Mandela's passing.

Engendering Transitions

As has been well documented elsewhere, transitional justice refers to an array of approaches undertaken by societies to address past human rights abuses. The field comprises both judicial and nonjudicial processes and may include criminal justice, truth seeking, institutional reforms, and reparative justice in a bid to right the wrongs of the past and "bridge the transition from apartheid, dictatorship, or communism to liberal democracy."[5]

However, despite increased attention by the international human rights community to the gender dimension of violations perpetrated during conflict, these experiences have generally received inadequate attention in transitional justice processes. Nonetheless, there is burgeoning literature on the potential and limitations of the field to promote gender justice. A number of analysts have questioned whether the focus of transitional justice processes (and international human rights law more broadly) on aspects of "extraordinary violence" obfuscates how violence, and in particular gender-based violence, can become ordinary. And as Pumla Gqola has noted, "gender based violence is very ordinary: it is everywhere, commonplace, made to seem normal."[6]

South Africa's decision to predicate its transition on a truth-seeking process should be framed within broader contestations over the efficacy of truth telling and the very concept of truth. As Orford notes, within the field of transitional justice truth telling is presented "at the individual level, in therapeutic terms, as a means of healing those who have been wounded by the violence of civil war, revolution, or despotism. At the collective level, establishing the truth of a contested history is understood as a necessary basis for moving forward as a nation and creating the conditions for a viable, shared life."[7] However, she suggests that appeals to truth in transitional contexts are in reality often mechanisms aimed at "an audience of liberal internationalists" to show that those "states undergoing 'transition' were also being produced as reliable subjects of the capitalist democratic order."[8] Ní Aoláin has also cautioned that "transitional justice discourse can reflexively deploy an uncritical, liberal, feminist positioning with little capacity to recognize its own hegemony and privilege."[9]

Numerous commentators, including those who adopt a feminist lens, argue that producing a "meaningful record of the past and . . . enabling healing are better met by the methods of truth commissions than by criminal prosecutions."[10] The record of failure by the international criminal tribunals and the International Criminal Court (ICC) to achieve convictions for more than a handful of gender-based crimes supports this assertion. Nonetheless, as Sarah Glatte has noted, existing unequal power relations between women and men are often perpetuated and reinforced by transitional justice, and so these processes often "inhibit meaningful and sustainable" transformation.[11] She contends that "the reinforcement of the public/private distinction through transitional justice processes and democratic transitions more generally has often led to situations in which political and economic structures (traditionally public) are fundamentally overhauled while the marginalisation of gender and equality concerns are reasserted."[12] This is apparent in South Africa where serious questions have been raised regarding the meaning of transformation and whether what has been achieved is merely a change of leadership instead of a more substantial metamorphosis of the political and economic order.

South Africa's Transition

The release of Nelson Mandela in 1990 and South Africa's subsequent democratization was accompanied by widespread commitments to create a nonracial and nonsexist society and, in so doing, to prevent a repetition of the past. This was always going to be a formidable task given the ways that race, class, gender, and sexuality were manipulated through apartheid's legal framework. But, as often occurs subsequent to regime change, mobilization by civil society occurred to ensure gender-sensitive policies and laws were enacted. Even before the first democratic elections in 1994, South Africa signed the UN Convention on the Elimination of All Forms of Discrimination against Women, an international treaty to protect and promote women's rights that has established standards for achieving gender equality.

Ní Aoláin and others have drawn attention to the unique and gendered ways authoritarian regimes such as the apartheid state were repressive. Following its election to government, the African National Congress (ANC) sought to demolish the repressive legal frameworks established by the prior apartheid government. In December 1996 a new constitution gave South Africa one of the most comprehensive frameworks in the world for the protection of human rights. It decrees: "The state may not unfairly discriminate directly or indirectly against anyone on one or more grounds, including race, gender, sex, pregnancy, marital status, ethnic or social origin, colour, sexual orientation, age, disability, religion, conscience, belief, culture, language and birth." In order to realize gender-based rights the constitution called for the creation of the Commission for Gender Equality, whose object was "to promote gender equality and to advise and to make recommendations to Parliament or any other legislature with regard to any laws or proposed legislation which affects gender equality and the status of women."[13] Indeed, Mandela made his commitment to gender equality apparent in 1995 when he noted: "As a tribute to the legions of women who navigated the path of fighting for justice before us, we ought to imprint in the supreme law of the land, firm principles upholding the rights of women. The women themselves, and the whole of society, must make this a prime responsibility."[14]

Beyond the constitution, other laws and policies have been implemented to address gender issues, such as the 1998 Domestic Violence Act and the 2007 Sexual Offences Act. In addition, one of South Africa's oft-cited achievements is the representation of women in public office, which has been achieved by the ruling party's own quota system. While women made up just 3 percent of parliamentarians during the last apartheid government, they now constitute 44 percent of the National Assembly. They are also well represented in cabinet positions, and at the international level South African women are in highly visible roles including at the helm of the African Union Commission and UN Women.

A number of analysts have bemoaned the sidelining of women in the aftermath of the Arab Spring and the failure of new regimes to recognize women's roles in the transition. Shireen Hassim and others have observed that, in South Africa, gender equality was won through "elite suasion" and "arose out of a commitment to human rights in the ANC, rather than out of a broad public deliberative process."[15] Indeed, we have seen the erosion of many of the gains made in the heady years of the 1990s. The increasing assertion of a heterosexist and patriarchal society under President Zuma has seen an emphasis on representation at the expense of "women's concerns about individual bodily integrity and authority over income and property."[16] As such, South Africa demonstrates that the liberal feminist ideal of women's increased representation as the key to transformation does not necessarily hold true.

Apartheid's Legacy

President Mandela was quick to see the need to address the structural and cultural obstacles to realizing gender equality in South Africa. In a speech on Women's Day in 1996 he observed: "The legacy of oppression weighs heavily on women. As long as women are bound by poverty and as long as they are looked down upon, human rights will lack substance. As long as outmoded ways of thinking prevent women from making a meaningful contribution to society, progress will be slow. As long as the nation refuses to acknowledge the equal role of more than half of itself, it is doomed to failure."[17]

However, despite the rhetoric, progress has been slow in addressing the profound inequalities within South African society. As noted above, South Africa is the most unequal nation in the world, and Human Rights Watch has noted that these inequalities remain largely determined by race: "Despite being a middle income country, the key indicators of poverty for the African population are equal to or worse than those for much poorer countries elsewhere in Africa."[18] Moreover, they continue, "95 percent of those in the poorest 40 percent of the population are African and 65 percent of Africans are poor, by the same measure."[19]

To fully assess the extent of these inequalities it is important to scrutinize them from a gender perspective, mindful of the fact that women are both the lowest-paid workers and the majority of the unemployed in South Africa. As Hassim notes: "Poverty and inequality are deeply-gendered and inextricable phenomena and to address them as if they were not is misguided to say the least."[20] African women have been bearing the brunt of the increasing feminization of poverty; human development indicators, such as those embodied in the UN Millennium Development Goals (MDGs), have, albeit inadvertently, highlighted African women's continued marginalization. While there is now generally parity in the educational achievement of men and women in South Africa, the majority of those living under the food poverty line—defined as less than R 305 per month—are African women. According to the government's 2013 MDG Report, women employees earn only 77 percent of the amount male employees earn. While 20 percent of women earned R 1,000 or less per month, only 10 percent of men did so.[21] Women form the majority of the unemployed, and in 2012 the ratio of female to male unemployment was two to one. The 2011 National Employment Equity Report noted that in the private sector women seldom held more than 12 percent of senior and top management positions. This was confirmed in a July 2013 report by audit firm PwC, which showed that women hold just 10 percent of executive-level positions in the companies listed on the Johannesburg Stock Exchange and on average earn 28.1 percent less than men. And although South Africa boasts progressive reproductive health laws (over 90 percent of pregnant women have access to antenatal care), levels of maternal mortality in South Africa had increased to 625 deaths per 100,000 live births in 2010. Given that the UN MDG target is 38 deaths per 100,000 live births by 2015, this figure clearly highlights the fact that changes to policies and laws alone are not enough to address legacies of inequality from the past.[22]

As discussed above, rates of gender-based violence are both contested and extraordinary. There are high incidences of sexual crimes—the South African Police Service (SAPS) received fifty-five thousand reports of rape in 2010, but the MRC claims that less than one in twenty-five rapes is reported to the police. In addition, the rate of teenage male homicide is extremely high but is nonetheless similar to the rate of adult male homicide.[23] While not a justification for the current levels of violence, there was an acceptance of violent behavior during apartheid and, consequently, widespread toleration of gender-based violence. A study by the MRC contends that the state-sponsored violence perpetrated during the apartheid era, in conjunction with societal responses to this violence, has meant that "for many people, physical violence has become a first line strategy for resolving conflict and gaining ascendancy."[24] Understanding the failure to have a national dialogue on this violence requires a meaningful discussion of the role of the TRC in South Africa's transition.

South Africa's Truth and Reconciliation Commission

The TRC was set up to investigate "the nature, causes and extent of gross violations of human rights" committed "within or outside" the country during the period from 1960 to 1994.[25] The premise of the South African TRC was that an alternative form of nonpunitive justice was necessary to enable the transition from apartheid to democracy. Moving away from earlier examples of what was perceived as victor's justice, such as the Nuremburg trials, the South African process operated to facilitate confessions, storytelling, and truth telling with the idea that justice and healing could be achieved through a national discourse about the past. As Dullah Omar, the minister of justice, noted, "A commission is a necessary exercise to enable South Africans to come to terms with their past on a morally accepted basis and to advance the cause of reconciliation."[26] Despite these lofty intentions, there was a pragmatic objective in prioritizing political justice over criminal justice, as Ugandan academic Mahmood Mamdani observes: "The rationale was simple: where there was no victor, one would need the cooperation of the very leaders who would otherwise be charged with war crimes to end the fighting and initiate political reforms. . . . Forgive all past crimes—in plain words, immunity from prosecution—provided both sides agree to change the rules to assure political justice for the living."[27]

The newly formed government argued that in order to achieve national unity and reconciliation there would be no pursuit of retributive justice, nor would there be a blanket amnesty for perpetrators of human rights violations. The TRC was thus intended to give victims an opportunity to present their truth without being subject to the interrogation that often accompanies prosecution trials. In turn, perpetrators were to be awarded amnesty if they made a full disclosure of violations they had committed with a political objective. This amnesty was offered to all perpetrators of political crimes, whatever their political allegiance. A public acknowledgment of the "untold suffering and injustice" endured by victims would help to restore their dignity and at the same time would "afford perpetrators the opportunity to come to terms with their own past."[28]

The TRC drew on the experiences of earlier truth commissions in Latin America and was composed of three committees: the Human Rights Violations Committee investigated human rights violations between 1960 and 1994, the Amnesty Committee considered applications by perpetrators, and the Reparation and Rehabilitation Committee formulated proposals to assist with reparation and rehabilitation. The commission was a major departure in both scale and ambition from previous commissions; it had a staff of three hundred and an annual budget of US$18 million. Between 1995 and 1998 some 21,298 statements were taken from victims detailing 38,000 violations of human rights. Of these, 2,000 of the most representative experiences were shared in public hearings.[29] Finally, on March 21, 2003, the seven-volume report of the TRC was handed over to the government.

Departing from the format of previous commissions, the South African process included hearings that were open to the public; these were recorded for both local and international radio and television. Victims of apartheid were actively encouraged to participate in the process, and input from all South Africans was facilitated through submissions and focused inquiries. It was claimed that by the time the TRC filed its final report in 1998 white South Africans could no longer claim ignorance about the atrocities committed in the name of apartheid.

As described earlier, the offer of a conditional amnesty was meant to provide perpetrators, particularly senior perpetrators, with the incentive to come forward and speak the truth. Unfortunately, this did not happen. Very few of those in senior roles came forward, and those who did provided largely sanitized versions of the truth. Thus, the bulk of the "truth" that constitutes the report of the South African TRC emerged from the work of the Human Rights Violations Committee, the research and investigation teams, and the statement taking and hearings rather than from the amnesty process. Making further mockery of the amnesty process, only a handful of the more than five thousand perpetrators who applied for—but were not granted—amnesty have since been prosecuted.

After the TRC opened its doors in 1995, a number of feminist activists engaged the TRC in discussions on the gendered nature of truth, arguing that the commission needed to address the systemic impact of apartheid on both men and women. Activists such as Sheila Meintjes and Beth Goldblatt argued that a truth commission's outcome is dependent on the input. When no information regarding gender-based crimes is provided, it is certain that gender will not emerge in the outcome of the process.[30] A survey of previous truth commissions indicated that the "truth" about legacies of human rights abuse may be slanted, distorted, or fashioned depending on the truth-telling process, the truth tellers who come forward, and the way in which a society responds to them. By paying attention to gender issues, truth commissions have the capacity to produce multiple truths, not a single unified truth, and they can expose the myths that sustain and legitimize the abuse of power.

In some regards, the South African TRC successfully included gender issues, particularly in terms of representation. Women were well represented on its staff, constituted nearly half of the seventeen commissioners, made up more than half of those who testified, and were the exclusive focus of three separate hearings. In addition, practical methods were employed to enable women's participation, such as hiring female statement takers and providing additional training on gender issues for commission staff. However, these aspects to the commission's work occurred only following the intervention of women's groups who organized a conference titled "Does Truth Have a Gender?"—a question that continues to be debated.[31]

Indeed, many gender activists have pointed to the failings of the TRC. First and foremost, women tended to speak only of the experiences of others rather than of their own experiences of violation. Despite women making up 54 percent of those providing the nearly twenty-two thousand statements, 79 percent of these women recounted the abuses suffered by their husbands and sons rather than their own experiences.[32] Of course it is essential to question more broadly whether the TRC was ever a viable mechanism to advance gender justice at that particular point in South African history, just two years into the new democracy. As Orford notes, in current transitional justice processes there often remains a "victim who refuses to be saved, the subject who will not speak of her suffering in the time and place and languages offered to her by the mechanisms of transitional justice. . . . [R]esponding to the call of the other may interrupt the process of transition, but it may also give us the opportunity to learn from her about justice."[33]

Although it has been widely understood that rape was used as a tactic by the apartheid security forces, both the Amnesty Committee and the Human Rights Violations Committee often struggled to draw a line between the political and personal motives behind sexual violence. As a result, a mere 158 women reported cases of sexual violence to the TRC.[34] This may in part be attributed to the fact that one commissioner argued rape was not a political crime and therefore not a crime for which amnesty could be awarded. As such, of the seven thousand amnesty applications only one was made regarding rape, and it was turned down.

In addition, the commission categorized rape as a form of "severe ill treatment," which was dramatically out of line with international developments toward recognizing rape as a form of torture, persecution, and indeed a crime against humanity. While the TRC held its hearings, significant strides in defining gender-based crimes were being made by the International Criminal Tribunal for Rwanda (ICTR) and the International Criminal Tribunal for the former Yugoslavia (ICTY). These were embodied in the 1998 Rome Statute creating the ICC. Further, this categorization occurred only after lobbying by civil society groups who were concerned about the low rate of women testifying about their own experiences and demanded that sexual violence be properly investigated.

Sexual violence was a widespread tactic used by the apartheid regime. According to Rashida Manjoo, among women detainees there were "reports of miscarriages in detention, torture using electric shock on pregnant women, [and] allegations of rape by police and soldiers."[35] And, as Hassim and Debby Bonnin have observed, during the apartheid era the rape of women "was a distinctive form of violence that was used not only against the political enemy but also within political groups," such as Inkatha and the United Democratic Front (UDF).[36] The introspection and reflection on gender discrimination that emerged in the 1996 film *Flame*, about the Zimbabwean liberation movement, was not possible in the TRC process because of its inadequate definition of rape and limited testimony of women about their own experiences of abuse.

Perhaps most seriously, the TRC failed to extend "ill treatment" to wider crimes of apartheid, such as forced removals and influx control, of which African women were arguably the primary victims. Thus, despite one chapter being dedicated to women in the final TRC report, the gendered nature of the country's past was only superficially recorded, and, as has been noted, the final report considered gender "in the narrowest possible terms."[37] Nonetheless, Ní Aoláin has noted that "while the TRC final report mutes women's voices throughout the narrative it endorses, grassroots activism around the TRC demonstrates the ongoing work of gendering the transition that occurs parallel to official transitional mechanisms in many societies."[38] This can perhaps be seen most clearly in the work of the Khulumani Support Group, the majority of whose members are women and which campaigns for the rights of victims of apartheid.

The third committee of the TRC, the five-member Reparation and Rehabilitation Committee, was dedicated to those areas often seen as central to addressing gender-based violations. The objective of the committee was "to provide victim support to ensure that the Truth Commission process restores victims' dignity; and to formulate policy proposals and recommendations on rehabilitation and healing of survivors, their families and communities at large."[39] The committee made "a wide-ranging series of recommendations relating to matters including reparations [and] provision of services" for those most affected by apartheid and legal reforms.[40]

Reparations, in the form of monetary compensation, were to be disbursed to those who had been named victims by either the Human Rights Violation Committee or the Amnesty Committee. The TRC has been widely criticized for its gender-blind approach to the delivery of reparations despite the fact that four women were on the Human Rights Violations Committee. When reparations were finally disbursed by the government in 2003, those identified as victims by the TRC received a one-time payment of R 30,000.[41] Some reparations—for example, the restoration of the women's jail in Johannesburg to house the Commission for Gender Equality—have acknowledged women's role in the struggle.

However, the small amounts of money disbursed were mostly symbolic in nature and made little impact in the lives of victims who continue to struggle in a discriminatory society. Of grave concern to feminist scholars was the failure to understand the relational factors in gender relations, which meant that issues faced by the families of victims were not recognized as an integral component of a comprehensive reparations program. In addition, the reparations program mirrored the failings of the TRC more broadly by only granting reparations to those who were recognized as victims of "gross violations of human rights" by the commission—that is, the twenty-two thousand who had provided statements. Thus, reparations did not acknowledge victims of sexual violence who had specific medical or psychosocial needs, nor did they acknowledge the broader gender-based crimes experienced under apartheid.

Mamdani has remarked that the TRC produced only a "diminished truth," and this is apparent with regard to the silences over gender-based violations committed during apartheid.[42] The focus of the TRC on issues of violence committed by individuals against individuals led to the neglect of deeper, and perhaps more subtle, crimes such as structural and cultural violence. Glatte notes that structural violence "is embedded in a country's social and economic structures and institutions and serves to leave the group of the exploited with perpetually constrained and unequal access to resources and power. The core of structural violence, in other words, is horizontal inequality."[43] By investigating only a limited range of violations, the commission neglected the violations created by structural violence, which was in reality the form of violence most widely experienced by the majority of black South African women under apartheid. As Graeme Simpson observes, "'Privileging' certain acts of political violence, and seeing race, class and gender as subsidiary to party-specific political motivations, had the ironic effect of shrouding rather than illuminating them as intrinsically political and self-explanatory characteristics essential to any understanding of the dominant patterns and experiences of violence under apartheid."[44]

Conclusion

Events during the Arab Spring have generated renewed calls for the promotion of women's rights through transitional justice processes, and South Africa provides a good example of the gap between legal (liberal) equality and lived realities. Hassim observes that while the "formal aspects of racism and institutional exclusions of the apartheid system have been eliminated, there has been minimal attention to the legacies of apartheid in the social fabric."[45] As Wendy Lambourne notes, it is important to evolve from the concept of " 'transition' as an interim process that links the past and the future" to that of " 'transformation,' which implies long-term, sustainable processes embedded in society and adoption of psychosocial, political and economic, as well as legal, perspectives on justice."[46] Any future transitional justice processes must be cognizant of the fact that violence does not occur in a vacuum, and thus "strategizing ways to end violence against women without discussing the wider social and economic disadvantages faced by women . . . [is like trying to] cut off the visible part of an iceberg without attending to the bit under the water."[47] Nelson Mandela argued that "there is no such thing as part freedom." Until South Africa combats structural inequalities and gender-based violence, the search for justice in postapartheid society will continue.[48]

Notes

1. Heidi Swart, "Will Anene Booysen's Brutal Rape and Murder Shake the Nation into Action?"

2. A coefficient of zero means all households earn exactly the same; one hundred means the most extreme inequality where one person holds all the income in a country.

3. Meintjes, Pillay, and Turshen, *Aftermath*; see also Manjoo, "South African Truth and Reconciliation Commission."

4. United Nations in South Africa, "United Nations Strongly Condemns the Rape and Murder of Anene Booysen."

5. Orford, "Commissioning the Truth," 861.

6. Cited in Hassim, "Democracy's Shadows," 66.

7. Orford, "Commissioning the Truth," 848.

8. Ibid., 851.

9. Ní Aoláin, "Advancing Feminist Positioning in the Field of Transitional Justice," 5.

10. Orford, "Commissioning the Truth," 857.

11. Glatte, "Structural Gender Violence and the South African Truth and Reconciliation Commission."

12. Ibid.

13. Human Rights Watch, *South Africa: The State Response to Domestic Violence and Rape*.

14. Mandela, "Message by President Nelson Mandela on Women's Day," August 9, 1995.

15. Hassim, "Democracy's Shadows," 66.

16. Walker, "Uneasy Relations," 79.

17. Mandela, "Speech by President Nelson Mandela on South African Women's Day," August 9, 1996.

18. Human Rights Watch, *South Africa: The State Response to Domestic Violence and Rape*.

19. Ibid.

20. Hassim, "Democracy's Shadows," 73.

21. See South Africa, *Millennium Development Goals: Country Report 2013*, 55.

22. See South Africa, *Millennium Development Goals: Country Report 2013*.

23. Sonke Gender Justice, "11 Reasons Why South Africa Needs a Fully Funded National Campaign to End Gender-Based Violence."

24. Outwater, Abrahams, and Campbell, "Women in South Africa," 139.

25. Truth and Reconciliation Commission of South Africa, *Truth and Reconciliation Commission of South Africa Final Report*.

26. Ibid.

27. Mamdani, "Beware Human Rights Fundamentalism."

28. Truth and Reconciliation Commission of South Africa, *Truth and Reconciliation Commission of South Africa Final Report*, 1.4.3.

29. See Truth and Reconciliation Commission of South Africa, *Truth and Reconciliation Commission of South Africa Final Report*, vol. 4, ch. 10, "Special Hearing: Women."

30. See Goldblatt and Meintjes, "South African Women Demand the Truth."

31. Meintjes, "Gendered Truth?," 110.

32. See Truth and Reconciliation Commission of South Africa, *Truth and Reconciliation Commission of South Africa Final Report*; and Kusafuka, "Truth Commissions and Gender."

33. Orford, "Commissioning the Truth."

34. Ibid.

35. Manjoo, "South African Truth and Reconciliation Commission," 6.

36. Hassim, "Democracy's Shadows," 66.

37. See Kusafuka, "Truth Commissions and Gender."

38. Ní Aoláin, "Advancing Feminist Positioning in the Field of Transitional Justice," 13.

39. Truth and Reconciliation Commission of South Africa, *Truth and Reconciliation Commission of South Africa Final Report*.

40. Orford, "Commissioning the Truth."

41. See Kusafuka, "Truth Commissions and Gender."

42. Mamdani, "A Diminished Truth," 38–41.

43. Glatte, "Structural Gender Violence."

44. Simpson, "Snake Gives Birth to a Snake."

45. Hassim, "Democracy's Shadows," 63.

46. Lambourne, "Transitional Justice and Peacebuilding after Mass Violence," 1.

47. Davis, "Analysis: Gender-Based Violence and the SA Women's Other Problems."

48. Askin, "Quest for Post-Conflict Gender Justice," 521.

Bibliography

Askin, Kelly D. "The Quest for Post-Conflict Gender Justice." *Columbia Journal of Transnational Law* 41(2003): 509–21.

Davis, Rebecca. "Analysis: Gender-Based Violence and the SA Women's Other Problems." *Daily Maverick*, August 22, 2013.

Glatte, Sarah. "Structural Gender Violence and the South African Truth and Reconciliation Commission." Working Paper, 2011. www.academia.edu/2394009/Structural_Gender_Vio lence_and_the_South_African_Truth_and_Reconciliation_Commission.

Goldblatt, Beth, and Sheila Meintjes. "South African Women Demand the Truth.'" In *What Women Do in Wartime*, edited by M. Turshen and C. Twagiramariya. London: Zed, 1998.

Hassim, Shireen. "Democracy's Shadows: Sexual Rights and Gender Politics in the Rape Trial of Jacob Zuma." *African Studies* 68, no. 1 (2009): 57–77.

Human Rights Watch. *South Africa: The State Response to Domestic Violence and Rape.* New York: Human Rights Watch, 1995. www.hrw.org/reports/1995/Safricawm-02.htm.

Kusafuka, Ayumi. "Truth Commissions and Gender: A South African Case Study." *African Journal on Conflict Resolution* 9, no. 2 (2009): 45–67. www.accord.org.za/images/downloads /ajcr/ajcr_2009_2.pdf.

Lambourne, Wendy. "Transitional Justice and Peacebuilding after Mass Violence." *International Journal of Transitional Justice* 3, no. 1 (2009): 28–48.

Mamdani, Mahmood. "Beware Human Rights Fundamentalism." *Mail and Guardian*, March 20, 2009.

———. "A Diminished Truth." *Siyaya!*, Spring 1998.

Mandela, Nelson. "Message by President Nelson Mandela on Women's Day." August 9, 1995. www.anc.org.za/show.php?id=3585.

———. "Speech by President Nelson Mandela on South African Women's Day." Pretoria, South Africa, August 9, 1996. www.anc.org.za/nelson/show.php?id=3334.

Manjoo, Rashida. "The South African Truth and Reconciliation Commission: A Model for Gender Justice?" United Nations Research Institute for Social Development, November 2004. www.unrisd.org/unrisd/website/document.nsf/ab82a6805797760f80256b4f005da1ab/f21 77ff8c83e0bb4c125723400591907/$FILE/Manjoo.pdf.

Meintjes, Sheila, Anu Pillay, and Meredeth Turshen. *The Aftermath: Women in Post Conflict Transformation.* London: Zed, 2001.

Meintjes, Sheila. "'Gendered Truth'? Legacies of the South African Truth and Reconciliation Commission." *African Journal on Conflict Resolution* 9, no. 2 (2009): 101–12.

Ní Aoláin, Fionnuala. "Advancing Feminist Positioning in the Field of Transitional Justice." *International Journal of Transitional Justice* 6, no. 2 (2012): 205–28.

Orford, Anne. "Commissioning the Truth." *Columbia Journal of Gender and Law* 15, no. 3 (2006): 851.

Outwater, Anne, Naeema Abrahams, and Jacquelyn C. Campbell. "Women in South Africa: Intentional Violence and HIV/AIDS: Intersections and Prevention." *Journal of Black Studies* 35, no. 4 (March 2005): 135–54.

Simpson, Graeme. "A Snake Gives Birth to a Snake: Politics and Crime in the Transition to Democracy in South Africa." In *Justice Gained? Crime and Crime Control in South Africa's Transition*, edited by Bill Dixon and Elrena Van der Spuy. Cape Town: UCT Press, 2004. www.csvr.org.za/docs/crime/snake.pdf.

Sonke Gender Justice, "11 Reasons Why South Africa Needs a Fully Funded National Cam- paign to End Gender-Based Violence." March 28, 2013. http://www.genderjustice.org.za /101692-11-reasons-why-south-africa-needs-a-fully-funded-national-campaign-to-end-gen der-based-violence-1.html.

South Africa. *Millennium Development Goals: Country Report 2013.* Statistics South Africa, 2013. http://beta2.statssa.gov.za/wp-content/uploads/2013/10/MDG_October-2013.pdf.

Swart, Heidi. "Will Anene Booysen's Brutal Rape and Murder Shake the Nation into Action?," *Mail and Guardian*, February 15, 2013. http://mg.co.za/article/2013-02-15-00-will-anene -booysens-brutal-rape-and-murder-shake-the-nation-into-action.

Truth and Reconciliation Commission of South Africa. *Truth and Reconciliation Commission of South Africa Final Report*. 7 vols. Cape Town, 1998–2002. www.justice.gov.za/trc/report/.

United Nations in South Africa. "United Nations Strongly Condemns the Rape and Murder of Anene Booysen." February 13, 2013. www.un.org.za/united-nations-strongly-condemns-the-rape-and-murder-of-anene-booysen/.

Walker, Cherryl. "Uneasy Relations: Women, Gender Equality and Tradition." *Thesis Eleven* 115, no. 1 (April 2013): 77–94.

5

Managing Transition

Lessons from Tunisia

IBRAHIM SHARQIEH

The sudden collapse in 2011 of President Zine el-Abidine Ben Ali's regime in Tunisia, one of the most robust security states in the Arab world, inspired protests from Egypt to Yemen. Some of these movements managed to topple entrenched autocratic rulers; others did not. Although Tunisia has its problems, the country is faring better today than most of its fellow Arab Spring nations. As interviews with senior government officials, heads of political parties, representatives of civil society organizations, academics and opinion leaders, and former political prisoners make clear, the Tunisian approach has distinguished itself in two areas: the sound management of its transition process and its rational, systematic approach. This approach has been largely successful. Tunisia has undertaken two productive national dialogues, and on January 26, 2014, its national assembly ratified a new constitution. A technocratic, caretaker cabinet, the result of a political compromise, will now govern the country until elections later this year. As countries throughout the region struggle to establish new social contracts, they should keep in mind the lessons learned in the Tunisian situation.

On July 25, 2013, a Salafi extremist assassinated Mohamed al-Brahmi, a member of the National Constituent Assembly (the interim parliament). In response, over fifty members withdrew from the assembly, demanding the dissolution of the existing government and the formation of a new, technocratic government to take over leadership of the continuing transition, at least until the next parliamentary elections. Rather than take up arms, opposition parties protested peacefully. Equally important, and unlike in Egypt, Tunisia's army remained committed to its professional role and refused to intervene between the opposition and the government.[1] Meanwhile, the government held intensive talks with all parties to try to end the standoff. As a testimony to its commitment to democratic principles in responding to the opposition's demands, the government has offered substantial concessions—including the formation of a national unity government and the suspension of sessions of the Constituent Assembly, which had been an opposition demand. Unlike in Egypt, no foreign mediation was required to reach these compromises. The fact that the two parties ultimately agreed about the need to form a new technocratic government presented a remarkable model for the post–Arab Spring Middle East. Indeed, the most powerful party in the Constituent Assembly—the Islamist Ennahda party—is leading the coalition troika to step down in order to work with the opposition and maintain a transition model that allows for power sharing and pluralism. Even more remarkable, Ennahda opted not to nominate a candidate for the new government and instead supported Ahmed Mestiri, the candidate of its coalition partner Ettakatol.

The fact that such a compromise was forged is a testament to the inclusive approach most Tunisians have taken to the transition from day one. As in Egypt, mainstream Islamists were poised to take power after the leader was overthrown. Just as the Egyptian Muslim Brotherhood made a strong showing in the first post-Mubarak vote, Tunisia's Ennahda Party won 41 percent of the seats in the Constituent Assembly in the first post–Ben Ali vote.[2] Rather than push out other parties, Ennahda politicians joined in a coalition troika with the Ettakatol Party and the Congress for the Republic, both center-left groups. Ennahda also decided to support the nomination of secularist Moncef Marzouki for the presidency. Marzouki, a human rights activist and detainee under Ben Ali, headed the Congress for the Republic, which had received only 13.4 percent of the assembly seats.[3] Despite the parties' ideological differences, the coalition has held together for almost two years now. For his part, Marzouki has managed to guide the coalition but has not established himself as an especially powerful leader on the national level, particularly amid political crises.

And Justice for Most

Tunisia's transitional government has made laudable progress toward a comprehensive, well-reasoned transitional justice law. Of the twelve members of the independent committee charged with drafting the law, only two represent the Ministry of Justice; the other ten come from various civil society groups.[4] Those members gauge popular opinion by meeting with people throughout the country and asking the victims of the Ben Ali dictatorship what they want and expect from the transitional justice process. The committee has also consulted with organizations specializing in transitions and transitional justice and has included them among its ten civil society members. The Al-Kawakibi Democracy Transition Center and the Tunisia Network for Transitional Justice, both represented in the committee, have played key roles.

Tunisia has chosen a middle path for dealing with former regime elements. It has avoided enacting anything resembling Libya's sweeping Political Isolation Law, which penalized almost anyone who held public office between 1969 and 2011.[5] Tunisia also opted for something more rigorous than did Yemen, where the immunity law that accompanied the country's Gulf-brokered settlement short-circuited any attempt at transitional justice and prevented prosecutions for past violations. Not one person in Yemen has been held accountable for past crimes, and the former regime has continued to govern without even minimal party reform. Tunisia's approach, on the other hand, has been termed *tahseen al-thawra* (fortifying the revolution). Some of the most senior former officials have been banned from public office for five years. But those who have not been tried or convicted will be permitted to participate in politics—allowing, for example, the Habib Bourguiba–era official Beji Caid Essebsi to lead the Nidaa Tounes Party. (Essebsi has also said he plans to run in the next presidential election.) Tunisians have emphasized a targeted process of transitional justice, prosecuting on an individual basis; otherwise, they are resolute that only the ballot box should exclude these figures from public life.

On institutional reform, meanwhile, the Constituent Assembly has adopted the approach of *gharbala* (sifting) rather than the full-scale *tathir* (purge) demanded in Libya. In reforming the judiciary, the priority will be to remove judges linked by hard evidence to corruption or misconduct. The security services, meanwhile, will be subject to oversight from new structures such as the National Authority for the Prevention of Torture, which will be in charge of monitoring and inspecting the country's prisons. It will also have the authority to enter any jail and interview its prisoners. In addition, although the government faces charges of restricting the media, the Constituent Assembly has at least formed special committees to inspect and reform both the state media, complicit for so long in glorifying the former regime, and the historically corrupt administrative apparatus.

All of the efforts to grapple with the legacy of the old regime have been complemented by parallel national dialogues, one put forward by the country's presidency and one by the Tunisian General Labor Union (UGTT). The dialogues aim to forge agreement on key challenges facing the country, including the nature of the state, elections, and basic elements of the constitution. More than sixty political parties and fifty civil society organizations are involved in one or the other of these dialogues.[6] They have already led to agreements on a number of key points: a firm rejection of violence, the economy as a government priority, a road map for the transition, consensus on major issues such as a civil state and a constitutional system, the independence of the judiciary, freedom of the press, and freedom of assembly. Further, the national dialogue formed a committee of seventeen political parties and four civil society organizations to implement all agreements.[7]

One of the greatest achievements produced by Tunisia's national dialogue is that the political standoff between the opposition and the troika government after the assassination of Mohamed al-Brahmi was fully mediated by UTGG's president, Hussein al-Abbasi. The national dialogue created an environment of cooperation conducive to successful mediation. The troika government, and Ennahda in particular, could have lost some privileges or political gains through the concessions made to resolve the crisis. However, the troika government's leaving power through a negotiated agreement with the opposition, mediated by Tunisia's civil society, is a great achievement for the process of democratic transition and successful compromise.

The Sources of Tunisian Settlement

There are several cultural and religious factors that have worked in Tunisia's favor throughout the transition. In conversation Tunisians frequently emphasize that most Tunisians reject radicalism and violence. Some, including Said Ferjani, an Ennahda politician, attribute that to the prevalence of the moderate Maliki school of Islamic jurisprudence, which has historically rejected extremism (a reported 98 percent of Tunisians adhere to Malikism).[8] Others point to President Bourguiba, who ruled from 1957 to 1987, and the cultural legacy of his centralizing and modernizing project. Tunisia also lacks the sharp ethnic, tribal, or sectarian-religious delineations that have proven so divisive elsewhere.

Structural factors, however, do not fully explain Tunisia's course. One important issue is the outlook of the Ennahda Party, which differs dramatically from that of Egypt's Muslim Brotherhood. Brotherhood leaders were subjected to decades of systematic repression and radicalization within Egypt; their political agenda was largely shaped in regime prisons. For example, Mohamed Badie, the supreme guide of the Muslim Brotherhood, was jailed from 1965 to 1974 under Egyptian presidents Gamal Abdul Nasser and Anwar al-Sadat. (And he has now been imprisoned again.) Ennahda leaders, on the other hand, spent the Ben Ali years in exile. From 1991 to 2011 Ennahda leader Rached al-Ghannouchi resided in London, as did many of the group's other top figures. The experience had a modernizing influence on Ennahda's political thought, pushing it to embrace and articulate a more inclusive and conciliatory model. In addition, Salafis have more political weight in Egypt, where they won 28 percent of the country's 2011 parliamentary vote and helped to polarize the country's political debate and drag the Egyptian Brotherhood further to the right.[9]

Tunisia also enjoys, contra Egypt, a professional, noninterventionist army with a commitment to republicanism. Egypt's army has historically wielded political power in its own right. It even has its own set of international allies: The military-to-military relationship between the United States and Egypt occasionally overshadows bilateral diplomatic relations. Tunisia's army, on the other hand, was decisive in Ben Ali's ouster and the subsequent transition in part because of its relative absence from Tunisian politics.

Tunisia has also benefited from having an intact Constituent Assembly for most of its transition, providing a broadly legitimate platform for debate. (The lower house of Egypt's parliament was dissolved by court order, leaving only the weaker upper house.) Although Tunisia's Constituent Assembly was also recently suspended, it is expected to return soon; most of the efforts to mediate the country's political crisis, which seem close to a resolution, have emphasized the resumption of the assembly's work. In addition, civil society has played a leading role in national dialogue and mediation.

The Tunisian Model

Of course, the Tunisian transition faces challenges, among them some continued popular protests and the desperate state of the economy. Transitions need substantial budgets; reconciliation is typically based in part on compensation for victims of the old regime—former prisoners, the families of the disappeared, and so on. Tunisia is resource poor, and its tourism industry has been hit hard by the revolution and its aftermath. It is not unusual to visit tourist destinations around the country and find them entirely deserted these days.

Tunisia also faces a difficult challenge to state authority and the rule of law: the Protection of the Revolution Committees (PRCs). These committees, which are composed of former revolutionaries, have taken it upon themselves to defend the revolution and agitate for old-regime elements to be held accountable. Although the transition is moving ahead, committee members fear the rise of a counterrevolution. In at least one instance a PRC has been accused of killing an opposition politician—Lutfi Naqeq of the Nidaa Tounes Party. PRCs have also been suspected of attacking UGTT in Tunis. Some opposition groups believe that the PRCs are the military wing of the Ennahda Party. In reality they are not, although they do include some party members. The challenge of revolutionary demobilization is one that faces most revolutions, and Tunisia's revolution is no exception. Still, determining the best way to deal with these committees has become divisive. Ennahda has argued that any political decision to dissolve the committees will undermine the transition and that, instead, committees linked to violence should be dissolved through the Tunisian courts. Others, though, argue that the license for vigilantism is intolerable and that protecting the revolution is the exclusive responsibility of the state.

Tunisia also faces at least one kind of polarization that is more extreme than in other Arab cases: the vast (and growing) divide between Tunisia's secularist liberals and its ultraconservative Salafi Islamists. Tunisian secularism is vibrant and unparalleled in the Arab world; under Bourguiba and Ben Ali, Tunisia was the only Arab country to ban the *hijab* in state institutions. Its Salafi jihadists, meanwhile, demand a purely religious state and have shown their willingness to attack cultural activities they deem un-Islamic. Tunisia is in sharp contrast with Egypt, for example, where there was basic consensus on the establishment of Islam as the state religion; in Tunisia the sheer distance between these two cultural extremes makes the chance that they will coalesce around one vision for the state rather slim. Moreover, Salafis, who were imprisoned or underground before the revolution, have been growing in strength. Jailed Salafi leaders—including Abu Ayadh, the leader of Ansar al-Sharia, a Salafi group in Tunisia—were released as part of the country's postrevolution amnesty and have since grown in influence. Ansar al-Sharia's annual conference in 2012 attracted roughly five thousand attendees; an estimated fifty thousand were expected to attend the 2013 conference in the city of Kairouan, but the government decided to block the roads leading to the city and prevented the conference by force.[10] The huge gap between liberals and Salafis has left the moderate Ennahda Party, almost by default, to occupy the Tunisian middle. The upshot is that one can witness Ennahda figures being tarred—often simultaneously—as closet fundamentalists by liberals and as infidels and tyrants by Salafis.

Moreover, security continues to emerge as another challenge to Tunisia's transition. In almost three years since the revolution, two Constituent Assembly members (Chokri Belaid —and Mohamed al-Brahmi) have been assassinated; tourists were targeted in October bombings in the cities of Sousse and Monstir; and a number of violent clashes between the Tunisian army and extremist groups in the Sha'anbi Mountain have taken place. Especially after the government labeled Ansar al-Sharia as a "terrorist organization," fears of an impending security crisis have become more pronounced among many Tunisians.[11]

Of course, the government has means of dealing with each of these problems. The ultimate solution for Tunisia's economic difficulties is progress on its political transition; as normalcy is restored, tourism can be expected to bounce back. In the meantime, however, the international community should financially support the transition, recognizing that they are not just investing in Tunisia but in a model for successful transitions that can be exported to the entire Arab region.

In the controversy over the PRCs, both sides have valid points and concerns. Here, the emphasis should be on bolstering and promoting the rule of law. PRCs should not all be treated as one; the choice should not be to either keep them all or dissolve them by political decree. Rather, any individual PRC that breaks the law or behaves in violation of its registered and declared goals should be immediately disbanded within the framework of the Tunisian judicial system.

Socioeconomic development can also help mitigate pockets of domestic radicalism. There is a reason that the poorest neighborhood of Tunis, Tadamon, witnessed violence when this year's Ansar al-Sharia conference was canceled. Tunisia can also rely on its legacy of Maliki jurisprudence. The Ez-Zitouna Mosque in

Tunis is one of the world's most important centers of Maliki thought. The mosque's Maliki scholars have worked hard to counter ultraconservative Wahhabi thought by putting forward an Islam based in knowledge and reason. They thus seem primed to repel a new surge in radicalism and help forge societal consensus.

Because of the challenges ahead, Tunisians seem to have little confidence in their transition. In conversation, they constantly ask how it compares to those in other countries. But the Tunisians really are a model for the Arab world's transitioning states. After all, they are not just building a new set of state institutions; they are forging a culture of accountability and the rule of law. This is how Tunisia can accommodate the political participation of prerevolutionary figures such as Essebsi and Kamel Morjane, around whom Tunisia is changing for the better. Although Tunisia benefits from some unique characteristics, other Arab countries should seek to emulate its homegrown national dialogue, its political coalition building, and its bottom-up approach to reform, best exemplified by the drafting of its transitional justice law. For Tunisia, this approach of steady, inclusive, and rule-based state building is allowing for broad reconciliation and a real evolution in Tunisian society. Tunisia may well show the rest of the Arab world the way forward.

Notes

1. Bellin, *Drivers of Democracy*.
2. Amara, "In Turnaround, Ruling Tunisia Islamists Will Meet Rivals."
3. Gamha, "Final Results of Tunisian Elections Announced."
4. Author's interview with members of the drafting committee of the transitional justice law, Tunisia, June 2013.
5. *Libya Herald*, "Political Isolation Law: The Full Text."
6. Author's interview with the UGTT Secretariat, Tunisia, June 2013.
7. Fikra Forum, "Tunisia's National Dialogue is the Last Hope for Solving Political Crisis."
8. Author's interview with Said Ferjani, Tunisia, June 2013.
9. Lacroix, *Sheikhs and Politicians*.
10. Saidani, "A Gathering Storm."
11. Aljazeera Center for Studies, *Tunisia: National Dialogue in the Context of Political and Security Challenges*.

Bibliography

Aljazeera Center for Studies. *Tunisia: National Dialogue in the Context of Political and Security Challenges*. Position Paper, November 2013. http://studies.aljazeera.net/en/positionpapers /2013/11/20131110123327549569.htm.

Amara, Tarek. "In Turnaround, Ruling Tunisia Islamists Will Meet Rivals," Reuters, August 18, 2013. http://mobile.reuters.com/article/idUSBRE97H0CN20130818?irpc = 932.

Bellin, Eva. *Drivers of Democracy: Lessons from Tunisia*. Middle East Brief, Brandeis University Crown Center for Middle East Studies, no. 75, August 2013. www.brandeis.edu/crown/publications/meb/MEB75.pdf.

Fikra Forum. "Tunisia's National Dialogue Is the Last Hope for Solving Political Crisis." October 24, 2013. http://fikraforum.org/?p = 3986.

Gamha, Eyman. "Final Results of Tunisian Elections Announced." Tunisialive, November 14, 2011. www.tunisia-live.net/2011/11/14/tunisian-election-final-results-tables/.

Lacroix, Stephane. *Sheikhs and Politicians: Inside the New Egyptian Salafism*. Brookings Doha Center, Policy Briefing, June 2012. www.brookings.edu/~/media/research/files/papers/2012/6/07%20egyptian%20salafism%20lacroix/stephane%20lacroix%20policy%20briefing%20english.pdf.

Libya Herald. "Political Isolation Law: The Full Text." May 14, 2013. www.libyaherald.com/2013/05/14/political-isolation-law-the-full-text/#axzz2mbcdnRSf.

Saidani, Monji. "A Gathering Storm." *Asharq Al-Awsat*, May 28, 2013. www.aawsat.net/2013/05/article55303311.

6

Is There a Center to Hold?

The Problem of Transition in Post-Qaddafi Libya

ASIF MAJID

After accepting responsibility—but not culpability—for the December 1988 bombing of Pan Am Flight 103, Muammar Qaddafi was received back into the international community in 2003. Libya paid compensation to the families of the 270 victims of the bombing, and sanctions were lifted against Libya as diplomatic relations were restored. Libya "bought peace," and the West was assured of open access to oil.[1] Fewer than ten years later, Qaddafi was overthrown in an uprising that received vast military support from the North Atlantic Treaty Organization (NATO). Found hiding in a drain, Qaddafi was assaulted and then killed. His body was buried in an unmarked grave somewhere in the Libyan Desert.

Today, Libya is in disarray. Islamist militias have taken over the nation's capital and captured the international airport in Tripoli. The elected Libyan government has fled from Tripoli to Tobruk, a third-choice city given control of Benghazi by Islamist militias. The Tripoli-based Islamists have set up their own parliament, such that the country now exists with two parallel government structures. These competing centers of power agreed to hold UN-facilitated talks in late September 2014; soon thereafter, militias in Tripoli rejected calls for a cease-fire that emerged from the discussions. The outcome remains to be seen.

Clearly, Libya faces immense challenges. Politically motivated armed conflict between Islamists and secularists and their respective militias, as well as growing lawlessness, have contributed to increasing criminal violence. Foreign interests and a readiness to pursue them in Libya add extra layers of complexity to an

The author acknowledges the important contributions of Tyrone Savage to this chapter. He has provided a detailed, in situ understanding of the current dynamics in Libya. This text would not be in its current form without his assistance and support.

already convoluted transition, while armed groups benefiting from a flood of heavy weaponry compete for internal power. This begs the question: Whither Libya?

Legacies of Deep Division

Libya's divisions are not new. Colonialism, manipulation, and depravation induced by foreign powers have a long history in what is today known as Libya. The country is split into three historic regions: Tripolitania in the northwest, Fezzan in the southwest, and Cyrenaica in the east. Attempting to unite these regions into a single state was a slow process, the bulk of which took place in the period from 1942 to 1951. During this time, the French ruled Fezzan while the British ruled Tripolitania and Cyrenaica. After a tumultuous period of political indecision, the allied forces of World War II united the three regions into one country, which became independent in 1951. Idris al-Senussi, head of the Senussi Sufi order, was installed as king; he thanked his benefactors with gifts of land, influence, and oil (after its discovery in the late 1950s). Wealth remained concentrated in the uppermost echelons of Libyan society.

Enter Muammar Qaddafi. Inspired by a coup d'état in Egypt led by Gamal Abdel Nasser, Qaddafi and his fellow Free Officers executed a peaceful coup in 1969, establishing the Libyan Arab Republic. He consolidated his power through a cultural revolution in 1973—the Jamahiriya, or state of the masses—and proclaimed the Great Socialist People's Libyan Arab Jamahiriya in 1977. While this masqueraded as a form of direct democracy that was free of political parties and that reflected the country's tribal divisions, it gave Qaddafi near total control.[2] Qaddafi pitted tribes against one another, made the armed services subservient to his personal needs, and imprisoned or exiled those who opposed him. Based on his reading of the Qur'an, he rejected both capitalism and communism.[3] At the same time, he developed extravagant manifestations of his Bedouin roots as well as an initial vision of pan-Arab unity.

Despite Qaddafi's authoritarian rule, Libyan opposition could not be silenced. From the mid-1980s onward, Qaddafi made some political concessions by restraining the power of the revolutionary committees he had established. He also yielded to demands for reform in the economy and allowed for modest private trade under the direction of his son Saif al-Islam Qaddafi, a process that further enriched the Tripoli-based elite.

Building on the December 2010 uprisings in Tunisia, Libyan opposition to Qaddafi intensified, leading to open rebellion in February 2011. Rebels received arms via ancient smuggling routes. In mid-March 2011, NATO initiated airstrikes to support the rebel cause. Qaddafi was killed in October 2011. The National

Transitional Council (NTC), the political face of the transition, gained international recognition before handing over power to the General National Congress (GNC) through elections in July 2012. Multiple civil society organizations emerged to take part in the political process upon Qaddafi's death. However, the collapse of Qaddafi's authoritarian state resulted in the disintegration of government institutions. This escalated distrust and suspicion between opposing groups as they fought to benefit from Qaddafi's demise.

Security became a major concern, leading the NTC and then the GNC to limit civil society activities. Armed groups proliferated, and attacks on both Libyan and international officials became commonplace. Though voices in Libya and beyond called for an inclusive national dialogue that reached across tribal, ideological, and class interests, such moderate viewpoints have been sidelined. At best, today Libya remains in a transition to a transition.

The Libyan Revolution

Dominant Arab Gulf States as well as the West, both of which played a major role in Qaddafi's exit, continue to be factors in the post-Qaddafi period. NATO and its allies underestimated the extent of Libyan sectarianism at the time of their 2011 intervention.

Opposition to Qaddafi's rule was deep-seated, resulting in everyday Libyan people in both urban and rural areas as well as organized rebel groups taking to the streets in 2011. Reports also indicate that the CIA and Britain's MI6 were involved in supporting the Libyan uprising.[4] Rebel groups also alleged that Qaddafi's troops had attacked unarmed civilians, which contributed to a situation that was interpreted as a justification for intervention. Alternate, nonviolent peace proposals forwarded by the International Crisis Group and the African Union (AU) called for negotiations and an immediate cease-fire, but leaders in Washington, Paris, and London brushed these aside.[5]

All of this contributed to Qaddafi's Libya becoming the latest victim in the Western tradition of eliminating unfriendly regimes around the world. NATO strikes and a no-fly zone were the order of the day, supported by Saudi Arabia and other powerful Gulf States. NATO's priority was regime change. Allegedly, this resulted in NATO pilots and strike commanders ignoring rebel requests for support in rural areas, preferring to focus their attention on the infrastructure on which Qaddafi depended to remain in power.

After Qaddafi was eliminated, direct military support was withdrawn and limited support for the reconstruction process was offered, leaving the NTC to deal with rebel forces. The West had learned its twenty-first-century lesson in interventionism the hard way in Iraq and was not about to repeat the mistake of a lengthy and costly restoration process. In the words of historian Hugh Roberts, "shadow play" limited Western liability.[6]

Libya's developing political structures reflect the country's deep divisions and fractures that had been held together by Qaddafi's strong hand; these fissures were not taken into account. NATO bombs were insufficient to establish a friendly regime in Libya or to create a context within which former enemies could develop a reconstructive environment. This placed the NTC and GNC in a power vacuum, the very situation that the AU's peace proposal sought to avoid.[7]

These circumstances serve Western elites and wealthy Gulf States in economic terms. With Qaddafi gone and the GNC on its way to disarray, economic and political interest groups are free to manipulate the country. As is discussed below, foreign oil companies increase their influence on Libya's future through funding and other forms of support for a cash-strapped and dependent government.

All of this leads to a question: To what extent was Libya's uprising a foreign intervention rather than a national revolution? Indigenous rebel forces were and are an inherent part of the continuing unrest in Libya, while the manipulation of the original uprising by outside forces has opened the door for foreign powers to reap the benefits. Whether from NATO, foreign intelligence sources, or politicians in far-off cities, interventions to refashion Libya have conspired to make it dependent on NATO countries and their allies.

Struggling with Leadership in a Power Vacuum

Libya is finding it increasingly difficult to forge national independence in the face of foreign pressure and in a declining security situation. Armed groups align themselves with external and internal sources of funding, promoting tribal allegiances and vying with one another to secure the support of different elements of the Libyan government. Reports identify approximately seventeen hundred armed groups that range in size and experience.[8] These include revolutionary groups that fought against Qaddafi during the 2011 uprisings as well as others that broke away from local military councils during and after the civil war. Beyond these recognized brigades, multiple criminal networks and extremist groups also exist, in addition to mercenaries who were once employed as security forces by Qaddafi.[9] At the same time, there is evidence that many of these armed groups have established relations with foreign governments and private funders. A US defense official noted that "just because someone is in a militia doesn't mean they can't participate" in training that meets "NATO standards."[10] As they grow, armed groups are looking beyond Libya, an orientation that is likely to escalate conflict within the country.

Libya's patchwork of armed groups represents a multitude of interests. The United States and the European Union (EU) have supported the integration of multiple brigades into Libya's government forces, while the wealthy Arab Gulf States and the United States have been involved in training Libyan government military recruits. Evidence points to the secular-leaning National Forces Alliance enjoying the support of Libya's Defense Ministry. Armed Islamist groups benefit from a closer relationship with private funders on the Arabian Peninsula via Libya's Interior Ministry, fueling the competition between Gulf and other Arab States in their quest to gain influence in Libya.

Complicating the situation is Operation Dignity, a military campaign launched by renegade general Khalifa Haftar in early 2014 with the stated aims of fighting terrorism and expelling Islamist extremists from the country. This resulted in early battles against Islamist militias in Benghazi, expanding to Tripoli by mid-2014. The GNC government insisted that Haftar had no authority to act, and the United States distanced itself from his actions. There is, however, evidence to indicate covert US support for Haftar, particularly in the form of aerial surveillance. Haftar, a one-time chief of staff in Libya's military, fell out of favor with Qaddafi and fled to the United States. Reports indicate that he underwent training with the CIA and acquired United States citizenship; he returned to Libya in 2011 to support the civil war.[11] Forces aligned with Operation Dignity stormed the GNC in May 2014 and pushed for its dissolution. Haftar has emerged as a military leader with significant support across the country. This backing includes disgruntled units of the Libyan security forces, the powerful Zintani militias from the Nafusa Mountains, councils of elders, and even the founder of the Islamist February 17 Brigade that Haftar's forces have been fighting in Benghazi.[12] Given Haftar's checkered history, he may well be an unacceptable leader to both Libyans and the international community. However, his rise to political visibility raises the question as to whether Libyans, NATO, and their allies will look for a strongman similar to Egypt's General Abdul Fatah al-Sisi, a figure discussed in chapter 7.

Leadership developments in Egypt and their relevance to Libya are part of a contentious debate that begins with the Political Isolation Law (PIL), which prevents Qaddafi-era officials from holding public office until ten years have passed. Fear of the emergence of a Qaddafi-era leader has resulted in multiple postponements of a final decision on the constitutionality of the PIL, which was made law in May 2013.[13] Critics of the PIL see it as an instrument of partisan national revenge that reduces institutional and administrative capacity while failing to make allowances for Qaddafi-era officials who criticized the regime and contributed to its downfall. In light of the PIL, Haftar's position as a former member of the regime presents a significant question mark.

Libya's leadership parallels to Egypt are obvious but should not be exaggerated. Egypt is a key player in the politics of the Middle East. Libya's influence on regional and global politics is of a different kind. Libya is a gateway to Europe that enables illegal migration across the Mediterranean; former Qaddafi and rebel fighters have been drawn into military conflicts in Syria, Iraq, Iran, and the Sahel;

and the country offers an accessible supply of oil. Further, while President Sisi has significant support through Egypt's military, corporate, and administrative infrastructure, whoever grabs power in Libya will have to (re)build the state, almost from nothing.

Despite the tendency to reject anything Qaddafi-esque, there is a realization that his policies—although unequal in application—led to literacy rates of 88 percent, an annual per capita income of US$12,000 (the highest in Africa), relatively good education, and adequate health care. Qaddafi also provided development and military aid to other African nations; his support for Pan-Africanism resulted in his being seen and treated as a cult hero by many across the continent. All of this, both at home and elsewhere in Africa, was possible because Qaddafi controlled oil revenue and used it to bolster his own agenda at the cost of democratic processes and human rights. Certain questions emerge in relation to current events: What are those everyday people who benefited from Qaddafi's favor prepared to do, and whom are they prepared to support, in order to recover those benefits? Is the war-ravaged public willing to follow any populist leader who has the military and material backing to promise peace?

There is growing support for forces loyal to Haftar, leaders of Zintani militias, and other rebel groups that feed off popular anger regarding the lack of adequate social services while exploiting Libya's history of entrenched sectarianism. This paints a dismal picture within the existing power vacuum. While competing militia groups provide a semblance of security for different sections of society in a country that suffers from a chronic absence of law, order, and normalcy, most of these militias are accused of human rights abuses, unlawful detentions, and vigilante justice. Dangerously, this escalates Libya's civil war.

Social Identity

Today's social identity struggle in Libya is embedded in yesterday's malady of colonialism that manipulated existing precolonial divisions between tribes. Colonial powers governed each tribal group according to distinct customary law that was executed by "loyal" and favored native chiefs. African nationalists had similar practices, cementing their position in the postcolonial period through the promotion of their own specific tribal allegiances and the exclusion of others.

Ironically, these loyalties, which entrenched divisions both before the rule of King Idris and throughout the Qaddafi years, may offer a semblance of hope in the lawlessness that is Libya. The residual persistence of patriarchal tribal authority, albeit with weakened control, provides a sense of constancy in parts of the country, even where traditional values have been depleted; nonetheless, equal inclusion of women remains a challenge. In reality, many armed groups have their roots in these structures. A good deal may hinge on whether tribal leaders have the will and capacity to reconcile with other tribal leaders and secular groups in the country. Effective leadership will need to appeal to communities steeped in tribal law and religion while at the same time accepting the agency of secular influences on government and business affairs.

In an attempt to reconcile the historic African tensions between tribal authorities and central government, Libya's original GNC was based on an electoral system that allowed for 64 constituency seats (for independent candidates only) and 136 seats for those nominated by political parties. However, the fact that 120 of the 200 seats in that GNC were held by independents—as opposed to the 64 seats designated for independents in the electoral law—suggests reluctance by political parties to include tribal leaders and hesitation by these leaders to engage in national politics. Evolving parliamentary formations, including the current iteration of the elected House of Representatives, furthers this historical tension.

Continuing contestation regarding the election of a prime minister is another indicator of ongoing instability in Libyan governance. In October 2013, a militia aligned with the Islamist-leaning Ministry of the Interior abducted Prime Minister Ali Zeidan; he was released the same day after Zintani and other militias intervened. Zeidan was ousted four months later. Abdullah al-Thinni was appointed caretaker prime minister, but he resigned from office after violence threatened his family. The GNC then appointed Ahmed Maiteeq as prime minister, but he was forced to resign after the selection was ruled unconstitutional. In June 2014, al-Thinni was returned to his former position. This means that post-Qaddafi Libya has changed prime ministers, on average, every five months. Each new figure has come via an alliance between numerous political parties, emerging from stormy and tumultuous conditions. GNC member Ahmed Langi highlighted this dynamism, calling for a "balanced cabinet team, consisting of members from Cyrenaica, Tripoli, and Fezzan."[14] The political tensions between regional and central interests in Libya need to be overcome.

Questions abound. Will the legacy of the Qaddafi years—in which civil society was sidelined, if not silenced—return to Libya? Will the upsurge of civil society seen in the immediate aftermath of Qaddafi's departure take root and create a culture of democratic participation? Will the involvement of powerful foreign countries result in the establishment of a client state in Libya that, once again, fails to enjoy the support of its people? Will Islamist forces establish an emirate governed by Islamic law? Or will the separate regions, tribes, and ideologies of Libya, each with diverse needs and interests, coexist in some form of federal government?

History suggests that people denied their basic rights have a capacity to renew themselves as they pursue those rights. This is seen across the Afro-Arab *ecumene*: Liberian women brought about the end of civil war in their country in 2003 through sit-ins and sex strikes. Fambul Tok in Sierra Leone has incorporated tribal divisions into its reconciliatory processes. The garnering of over a million votes in the South African national elections by the new Economic Freedom Fighters (EFF) party indicates restlessness among that country's poor. Popular protests continue to be a significant factor in Egyptian politics, while Tunisia, despite its progress in governance, continues to face demands for broader democratic inclusion. Demonstrations continue in other parts of Southwestern Asia and Africa. The list of successful civil society movements across Afro-Arab nations is long and growing.

Building a new Libyan state requires the integration of government, tribal, and other structures. Indeed, the involvement of elites from the West and Arab Gulf States, as well as other global powers, is likely to increase. Time is the greatest of teachers, and it is still too early to predict the outcome of developments in Libya. However, ineffective understanding of on-the-ground complexities could generate more violence in an already broken country.

Oil

Oil has long been seen as both a blessing and a curse for developing countries. In Libya, oil is a lure that can exacerbate the involvement of industrialized nations in the country's struggle to find a common center. Qaddafi's ousting has given rise to a new Libyan era, one twisted by international oil needs. Export figures from 2010 reflect that year's flow of Libyan oil: 27 percent to Italy, 16 percent to France, 10 percent to Spain, 10 percent to Germany, 5 percent to Greece, 4 percent to the United Kingdom, and 3 percent to the United States. With Europe and the United States receiving 75 percent of Libya's 2010 oil output, it could ill afford to leave their supplies dependent on the whims of Qaddafi, a man they dismissed as an impulsive dictator.[15] The Iraq war and its implications for the Arab Gulf States, as well as deteriorating relations between the European Union and Russia and increasing Chinese demands for oil, complicate matters further. International dependence on Libyan oil reflects one of the vested foreign interests that impacted Libya's past and continues to govern its future.

Just after the NATO strikes on Libya, oil production dropped at least 10 percent. Oil and gas, however, continued to be in high demand across the developing world. Saudi Arabia, the only country in the world with the capacity to turn production on and off at will, added over 150,000 barrels per day to global output almost overnight. Iraq played its part as well, contributing an additional 200,000 barrels per day during August 2013.[16]

By increasing world supplies, Saudi Arabian oil reported record profits in 2012. The big five oil companies (BP, ConocoPhillips, Chevron, ExxonMobil, and Shell) also reported massive profits nearing US$20 billion during the second quarter of 2013.[17] Furthermore, a recent report from the Kurdish magazine *Lvin* shows that well-placed retired generals and politicians—former British Prime Minister Tony

Blair apparently among them—are benefiting from the establishment of multiple oil contracts in Kurdish parts of Iraq.[18]

Threats by Ibrahim Saeed Jdharan—head of Cyrenaica's political bureau—regarding oil-rich Cyrenaica's intention to secede from the national state have important implications for both the country's level of oil production and its political stability. While the now Tobruk-based government seeks to restore war-damaged ports in Cyrenaica to ship oil from the multiple oil fields in the area, armed tribal groups with the capacity to sabotage national reconstruction and restoration processes are demanding a share of oil revenues.

This conflict between Tripoli and Cyrenaica is of particular importance to oil companies interested in Libya. The country's major pipelines, as well as a number of the most prominent oil fields, are in Cyrenaica. In addition, most of Libya's ports for shipping oil are in the Cyrenaica region. Oil companies are thus forced to renegotiate their relationship with multiple centers of influence in Libya, among them the Libyan government, Cyrenaica's political bureau, and rebel groups. Whatever the outcome of the Cyrenaican threat to secede, the involvement of oil companies in Libyan political developments is likely to increase in the future, as is the role of foreign states.

At the same time, there are other suitors such as Russia, some of the Arab Gulf States, and China. Each is competing for varying degrees of influence in Libya, particularly in terms of access to oil and the sale of military equipment. Other countries in North Africa, including Morocco and Algeria, are also keen to provide military support to the government and rebel groups in the country. In turn, Egypt under Sisi's rule may support a strong Libyan ruler who has the ability to impose law and order, regardless of the circumstances under which he may come to power. The intersection of external and internal trade factors will, most likely, make these countries important contestants in the struggle for political influence in Libya.

The Way Forward

Extended political and sectarian violence makes structured dialogue increasingly difficult, yet this may be the only alternative to further violence. To succeed, the ground rules for such a dialogue will need to involve a commitment to address all issues of accountability for past and present human rights violations, involving people engaged in all sides of the conflict.

This makes the issue of purging, embodied in the PIL, an increasingly contentious matter. A policy of excluding those affiliated with a past regime was adopted in Iraq after the removal of Saddam Hussein. It escalated political conflict there, with the present disarray in Iraq indicating the importance of including all sections of a nation in any reconstruction program.[19] Though the PIL is a major concern in this regard, Haftar's military operations and desire to rid Libya of any Islamist influence represent a more direct form of purging.

Qaddafi's rule resulted in serious repression—from the Ownership Law of 1978, which encouraged mass seizure of private property such as homes and businesses, to the infamous massacre at Abu Salim Prison. In 1996, 1,270 prisoners were killed at Abu Salim after they sought improved living conditions.[20] Families of the deceased have not received reparations or assistance from the state in dealing with their losses, nor have they obtained the basic information required for them to have a measure of closure in their lives. Any national dialogue process in Libya would have to consider these elements of Libya's past.

National dialogue is also required in order to handle questions of providing immunity to those responsible for the implementation of Qaddafi-era policies and to revolutionary brigades and rebel armies for crimes committed in the context of efforts to oust Qaddafi. Part of the problem with establishing a national dialogue is that there is no precedent for such conversation in Libya. Qaddafi's decentralization of power outlawed Libya's political parties, which resulted in the Libyan people's lack of familiarity with constructive national debate. Inclusive reconciliation, however, requires that the nation's multiple stakeholders engage one another regarding the most controversial issues facing the nation. This means that transitional justice structures in Libya will need to equip the country with checks and balances that facilitate an inherently difficult dialogue, a process that is growing more convoluted by the day. Whatever the underlying causes of Qaddafi's overthrow and the nature of external forces in the final demise of his regime, Libyans must find a method of coexistence if they are to build a post-Qaddafi state.

Including members of Qaddafi's regime, minority groups, tribal leaders, youth, and women in national conversation is an important step forward in this regard. However, the process of the elections in early 2014 for the Constitutional Drafting Assembly (CDA) suggests that the participation of female candidates in the constitution-making process will be limited. As Lawyers for Justice in Libya articulated:

> Despite representing 49% of the population, women's participation is likely to be limited to the six reserved seats. Female representation in the constitution-drafting process is likely to be further hampered due to an asymmetrically implemented electoral system. As a result, only a few sub-constituencies will have separate lists for women candidates and many will, therefore, be left with no choice as to which women will represent them in the CDA. While women candidates could theoretically still be elected into the assembly via the general lists, this is unlikely to happen due to the limited number of female candidates on the general lists. The elections for the General National Council in 2012 also demonstrated that women candidates are currently unlikely to win seats through the general ballot.[21]

Change in Libya will require a level of political inclusion in the GNC that the broader Libyan political apparatus, at present, fails to reflect.

For a sustainable peace, Libyans must reach beyond the categories of those who supported and those who opposed Qaddafi's rule. Such a task demands a commitment to dialogue and national reconciliation as captured in the September 2013 report to the UN Security Council from UN Secretary-General Ban Ki-moon. The report highlights the importance of tackling security concerns, recognizing interconnected foreign and domestic factors, addressing the challenge of internally displaced persons, disarming militia groups, building state institutions, and implementing transitional justice programs.[22]

A meaningful and comprehensive response by a broad cross section of Libyans to Ban Ki-moon's report could go a long way toward determining the country's future direction. In what the UN report refers to as a "stalled transition," the worst-case scenario for Libya could be either a foreign-dominated client state or a Somalia-like disintegration. Indeed, continuing uncertainty is today's only certainty.

Notes

1. BBC News, "Full Transcript: Libyan PM Interview."
2. Libyan tribes include: Major Libyan Tribes (Gadhadhfa, Warfalla, Magarha, Firjan, Hasawna, and Sweia); those found in the Cyrenaica Region (Al-Awagir, Al-Abaydat, Drasa, Al-Barasa, Al-Fawakhir, Al-Zuwayya, and Al-Majabra); those in the Tripolitania Region (Warfalla, Awlad Busayf, Al-Zintan, and Al-Rijban); those in the city of Sirte (Al-Qaddadfa, Al-Magarha, Al-Magharba, Al-Riyyah, Al-Haraba, Al-Zuwaid, and Al-Guwaid); and those in the Fezzan Region (Al-Hutman, Al-Hassawna, Toubou, and Tuareg).
3. Bruce St. John, *Libya: From Colony to Revolution*, 157–59.
4. Azikiwe, "CIA & MI6 in Libya: U.S.-British Covert Operations Exposed."
5. Roberts, "Who Said Gaddafi Had to Go?"
6. Ibid.
7. De Waal, "The African Union and the Libya Conflict of 2011."
8. BBC News, "Guide to Key Libyan Militias."
9. McQuinn, "After the Fall: Libya's Evolving Armed Groups."
10. Hauslohner and DeYoung, "U.S. Plan for New Libyan Force Faces Obstacles."
11. Lacher, "Libya's Transition: Towards Collapse."
12. el Gomati, "Khalifa Haftar: Fighting Terrorism or Pursuing Political Power?"
13. Amirah-Fernández, "Libya and the Problematic Political Isolation Law."
14. Abdallah, "Libya's New Prime Minister."
15. Energy Information Administration, "Libya."
16. Faucon and Said, "Saudi, U.S., Iraq Step in to Plug Libya Oil Gap."
17. Weiss and Weidman, "Big Oil Rakes in Huge Profits, Again."
18. McEwan, "Retired US Generals and Politicians Reaping Oil Profits from Iraq's Kurdistan."
19. Stover, Megally, and Mufti, "Bremer's Gordian Knot: Transitional Justice and the US Occupation of Iraq."
20. Human Rights Watch, "Libya: June 1996 Killings at Abu Salim Prison."

21. Lawyers for Justice in Libya, "LFJL Acknowledges the Constitutional Drafting Assembly Elections."
22. Ban, "Report of the Secretary-General on the United Nations Support Mission in Libya."

Bibliography

Abdallah, Kamel. "Libya's New Prime Minister." *Al-Ahram Weekly*, May 8, 2014.
Amirah-Fernández, Haizam. "Libya and the Problematic Political Isolation Law." Real Instituto Elcano, June 20, 2013. www.realinstitutoelcano.org/wps/portal/web/rielcano_en/conte nido?WCM_GLOBAL_CONTEXT = /elcano/elcano_in/zonas_in/mediterranean + arab + world/ari20-2013-amirah-fernandez-libia-ley-aislamiento-politico/.
Azikiwe, Abayomi. "CIA & MI6 in Libya: U.S.-British Covert Operations Exposed." International Action Center, April 7, 2011. www.iacenter.org/africa/libya-cia-m16-040911/.
Ban Ki-moon. "Report of the Secretary-General on the United Nations Support Mission in Libya." United Nations Security Council, S/2013/516, September 5, 2013. http://unsmil.un missions.org/Portals/unsmil/Documents/UNSG%20Report%2005092013_EN.pdf.
BBC News. "Full Transcript: Libyan PM Interview." February 24, 2004. http://news.bbc.co.uk /2/hi/uk_news/politics/3517101.stm.
———. "Guide to Key Libyan Militias." May 20, 2014. www.bbc.co.uk/news/world-middle -east-19744533.
Bruce St. John, Robert. *Libya: From Colony to Revolution*. Oxford: Oneworld, 2012.
de Waal, Alex. "The African Union and the Libya Conflict of 2011." World Peace Foundation, December 19, 2012. http://sites.tufts.edu/reinventingpeace/2012/12/19/the-african-union-and -the-libya-conflict-of-2011/.
el Gomati, Anas. "Khalifa Haftar: Fighting Terrorism or Pursuing Political Power?" Al Jazeera English, June 10, 2014. www.aljazeera.com/indepth/opinion/2014/06/khalifa-hifter-opera tion-dignity-20146108259233889.html.
Energy Information Administration. "Libya." US Department of Energy, June 2012. http:// www.eia.gov/countries/analysisbriefs/cabs/Libya/pdf.pdf.
Faucon, Benoît, and Summer Said. "Saudi, U.S., Iraq Step in to Plug Libya Oil Gap." *Wall Street Journal*, September 10, 2013.
Hauslohner, Abigail, and Karen DeYoung. "U.S. Plan for New Libyan Force Faces Obstacles." *Washington Post*, December 1, 2013.
Human Rights Watch. "Libya: June 1996 Killings at Abu Salim Prison." June 27, 2006. www.hrw.org/news/2006/06/27/libya-june-1996-killings-abu-salim-prison.
Lacher, Wolfram. "Libya's Transition: Towards Collapse." *SWP Comments* (German Institute for International and Security Affairs), no. 25 (May 2014). www.swp-berlin.org/fileadmin /contents/products/comments/2014C25_lac.pdf.
Lawyers for Justice in Libya. "LFJL Acknowledges the Constitutional Drafting Assembly Elections." July 18, 2013. www.libyanjustice.org/news/news/post/98-lfjl-welcomes-start-of-consti tutional-process-calls-for-more-representation-and-public-engagement.
Mamdani, Mahmood. "Beyond Settler and Native as Political Identities: Overcoming the Political Legacy of Colonialism." *Comparative Studies in Society and History* 43, no. 4 (October 2001): 651–64.
McEwan, Dale. "Retired US Generals and Politicians Reaping Oil Profits from Iraq's Kurdistan." *PressTV*, June 8, 2013. www.presstv.com/detail/2013/06/08/307889/retired-us-generals -and-politicians-reaping-oil-profits-from-iraqs-kurdistan/.

McQuinn, Brian. "After the Fall: Libya's Evolving Armed Groups." Small Arms Survey, Working Paper 12, October 2012. www.smallarmssurvey.org/fileadmin/docs/F-Working-papers/SAS-WP12-After-the-Fall-Libya.pdf.

Roberts, Hugh. "Who Said Gaddafi Had to Go?" *London Review of Books* 33, no. 22 (November 17, 2011).

Sharqieh, Ibrahim. "Reconstructing Libya: Stability through National Reconciliation." *Brookings Doha Center Analysis Paper*, 2013. www.brookings.edu/research/papers/2013/12/03-libya-national-reconciliation-sharqieh.

Stover, Eric, Hanny Megally, and Hania Mufti. "Bremer's Gordian Knot: Transitional Justice and the US Occupation of Iraq." *Human Rights Quarterly* 27 (January 2005): 830–857.

Weiss, Daniel J., and Jackie Weidman. "Big Oil Rakes in Huge Profits, Again." Center for American Progress, August 2, 2013. www.americanprogress.org/issues/green/news/2013/08/02/71386/big-oil-rakes-in-huge-profits-again/.

7

The Pharaoh Returns

The "Politics of Order" and the Muslim Yearning for Freedom

EBRAHIM RASOOL

History records a tragedy that played out in a newly free and independent country on the African continent, where after decades of authoritarian rule its first democratically elected head of government was overthrown in a coup d'état shortly after his election. He was incarcerated at the hands of the man he appointed as the head of the military. Prior to the coup, Western countries actively cultivated a variety of oppositional forces because of the presumed ideological disposition of the ruling party and its leader, and the country involved became the base from which the quest for freedom, independence, and democracy in the other regional countries was thwarted.

This is the story of Patrice Lumumba and the Congo of 1960.

The Congo gained its formal independence from Belgium on June 30, 1960, and Patrice Lumumba was elected the country's prime minister. Two months later the head of the military, Colonel Mobutu, overthrew the democratically elected government of Patrice Lumumba with the participation of Belgium and the collusion of the White House and 10 Downing Street. On January 17, 1961, Patrice Lumumba was assassinated by a Belgian hit squad. The Democratic Republic of the Congo, as we know it today, and other sovereign states in the African Great Lakes region tragically continue to suffer the fallout of Mobutu's rule.

It is worth recording the story of Patrice Lumumba to establish the template for coup d'états engineered by Western powers in many parts of the world to refute the theory of uniqueness invoked by some Egyptians. Until recently they supported the uprising against Mubarak's oppressive rule but have now become apologists for the military coup against Mohamed Morsi. This has emboldened the forces of reaction in Egypt and elsewhere who employ the ruse of a popular mandate to justify a military intervention against a democratically elected govern-ment. Monarchs in the region justify their heavy hand against their own people by raising the specter of a failed Brotherhood and chastise the West for suggesting there can be democracy in the Middle East, while those in the West berate them-selves for their naïveté in thinking that Islamists can be peaceful or democratic.

Anatomy of a Coup

If silence can be a lie, it is the refusal to name the Egyptian tragedy of 2013 a coup d'état. Whatever its unique narrative and mythology, the overthrow of Morsi is a twenty-first-century imitation of the coups that took place in Iran in 1953, the Congo in 1960, Chile in 1973, Haiti in 1991, Turkey in 1997, and Haiti again in 2004. Egypt has elements of each one. When deconstructed, the Egyptian coup shares the essential DNA of these other coups. This dispels the idea—claimed by some Egyptians and their supporters—that the Egyptian coup was in some way unique. The similarities among the coups are numerous.

To begin with, these coups were designed to replace democratically elected leaders, not autocrats. Egypt's Morsi found himself in the good company of leaders such as Mossadeq in Iran, Lumumba in Congo, and Aristide in Haiti, all of whom were the first fully democratically elected leaders of their countries after a long history of dictatorship. They all made mistakes, but all were elected to power—and the citizens of these countries were denied the opportunity to remove them from power through the ballot box if they so desired.

The existence of freedom and democracy in these countries was also painfully short-lived—from two months in the Congo to little more than two years in Iran and one year in Egypt. In all of these cases it is clear that the military and their backers opposed the prospect of freedom and democracy taking root. They needed to kill democracy while a residual memory and tolerance of dictatorship still remained.

In addition, the choreographies of these coups are remarkably similar, led by the military, often through a general trained in the West, loyal to it, and dependent on the West's continuing technological and financial support. Mobutu spent seven years being trained in Belgium's Force Publique. Raoul Cedras, who overthrew Aristide in Haiti in 1991, was educated in the United States and was a member of the US-trained Leopard Corps. Egypt's General Sisi studied at the US Army War College in Carlisle, Pennsylvania.

In most of the coups there is the lingering suspicion of the hidden hand of the United States or British intelligence. In the cases of Iran and the Congo, the role of the Central Intelligence Agency (CIA) is well documented in declassified CIA documents and records. The Investigative Reporting Program at the University of California, Berkley points to evidence, obtained under the Freedom of Information Act, that the United States channeled funds to anti-Morsi groups in Egypt and the United States.[1] Recently the hidden hands of some Gulf States in support of anti-Morsi groups in the Egyptian coup have also become more visible.[2]

These coups were politically justified. Necmettin Erbakan's removal in 1997 by the military in Turkey was hailed by secular liberals in the name of defending secularism against democratically elected Islamists, as in Egypt. Earlier coups in Iran and the Congo, as well as in Latin American countries such as Argentina, Chile, and elsewhere, were driven by the West's commitment to dispose of leftist governments.

Just like Allende in Chile before him, Morsi in Egypt who received 51 percent of the vote was charged with not governing inclusively and democratically. President Obama, who received approximately 51 percent of the vote and presides over a dysfunctional Congress in the United States, amplified this theme in the UN General Assembly in September 2013 when he said: "Mohammed Morsi was democratically elected, but proved unwilling or unable to govern in a way that was fully inclusive."[3] By implication and in one sentence, a coup was justified.

The coups under consideration fed off either an orchestrated uprising or the intervention of the military to restore public order. Mobutu is said to have restored order after an army mutiny. In 2004 Aristide was forced to leave after Buteur Métayer led the criminal Cannibal Army on a three-week rampage through Port-au-Prince, ostensibly to avenge his brother's death, which he blamed on Aristide.[4] On August 19, 1953, a mob, recruited by Kermit Roosevelt and paid by the CIA, consisting of some of Tehran's most feared gangsters, clergy, military officers, and local politicians, brought in by buses and trucks hired by the CIA, marched to Mossadeq's home and staged pro-Shah riots in which hundreds were killed and injured. Mossadeq was removed and the Shah returned to power.[5]

In Egypt, nothing demonstrates more cynically the military's sophisticated grasp of how to manipulate public sentiment than General Sisi's speech calling for a mandate to crush the Brotherhood. This he did at a military parade on July 24, 2013, in the name of opposing terrorism.[6] The crackdown came after the claim that more people were in Tahrir Square protesting against Morsi on the anniversary of Morsi's election than had apparently voted for him. As General Somoza of Nicaragua once said: "You won the election, but I won the count."

Coups rarely give rise to freedom and democracy. Iran's coup gave rise to the Shah who ruled as an absolute monarch, imposing his will through the dreaded Savak until the revolution in 1979. Congo got Mobutu's dictatorship for the next thirty years, Chile ended up with Pinochet and repression for the next decade and a half, and Haiti had General Cedras entrenched behind the scenes of public office. Abdul Fatah al Sisi is no exception to the rule. Like Mubarak before him, he was elected president with 94 percent of the vote—the sign of a bullied society—in a claimed voter turnout of under 50 percent. Egypt's future looks ominously like its past. Since the coup, Egypt has experienced killings, detentions, repression, and outlawing of media organizations and political parties, including the Muslim Brotherhood. Sisi insists that "there will be no place for the Muslim Brotherhood" during his presidency.[7] The judiciary—with its willing compliance—has also been debased, as seen in the travesty in which it collectively condemned over twelve hundred of Sisi's opponents to death and upheld the ongoing state of emergency. These already outweigh any mistakes Morsi may have made and contradict any pretense at laying democratic foundations for the future. These coups were repressive, best characterized in the chilling words of Chile's General Pinochet: "Sometimes democracy must be bathed in blood."

The Politics of Order: A New Application

The anatomy of the coups of the twentieth century reveals a systematic methodology shaped by the Cold War in pursuit of a set of ideological and strategic objectives in a war against communism. Samuel Huntington, in his work *Political Order in Changing Societies*, articulated this policy as follows: "The most important political distinction among countries concerns not their *form* of government but their *degree* of government."[8]

The politics of order is transforming itself from an essentially anticommunist, antileftist weapon into a weapon nimble enough to be applied with greater sophistication to meet the challenges of the twenty-first century. Huntington used the term "institutionalization" to describe the most important objective for the developing world: strong government institutions able to ensure political stability and order through the military, bureaucracy, and even vanguard single parties. Huntington justifies this by saying, "They may not provide *liberty*, but they do provide *authority*; they do create governments that govern."[9]

During much of the twentieth century, societies in Africa, Latin America, Asia, and the Middle East were the theater of the Cold War. Today, some of these regions are the theater for the War on Terror. Freedom is not on the agenda if it threatens law and order. Democracy is feared as the precursor to political instability. When comparing Egypt 2013 to its antecedents in the twentieth century, the rulebook for a politics of order remains essentially the same, and the supporters of Sisi have an intimate grasp of it. They lure the consent from Europe and America by offering the tenets of this rulebook: strong rather than democratic government; a coercive rather than open state; law, order, and stability rather than freedom, democracy, and human rights. In the few interviews Sisi granted ahead of the presidential election, his consistent message was that law, order, and stability were more important than freedom. For him this means the elimination of opposition and the suppression of protests.

The Coup: Self-Fulfilling Prophecy or Strategic Naïveté?

When considering what went wrong in Egypt 2013, why the conditions were ripe for the coup that removed the Muslim Brotherhood from power, and what allowed the return of the generals with the permission of the secular liberals, it would be tempting simply to say that the coup was preordained. Such inevitability would be especially tempting to the leaders of the Muslim Brotherhood who would see in it an absolution from any responsibility for the coup.

The Muslim Brotherhood should have committed themselves to the consolidation of democracy as the antidote to counterrevolution. The secular liberals had suffered surprising electoral defeats. The military was still firmly in control and had signaled an intent to maintain dominance in Egypt even though Mubarak had been ousted. This they did by foisting the Silmi document on Egyptians even before parliamentary elections in 2011.[10]

The military declared that the Supreme Council of the Armed Forces (SCAF) "is solely responsible for all matters concerning the armed forces, and for discussing its budget . . . [and] is also exclusively competent to approve all bills relating to the armed forces before they come into effect."[11] Stepan and Linz argue that the Brotherhood, isolated from the secular liberals, may have drawn closer to the military and allowed the military a larger-than-usual role in society, as well as special concessions such as drawing the defense minister from military ranks and granting the military the right to try civilians in military courts.[12]

That the military sought to retain as much power as possible is understandable, but that the Brotherhood acceded to some of the military's requests speaks either to a strategic miscalculation, strategic naïveté, or the absence of choice that emerges as a result of being isolated politically and institutionally. Was the Brotherhood prepared for the task at hand? Did they understand what was being offered to them and what was required of them? Did they know what odds were stacked against them, domestically and internationally? Did they trust the military too much and did Morsi think, naively, that Sisi was with him? Did Morsi think that Obama was an ally after cooperating to temper Hamas? This naïveté may have been born from what Tariq Ramadan calls "political intoxication."

Ramadan argues that the West needed reform that improved global economic integration of the Middle East and North Africa (MENA) in their competition against emerging markets. New rules were needed for more open, but not unstable, societies.[13] In referring to the uprisings and national enthusiasm that brought Morsi and the Brotherhood to power, Ramadan concludes that such uprisings "without taking regional realities into account would be a risky proposition: in a state of political intoxication, it is often difficult to distinguish between a historical opportunity for liberation and cynical manipulation."[14]

The War of Position

There is no doubt that the Brotherhood had been outmaneuvered in the war of position in Egypt. They could not prevent the overweening presence of the military, nor did they resist being drawn into the false binary of Islamist versus secular liberal as the new divide in Egypt. The Brotherhood, therefore, could not present Egyptians with a balanced government of unity that included the important forces in Egypt without compromising the middle ground and the moderation required.

In Tunisia, Ennahda's leader Rached Ghannoushi, the secular human rights leader Moncef Marzouki, and their respective parties knew each other and had discussed their differences long before the uprising, so they had sufficient common ground at the moment of governance. The groups gathered on Tahrir Square in Egypt at the time Mubarak was overthrown had had no such contact. Years of distrust and conflict had eroded the possibility of building the level of cooperation witnessed initially in Tunisia. Ramadan suggests Egyptians may have missed "a historical opportunity for liberation."[15] Instead, both the Brotherhood and the secular liberals—the forces for change—appear to have believed that the way forward was through proximity to the military: the Brotherhood through the de facto acceptance of the military's terms and the secular liberals, according to Stepan and Linz, by arguing that "the Muslim Brotherhood was so strong and fundamentally undemocratic that core liberal-democratic values could only be saved if secular liberals cut a deal with a non-democratic source of power—the military."[16]

In the absence, therefore, of a broad vision, a minimalist unifying program of action, and a healthy measure of inclusive governance fashioned by the forces for change, the transition would be dangerously unstable and fertile for intervention in the name of the politics of order. Egypt would become a site for contesting interests—not only between the forces for change and the status quo, but also within the forces for change. The secular liberals, after electoral defeat, would tactically avoid the responsibility for the first round of governance and focus rather on the subsequent election to feed off the inevitable weaknesses of the first government while the military waited in the wings as the source of stability. However, it is now apparent that the secular liberals themselves had miscalculated in this war of position. Instead of providing a democratic alternative to a failed Brotherhood, they deified Sisi and entrenched yet another era of military dictatorship.

The Muslim Brotherhood, in addition to facing the ever-present threat from the politics of order, became a victim of both a series of self-fulfilling prophecies and a remarkable lack of strategic and tactical ability and wisdom.

On the one hand, the prophecies were self-fulfilling in that the opposition blamed the Brotherhood for being exclusivist in government appointments yet promptly refused any offer made to join the government, as at the Kempinski meeting on June 5, 2012. The opposition predicted a worsening economy under the Brotherhood, yet through their actions discouraged investments and transfers of grants and loans from their allies in the Gulf and the West that materialized immediately after the coup. Morsi was accused of governing badly, yet Egypt had for decades been governed under successive states of emergency that denatured and eroded any institutional basis from which to govern.

On the other hand, President Morsi failed to seize the opportunity to unite Egyptians around either an inclusive coalition government or the process of writing a new constitution. He let the secular liberals abdicate their responsibility to join a government of unity. He wanted the constitution to be set in place quickly and thus lost the opportunity for inclusivity; in contrast, Nelson Mandela's first two years as president of South Africa were under an interim constitution while he mobilized popular ownership for the constitution passed in 1996. Additionally, Mandela also appointed the last apartheid president, F. W. de Klerk, as his deputy president through a constitutionally mandated coalition.

Implications for Freedom and Democracy in the Muslim World

The setback in Egypt must be evaluated not simply in terms of the specificities of Egypt in 2013, nor by its strategic errors in alliances and choices, nor by the degree of autonomy enjoyed by the Brotherhood and the other forces for change in the overarching paradigm of the politics of order. Rather, it has to be assessed against what remains possible in pursuing the agenda of freedom, democracy, and human rights in the broader Muslim world, and in the Middle East and North Africa in particular. Under despotism for so long, this region, as seen in Egypt, continues to display a predisposition to authoritarianism. Morgan Freeman in his epic film *The Shawshank Redemption* describes his desire to return to the familiarity of prison by saying that he's been "institutionalized"—he could not manage the complexity of freedom.[17]

Theologically understood, the Muslim yearning for God should be a yearning for peace, justice, and coexistence. These are the great normative values for which the mainstream of the Muslim community strives. The word "Islam" derives from the word "peace." The essence of the Prophet Muhammad's mission compels his followers to promote compassion and mercy in the world. And the defining characteristic of the global Muslim community is to occupy the middle ground, allowing for common ground to emerge between opposing views. Any deviation from these ought to be exceptions rather than the norm. The question is how best to inculcate this balance into the Muslim psyche and how best to carve out a space in the world where such a vision can be established free from—or, probably, despite—the imperatives of the politics of order. The success of this project could usher in an era of freedom, democracy, dignity, and peace for Muslims, as well as their fellow citizens across the world.

It is for such ends that we need to learn the lessons of Egypt 2013. If we do not call it a coup, we will not admit that domestic and global forces conspired to stymie an emergent democratic experiment in governance following an uprising against a dictator and an expression of the popular will. We cannot afford to create an image of democracy as dispensable and expedient. Nor will we admit, if we do not call it a coup, that the opportunity for liberation and transformation may have been lost because of strategic shortcomings in the face of the overwhelming odds faced by this experiment. Defeat and setback must result in lessons learned.

Several concerns are being expressed concerning Muslim and Western political agendas in the aftermath of the coup in Egypt. These raise questions about whether democratic ideals will take root in the Muslim world and, conversely, whether the democratic model of the West can be adapted to take account of realities peculiar to Islam and the Muslim community. These are questions that have been subliminal for a while but that scream out for debate following the Egyptian coup.

Debating these questions will in itself be an act that boosts confidence in democracy and freedom and hopefully drowns the siren songs of those who see the coup in Egypt as an opportunity to reassert the idea that the West has no use for democracy if it does not produce the outcomes it desires and suit its interests. Already Ayman al Zawahiri, the leader of al-Qaeda, has called on Egyptians and Muslims to give up on democracy and speak to those in the West only in the language they respect: the language of jihad, the language of war. The early signs—as with the Mansoura Bombing—are that he may gain support among less committed members and supporters of the Brotherhood who have not had years of the legendary discipline training, as well as among committed Muslims who have had their historical distrust of democracy confirmed. This is precisely the response Sisi wants to justify the coup and its attendant repression. He is decimating the leadership of the Brotherhood in order to provoke either or both of these responses from the fourth-tier Brotherhood leadership left on the ground in Egypt. He is inviting them onto his terrain of strength—military engagement—so as to avoid the moral and political terrain, where he is weaker internationally. Can the Brotherhood resist his terrain, engaging him on their own terms?

Europe and the United States, in their desire to normalize relations with Sisi's regime, must act to blunt the implications of the shortsighted tactics of General Sisi and his government. Sisi and his government assure the world that they are committed to democracy through a referendum for a new constitution and elections for a new government, but they do so only after bludgeoning meaningful opposition out of the race by both legal and repressive means. They claim that they fight terrorism but end up promoting extremism in Egypt and elsewhere by driving the Muslim Brotherhood underground, removing three tiers of its leadership, closing its historical social activism, and even proscribing nonviolent protest. Even the secular liberals are no longer immune to repression, and in this lies the possibility of a broad, nonideological front to restart the long walk to freedom in Egypt. But it needs a new set of ideas.

A New Set of Ideas

We may not be able immediately to answer eloquently and persuasively the key questions raised by the coup in Egypt, but the following are some key implications, issues, and debates that emerge from the coup.

Religion as Reference

The West needs to accept that, for the foreseeable future, religion will remain the crucial reference for Muslims, individually and collectively. Despite not initiating the uprisings in Egypt, the Muslim Brotherhood and Al Nour gained a combined 68 percent of the popular support (43 and 25 percent, respectively) within the People's Assembly, which was subsequently dissolved. These were votes for parties with explicit Muslim identities and with an Islamic appeal, differing insofar as the former were seen as Islamist and the latter as Salafist. This outcome echoed elections in Tunisia where the Islamist Ennahda won 89 of the 217 seats, the consolidation of Prime Minister Erdogan's AK Party in Turkey and his later election as president, as well as victories for Hamas in 2006 in Palestine, the Islamic Salvation Front (FIS) in 1991 in Algeria, and the Islamists in Iran since 1979.

In trying to fathom this phenomenon, Stepan and Linz argue that "religion was under-theorised in scholarly writing about the third wave (attempts at democratic transition)."[18] Yet the hegemony, perceived or actual, of religious forces over much of civil society in the Arab world, especially in the countryside, had no parallel in the third wave. Thus the central role that Islam has played in the Arab Spring presents students of democratization with a novel phenomenon, and prompts them accordingly to come up with new concepts and fresh data to shed light upon it.

The challenge to those in the West is to be consistent and thoughtful in their approach to the debate. The West cannot by omission or, even more, by commission allow the overthrow of the Brotherhood—thus making no distinction between the Brotherhood's Islamism and the extremism of others—while at the same time being quite supportive of political Islam where it serves their interests in several Middle East countries. Tariq Ramadan makes this point caustically when he says that the West's "alliance with the Kingdom of Saudi Arabia, where Islam is the state religion, and where the ruling monarchy claims that Islam is, by

its essence, opposed to democracy, offers proof positive that the West has no problem with political Islam as such, as long as Islamist leaders promise to protect its
economic and political interests. . . . They may be dictators or Islamists, but Western governments' best friends are those who best serve their interests."[19]

Secularism as Precondition for Democracy

Islam is not incompatible with democracy, freedom, and human rights, and clearly
secularism cannot be regarded as a precondition for the realization of democratic
values in the Muslim world.

It is crucial that the West reevaluate its historical skepticism about Islam, inherent in the persistent orientalism, most crudely articulated by Ernest Renan in an
1883 lecture at the Sorbonne: "Islam has brought nothing but harm to human
reason. The minds it has closed to light may already have been closed by their
own internal limitations, but it has persecuted free thought. . . . It has transformed
the lands it has conquered into a field closed to the rational culture of the mind."[20]

Samuel Huntington, among others, built on Renan's sentiment under the
rubric of a politics of order, within which he argues that Islam limits the advance-
ment of democracy, freedom, and human rights. Any tendency toward collective
behavior, including religious codes by which to regulate societies, should not be
allowed to reemerge. Friedrich von Hayek in *The Political Order of Free People*
asserts: "The only moral principle which has ever made the growth of an
advanced civilisation possible was the principle of individual freedom. . . . No
principles of collective conduct which bind the individual can exist in a society of
free men."[21]

Precisely because of a fear that Islam cannot coexist with reason, democracy,
and individual freedom, secular liberals have both the sympathy and support of
the Western world, which results in the turning of the proverbial blind eye to the
subversion of democratically elected Islamist governments, justified in the name
of secularism. Secularism, a necessary bulwark against the impact of religion, thus
emerges as the precondition for democracy. Stepan argues, however, that "neither
laicite of the French sort (generally recognized not merely as secularist but as
positively antireligious), nor a type of secularism that decrees a complete separation between religion and the state, was empirically necessary for democracy to
emerge." The question for him was rather: "What was needed for both democracy
and religion to flourish?"[22]

Against the secular fundamentalist models are other models of secularism that
should be thought through for aspirant or emergent democracies in the Muslim
world. The postapartheid South African experience is a step ahead of the positive
accommodation or twin toleration models of Western Europe that fashioned a
cooperative relationship with their previously dominant Christian institutions but
excluded other religions. South Africa is closer to the Muslim experience outside

the MENA region, such as in Indonesia, Senegal, and Albania, where there is not only accommodation and recognition of the majority religion, Islam, but also accommodation of and recognition for the minority religions, whose holy days are part of the public holiday calendar, for example. India under Mahatma Gandhi's influence is an example in which a Muslim minority benefits from secularism. Muslims in South Africa have benefited from secular rule in a similar manner.

In these secular situations Muslim attitudes toward democracy and freedom are overwhelmingly positive because they experience an appreciation for both their individual worth and their collective identity. Rached Ghannoushi, leader of Tunisia's Ennahda Party, spoke recently at a colloquium of Muslim minority leaders of the need in such contexts for a civil state (*dawla madiniyyah*) that is neither secular nor Islamic. His concern is to see the emergence of a state that respects democratic principles such as the popular will, equality between men and women, the rights of those affirming minority religions, and the sovereignty of institutions such as parliament and the judiciary. Ghannouchi's concerns are in direct continuity with Amien Rais, an Indonesian political scientist who asserts, "The Quran does not say anything about the formation of an Islamic State, or about the necessity and obligations on the part of Muslims to establish a Shariah or Islamic State."[23]

The strategic challenge faced by these and other Islamic scholars opens up an important debate on the need for Islamic values to be viewed and promoted within the context of democratic debate and for coexistence with people of other faiths. It allows for the recognition of Islamic prerogatives in the public sphere, but insofar as they refer to Islamic principles, objectives, and values, not the rules and regulations that themselves may be in need of review.

The Civil State

Constructing a civil state may well be the balanced middle ground between secular fundamentalism and the totalizing Islamic state, recognizing religion as critical to identity and to reconciling the Muslim world with the values of freedom, democracy, and human rights.

Whenever a party with a Muslim identity wins power, there is some popular expectation and some pressure from Salafi or fundamentalist groups for a program to implement Sharia, Islamic punishment, personal law, and a clampdown on matters considered anathema to Islam. At the very least there is an expectation that a basic Islamic identity will be maintained. Egypt is not exempt from these expectations, which vary between maximalist incorporation of Islam and a minimalist compliance with it. Nothing illustrated the tension between Islamists and Salafists in Egypt more than when the first democratic parliament was inaugurated on January 23, 2012. The Brotherhood followed the prescribed oath of allegiance to the republic, the constitution, and the law. The Salafists defiantly added: "In whatever does not contradict God's law."

The preceding discussions show that Muslim leaders and theorists are seeing the limitations of the theocratic, religiously founded model of the Islamic state, and emergent thoughts around the civil state are gaining traction. The Brotherhood in Egypt may not have had a full and adequate understanding of the civil state, but its overall history does not suggest that it sought to establish a state that would totalize Islam. It suggests rather that the Brotherhood was somewhat behind Ennahda in Tunisia, whose followers were slowly making their way toward an appreciation of the civil state. They were starting to identify the salient aspects of the Islamic ethical framework, determining how this would manifest a form of secularism that allows for an affirmation of religious beliefs and practice.

The Brotherhood, on the other hand, having been repressed and proscribed for decades, was thrust into government by the popular will. It was finding its way ponderously toward a civil state: committed to doing good but locked in its experience of welfare, open to other faiths but unable to transcend the classical approach of "the people of the Book," less misogynistic than many others but unable to move beyond the paradigm of kindness to women, and willing to embrace freedom and democracy but unable to reconcile some of the practices of freedom with Islam. The Brotherhood was naive in the art of practical and strategic politics: Pressured by the Salafis, outmaneuvered by an entrenched military, besieged by a fearful secular liberal community, and mistrusted by a suspicious West, it suddenly had to find an answer to the piercing challenge posed by Stepan and Linz: "What was needed for both democracy and religion to flourish?"[24]

If the Brotherhood's path to the coexistence of democracy and religion was impeded by a coup, the military, the West, and secular liberals have their own challenge concerning the coexistence of democratic ideals and the need for political control. Some analysts point to the painfully long transition in Brazil through the decade of the 1970s to make the point that coexistence between democratic ideals and control can ultimately yield viable forms of participatory democracy. Brazil also teaches us that interventions to remove democratically elected leaders and governments through coups have had painfully long authoritarian interregnums, promoted under the promise of a democratic objective but always with the reality of long, brutal dictatorships, as the earlier discussion of Chile, the Congo, Iran, and elsewhere also demonstrates. In Egypt it appears that the proposed path to democracy is through, first, the complete suppression of the Brotherhood in the name of fighting terrorism and, second, the anointing of the "hero" of that fight by instigating a popular clamor for him to lead. In turn, the hero is fully prepared for the long Brazilian interregnum. Sisi is of the view that Egypt would require "20 to 25 years to achieve true democracy."[25]

A little more than three years ago the Egyptian situation reached a breaking point with the overthrow of Mubarak, a corrupt military man who had ruled the country for thirty years. Egyptians have again placed their trust in a former army chief, who has since the overthrow of Morsi in July 2013 again resolutely moved the country to authoritarian rule. His promise of iron rule under the guise of democratic legitimacy is unlikely to endure for thirty years, especially since he fell significantly short of the 80 percent electoral turnout he indicated would be required for his own electoral legitimacy. He fell short despite all incentives and threats to the electorate.

The Way Forward

The challenge is to ensure that Muslim cynicism regarding the promotion of democracy becomes neither a permanent barrier to democratic values in the Muslim psyche nor the fertile breeding ground for the next generation of fundamentalist extremists. The antidote to this scenario is greater discernment in the analysis of the contending forces in the Muslim world. Muslims are not homogeneous. This is increasingly acknowledged. But the divides are not simple: They are not just Sunni and Shi'a, and they certainly are not just extremists and moderates. Such simplicity has been at the core of a number of miscalculations in the fight against extremism. We need a new and more nuanced reading of the contestants for power in the Muslim world in order to recalibrate a new set of alliances, coalitions, or even just tolerations.

The world after 9/11, following the lessons learned in the war on terror and the energy displayed in the Arab Spring, has shown that the Muslim middle ground is asserting a new set of ideas. These respond to the impulse for freedom and human rights, which are yearned for by Muslims along with all other citizens of the world. Muslims are overcoming the notion that these are Western constructs and are actively seeking synergies between these values and the overarching principles and objectives of Islam. The notion of the civil state is challenging the core Muslim idea of the twentieth century that the apotheosis of Islam's principles and objectives is the establishment of the Islamic state and the institutionalization of Sharia.

Time will tell whether the coup in Egypt constitutes a setback for the Muslim yearning for democracy, freedom, and human rights.

Notes

1. Emad Mekay, "Exclusive: US Bankrolled Anti-Morsi Activists."
2. Samira Shackle, "Did the Gulf Kingdoms Engineer Morsi's Demise?"
3. Barack Obama, "Remarks by President Obama in Address to the UN General Assembly."
4. Marx, "Haitian 'Cannibal Army' Leader Orchestrates Chaos to Force Aristide's Ouster."
5. Kinzer, *All The Shah's Men*, 169–72 and 210–11.
6. Beach, "Showdown in Cairo."

7. Atlantic Council, "Top News: Abdel Fattah al-Sisi Gives First Ever TV Interview."

8. Huntington, *Political Order in Changing Societies*, 1; my emphasis.

9. Ibid., 8; my emphasis.

10. Drafted by Ali Al-Silmi, deputy leader of the secular Al-Wafd Party, the document calls for a creation of a civil state that effectively excludes the influence of religious groups such as the Muslim Brotherhood. The document is in contradistinction to the Al-Azhar document that enjoyed support across political and religious divisions in Egypt.

11. Stepan and Linz, "Democratization Theory and the Arab Spring," 15–30.

12. Ibid.

13. Ramadan, *Islam and the Arab Awakening*, 55–56.

14. Ibid., 41.

15. Ibid., 55.

16. Stepan and Linz, "Democratization Theory and the Arab Spring," 21.

17. See Kevin Polowy, "Role Recall: Morgan Freeman Narrates His Own Journey through *Glory, Shawshank*, and More."

18. Stepan and Linz, "Democratization Theory and the Arab Spring," 15–16.

19. Ramadan, *Islam and the Arab Awakening*, 14.

20. Renan and Psichari, *Oeuvres Completes Vol. 1*, 901.

21. Von Hayek, *Law, Legislation and Liberty*, 3:152–53.

22. Stepan and Linz, "Democratization Theory and the Arab Spring," 17.

23. Stepan and Kunkler, "Interview with Amien Rais," 205.

24. Stepan and Linz, "Democratization Theory and the Arab Spring," 17.

25. Al Jazeera English, "Egypt's Sisi Chooses Stability over Freedoms."

Bibliography

Al Jazeera English. "Egypt's Sisi Chooses Stability over Freedoms." May 11, 2014. www.aljaze era.com/news/middleeast/2014/05/egypt-sisi-chooses-stability-over-freedoms-201451197174 30958.html.

Atlantic Council. "Top News: Abdel Fattah al-Sisi Gives First Ever TV Interview." May 6, 2014. www.atlanticcouncil.org/blogs/egyptsource/top-news-abdel-fattah-al-sisi-gives-first -ever-tv-interview#r.

Beach, Alastair. "Showdown in Cairo: Egyptians General Demands Permission to Take on the 'Terrorists.'" *Independent*, July 24, 2013.

Huntington, Samuel. *Political Order in Changing Societies*. New Haven, CT: Yale University Press, 2006.

Kinzer, Stephen. *All the Shah's Men: An American Coup and the Roots of Middle East Terror*. Hoboken, NJ: John Wiley, 2008.

Marx, Gary. "Haitian 'Cannibal Army' Leader Orchestrates Chaos to Force Aristide's Ouster." *Chicago Tribune*, February 12, 2004. www.highbeam.com/doc/1G1-118751501.html.

Mekay, Emad. "Exclusive: US Bankrolled Anti-Morsi Activists." Al Jazeera English, July 10, 2013. http://www.aljazeera.com/indepth/features/2013/07/2013710113522489801.html. .

Obama, Barack. "Remarks by President Obama in Address to the UN General Assembly." United Nations, New York, September 24, 2013. www.whitehouse.gov/the-press-office/2013 /09/24/remarks-president-obama-address-united-nations-general-assembly.

Polowy, Kevin. "Role Recall: Morgan Freeman Narrates His Own Journey through *Glory*, *Shawshank*, and More." Yahoo Movies, April 8, 2014. https://movies.yahoo.com/blogs/yahoo-movies/role-recall-morgan-freeman-narrates-own-journey-glory-190011415.html.

Ramadan, Tariq. *Islam and the Arab Awakening*. Oxford: Oxford University Press, 2012.

Renan, Ernest, and Henriette Psichari. *Oeuvres Completes Vol. 1*. Paris: Calmann-Levy, 1961.

Shackle, Samira. "Did the Gulf Kingdoms Engineer Morsi's Demise?" *Middle East Monitor*, July 12, 2013. www.middleeastmonitor.com/articles/africa/6556-did-the-gulf-kingdoms-engineer-morsis-demise.

Stepan, Alfred, and Mirjam Kunkler. "An Interview with Amien Rais." *Journal of International Affairs* 61 (2007): 205–16.

Stepan, Alfred, and Juan J. Linz. "Democratization Theory and the Arab Spring." *Journal of Democracy* 24 (2013): 15–30.

Von Hayek, Friedrich. *Law, Legislation and Liberty*. Volume 3, *The Political Order of Free People*. Chicago: University of Chicago Press, 1981.

8

Political Theology in the Aftermath of the Arab Spring

Returning to the Ethical

EBRAHIM MOOSA

O ptics in politics is like a picture. It is worth more than a thousand words. On June 30, 2013, Egypt's new military strongman, General Abdel Fattah al-Sisi, installed himself as president after deposing the democratically elected president Mohamed Morsi. This signaled a major turning point in that country's political theology. At his inauguration Sisi was flanked by three important religious figures: Ahmed el-Tayeb, the president or *shaykh* of al-Azhar, the most reputable Islamic university; Pope Theodorus II, the Coptic archbishop; and Younis Makhyoun, the leader of the Salafi al-Nur party. Blessed by three distinct theologies, the general then acted with unrestrained brutality: Under his orders hundreds of protesters were killed during the evacuation of Cairo's streets, followed by ruthless repression of the once-ruling Freedom and Justice Party (FJP) allied to the Muslim Brotherhood. Reports of human rights abuses against political prisoners in Egyptian prisons abound.

The headline story is the return to authoritarianism, although some Egyptians dispute that and call the return of the army a step toward democracy. My goal is to identify the sources of authoritarianism in Arab-Islamic politics. My hypothesis is that while political and economic factors clearly drive politics, there is also a distinct Muslim political theology that lends itself to an authoritarianism that infects both secular and religious regimes. How could it be that the same protesters, by and large, who had taken to the streets and ousted an authoritarian Hosni Mubarak from power barely three years earlier now urged the army to return? And how was it that they chose an army general who was cut from the same cloth as Mubarak to take the reins of power? Why do religious authorities condone the return of authoritarianism? Why did Islamic groups such as the FJP and the

101

Muslim Brotherhood, who were once victims of authoritarianism, also show during their brief rule of Egypt that they had the capacity to be authoritarian?

Miscalculations of Revolution

Revolutions and counterrevolutions are bloody and brutal affairs. In Egypt the national psyche is divided as to whether the ousting of the democractically elected Morsi of the FJP was a good or a bad thing. Elements of the Egyptian public were sufficiently alarmed by what they had experienced of Morsi's government to want to return to the devil they knew—namely, the military—rather than to follow the devout Morsi whom some suspected to be a wolf in angel's garb. The Egyptian political process has since become so riddled with contradictions and complexity as to make most political analysts scratch their heads. Political psychologists might be in a better position to diagnose the national pathology.

In Libya a stable state apparatus has yet to take charge of the situation. Syria is not only disintegrating under the burden of a civil war but a militant insurgency group known as ISIS, the Islamic State of Syria and Iraq, has proclaimed a caliphate and has taken large chunks of Syrian and Iraqi territory. In Bahrain the lid is brutally shut on all forms of political protest. Only in Tunisia are signs of stability and a gradual movement toward democracy evident. For those whose hopes for an Arab Spring were dashed by the setbacks, the very causes of darkness may someday yield a dawn. As the French political theorist Jacques Rancière points out, "politics is a paradoxical form of action."[1] The line between the power to rule, freedom, and the polis "is not straight but broken."[2]

Not only did Morsi's epic power grab in some manner facilitate the counterrevolution, but he critically misunderstood several issues. The first is fairly obvious. Morsi and the Muslim Brotherhood were clueless about the layers of power held by the "deep state" in Egypt. The military in Egypt has the resources, power, and patience to play the long game and use brutal force domestically. When Morsi dismissed General Mohammed Hussein Tantawi as soon as he took power, he was convinced that he had defanged the military establishment and was convinced that he had neutralized their economic interests. He was yet to learn that there is more to democracy and the taking of power than counting the ballots. Morsi so gravely offended the military establishment that they silently vowed to humiliate him even while they were pledging loyalty to him. As importantly, we can see with the advantage of hindsight that the deep state had co-opted an influential section of the religious authorities in Egypt.

Second, the Muslim Brotherhood and other Islamists in the region were blissfully unaware of the deep skepticism political Islam has evoked not only among secular Muslims but also among devout traditional Muslims. For almost a century Muslim thinkers, activists, and those involved in various social movements have agonized over ways to reshape their societies. Political Islam has emerged as the only political movement with the stamina to reform society into its perception of the demands of Sharia. But the brief reign of political Islam in the Arab Middle East and a glimpse of its potential for authoritarianism might have also signaled its death. Neighboring Tunisia learned from Egypt's failure, and the Renaissance Party there wisely took Sharia debates off the table and withdrew from running the government.

In the future Field Marshal Sisi's jubilant supporters in Egypt might come to regret their decision to oust Morsi from power and opt for the devil they knew—namely, the dictatorial army. Public sentiment can be manipulated in such a way that fear of political Islam carries greater weight than fear of the brutal military power that had ruled Egypt for decades.

The third issue was Morsi's inability to gauge the destabilizing effects of the ever-shifting power contest between Sunni Saudi Arabia (together with Turkey, Jordan, and other Gulf States) and Shia Iran. Iran is viewed as the mortal political enemy by some Sunni majority states. Its nuclear ambitions and its ability to act as a regional power via its proxy, the Lebanon-based Hizbollah, give it military hegemony over Sunni states that have been wary of what they describe as the growth of the "Shia crescent." Iran's political and logistical support for Syria's Bashar al-Asad in a bloody civil war, begun by an uprising of the majority Sunni, all but confirms the sectarian polarization in the region. Because the Sunni states wish to isolate Iran, Morsi's rapid opening of diplomatic ties with Iran might not have endeared him to the Saudis either.

Sedimented Theologies

Deeply embedded in the political practices and actions of Muslim societies are the unspoken and inarticulate sedimentations of different Muslim political theologies. These are not extinguished theological volcanoes. They are active volcanoes—narratives that give coherence to prevailing political behavior. They blend economic and political concerns with vibrant memories and theological discourses that provide answers to deep unresolved aporias in society. The quest for politics within a salvation narrative has been part of Islamic discourse for centuries and has featured prominently in the colonial and postcolonial eras of the twentieth century.

It began with nineteenth-century Muslim reformers who were determined to end external colonial occupation and break the yoke of internal authoritarianism. If the Arab and Muslim peoples freed themselves to some extent from the burden of colonialism, then the challenge awaiting them was to rid themselves of the scourge of political authoritarianism that stalked their lives. Throughout the twentieth century scholars debated the viability of nonauthoritarian models of governence. But in most cases liberal governance failed to become a serious work in progress.[3] However, two distinct as well as overlapping political theologies, each with its own inner diversity, coexisted side by side: secular and Islamist. The secular narrative of salvation was focused on the existence of a strong state, control of religion by the state, and the demands of modernity initially conceived as a socialist economy but later replaced by a liberal political economy. The Islamist narrative of salvation was focused on the supremacy and legitimacy of the Sharia, a strong state, selective use of modernity, and a liberal, if not free-market, political economy.

During the postindependence period, efforts to attain democracy were often derailed. In the context of rising levels of public desperation in several countries plagued by poverty, a growing proportion of youth in the population, and rising unemployment, the 2011 Arab Spring was enthusiastically welcomed. Yet, the Arab Spring also revealed several areas of vulnerability, one of particular importance: the absence of an Islamic political theology compatible with democratic transition. The setbacks and reversals in several countries were caused, among other reasons, by the ruling elites' lack of a deep cultural and political sense of human dignity and their failure to appreciate the value of nonviolent politics and the possibility of reasonable political discourse. In Egypt, one of the largest and most influential Arab countries, the brief Arab Spring heralded a possible end to authoritarian rule that could have influenced other regions. As the draconian political measures now adopted show clearly, Egypt is back in the bosom of authoritarianism. Yet all is not lost.

Sane political calculations in Tunisia enabled the Renaissance Party (Ennahda) to read the tea leaves and retreat from government. They did so in order to reassure a skeptical public who feared they might face an Islamist political agenda.[4] Tunisia's Islamists were also realists who knew they did not have a silver bullet to solve intractable political and economic challenges. If they did govern, they were bound to fail and thus would gain a reputation of being inept and lacking the imagination to govern effectively.

Muslim Politics

Today's political harvest goes back at least a century, if not longer. A group of Muslim reformers based in Egypt in the last quarter of the nineteenth century contemplated a political future for the Arab Muslim people that would replace the waning Ottoman power and retreating European colonial powers. In reformist circles—in particular the movement of the Iranian thinker known as Jamal al-Din al-Afghani (d. 1897), his Egyptian counterpart Muhammad Abduh (d. 1905), and the Syrian Rashid Rida (d. 1935)—the end of the Ottoman caliphate was viewed as a major blow to pan-Islamic aspirations. While these reformers did not always find Turkish domination comfortable, they did believe that a reformed caliphate could steer Muslim nations in the direction of progress. Rashid Rida viewed the founding of the secular Turkish Republic in 1923 as a crushing blow to his hopes of Islamic reform, and it led him to adopt a very critical and increasingly hostile attitude toward secular government.

The reformers nevertheless sought ways to indigenize modern political systems. Their project was to find a modernizing rationale for Islam's moral philosophy, theology, and law. They generated readings of traditional Islamic teachings in order to make these compatible with the demands of a modernizing Muslim public as well as to meet the needs of Muslims with changing experiences. One outcome was to encourage lay Muslims to increase their knowledge of scripture. The reformers also challenged the Muslim clerics, the *ulama*, for being stubborn, resistant to change, and wedded to a static notion of tradition. The reformers petitioned for new investment in intellectual effort (*ijtihad*) to kick-start new modes of thinking and creativity in Islamic theology and juridical ethics, often referred to simply as Islamic law. New pathways in Islamic law often resonated with the rise of scientific cultures and made some headway. But while Muslim societies cautiously embraced science and technology, religious thought itself remained impregnable to innovation and creativity.

One area of thought that did receive some, but clearly not sufficient, attention was Islamic politics. Proposals for a new political order based on Islamic values that resonated with the demands and needs of Muslim communities were in short supply. The political model most Sunni Muslims were familiar with was the caliphate. (It took the 1979 revolution in Iran to stimulate Shiite political thinking, which had been in a quietistic mode for some time.) Simply put, the caliphate was ruled through the personal authority of a legitimate and qualified Muslim leader who sought to impose political order, secure peace, and establish security in Muslim territories. Over the centuries scholars debated the source of the caliph's authority: Was it a divinely ordained office or was the caliph delegated by the Muslim community? This conundrum was not easily resolved; in Sunni thinking it was an office established by tradition whereas in Shia thinking it was an office appointed by divine sanction.[5] Yet most scholars held the caliphate to be a legitimate political model enjoying the sanction of tradition, the consensus of the community, and the support of the experts in law and theology who derived their ideas from the exemplary practices of the Prophet Muhammad and successive generations of the Muslim community after his death. Doctrinally, the caliphate as a political structure was imagined to substitute for the authority of the Prophet in order to preserve religion and ensure earthly governance.[6] In other words, the caliphate was viewed as a necessary means for the earthly and otherworldly salvation of Muslims; retaining it was seen as a secular obligation by some and a religious obligation by others. But given the aspiration of some forms of Islamism for world domination, the caliphate and caliphate-like political models always ran the risk of becoming stranded on the shores of authoritarianism, as Hannah Arendt soberly warned about political regimes heading toward totalitarianism decades ago.[7]

So when Hasan al-Banna (1906–1949) founded the Muslim Brotherhood in 1928, he articulated Islam as both a social gospel and a political movement. His was one of the most powerful articulations of Islam at the popular level and took everyone by surprise: the colonial powers, their governing allies, and the traditional religious leadership of the Muslim world. "Whoever thought that religion, more specifically Islam, is unfamiliar with politics or thinks that politics is not part of its debates," wrote Banna, "then such a person had wronged himself and his knowledge of this Islam."[8] With that announcement Banna not only fueled the debate about Islam and politics in a way that an earlier generation could not do but also polarized Muslim communities into secular and Islamist segments. Of course, Banna's message was focused on reforming society and retrieving authentic Islamic values in the face of a hegemonic West and its secular cultural imprint on Muslim societies.

Banna's message, as well as those of the more influential ideologues who succeeded him, such as Sayyid Qutb (d. 1966), injected a theological rhetoric into the political. Those Muslims at the helm of secular governance in twentieth-century Egypt, for instance, became the target of the Brotherhood's ideology-filled rhetoric decrying their lack of Islamic legitimacy. They were subject to imprecations of theological anathematization (*kufr*) for not implementing God's law, the Sharia, in the public sphere. With the rise of Qutb's influence the doctrine of the sovereignty of God and the Sharia became a vital element in the rhetorical toolkit of the Brotherhood. By the 1970s the Islamists began to question the secular foundations of the state. In 1971 Egypt's secular government had to placate religious fervor by amending article 2 of the constitution, explicitly acknowledging that "the principles of the Sharia are *a* chief source of legislation" in Egypt. The credibility of the Islamic social movements was boosted by the successive military losses and the loss of territory that the Arab-Muslim armies faced at the hands of Israel. Secularists and secular ideology were identified as the weakness and were blamed for the failure of Arab-Muslim will to stand up to their political adversary. By 1980 article 2 was again amended to make Sharia "*the* chief source of legislation." Egypt served as a weathervane: The pendulum of political theology in the Islamic world swung away from an aspiration for secular governance and toward Islamism. Repression of Islamism and the brutality meted out to Islamists in Egypt, Syria, Algeria, and Tunisia only made things worse. In the end those who would emerge with the least credibility were the secularists, who left a legacy of monumental failures in governance and are best remembered for their singular contribution to totalitarianism and brutality.

But the place of religion in politics was debated well before the rise of the Muslim Brotherhood in Egypt and should serve as a backdrop to current developments.

Governance in Islam: Theological or Pragmatic?

Calls for Islamic governance in Egypt in 1928 might have been in response to two major events prior to the formation of the Muslim Brotherhood: the publication of a book and the abolition of the caliphate in Turkey. In 1925 a prominent Egyptian thinker, Ali Abd al-Raziq (1888–1966) wrote a book titled *Islam and the Principles of Governance (Islam wa usul al-hukm)*. Abd al-Raziq was a graduate of the famous bastion of Sunni Islamic orthodoxy, al-Azhar University. At the time he was head of the Islamic Sharia courts of Egypt and was also familiar with elements of Western intellectual discourse. His purpose for penning the book, he explained, was to reflect on the history of Islamic law and constitutional jurisprudence.

His book was published a year after Mustafa Kemal Ataturk of Turkey abolished the caliphate, the office of the titular head of the Islamic domains, and declared Turkey a republic on March 3, 1924. The abolition of the caliphate was greeted with different responses in the Muslim world. For many it was a day of mourning because it signaled the end of Islam as empire, despite the fact this empire had been in dire straits for some time. Even prominent Indian figures like Mahatma Gandhi threw their weight and authority behind Indian Muslims who mobilized the Khilafat Movement in an effort to rescue the caliphate, but to no avail. Other Muslims, especially some secular Arabs, were delighted to finally get rid of Turkish domination and were happy to close this chapter in favor of secular options for state formation. But that was by no means a uniform reaction.

Abd al-Raziq's book served as a lightning rod in the traumatic postcaliphate environment. He was viciously criticized, defrocked of his al-Azhar title, and rendered jobless. He raised the fundamental question about the nature and relationship of the Prophet Muhammad's prophetic mission to his political career. The Prophet exercised multiple kinds of authority, he argued. Politics was in his view incidental, not essential, to Muhammad's career. Muhammad engaged in extensive political activities as a prophet. He was at first persecuted in his native city of Mecca and later became the leader of the city of Medina and imposed Islamic suzerainty on neighboring territories. Nevertheless, Abd al-Raziq argued fervently that one had to distinguish between Muhammad's prophecy and his policy as two different and separate types of authority. Muhammad's religious message was inspired by revelation. His political message, while leavened by his religious message, could not equal his moral authority as a prophet. At best one could argue that Muhammad exercised a kind of political leadership, but he did not enjoy a divine mandate for his political office. When pressed, Abd al-Raziq conceded that Muhammad exercised a monarchical function, like some biblical prophets, but even such a function was not essential to his propehcy.

In short, Abd al-Raziq wished to overturn the idea that the office of a caliph was essential to Islam as a religion. While some medieval scholars also held this view, they favored the caliphate on grounds of tradition.[9] The term *khalif* in Arabic means successor. Abd al-Raziq argued that Muhammad was never addressed as a *khalif* since he was the Messenger of God. Those who succeeded him were known as *khalif* (pl. *khulafa*)—hence the designation of the long-standing caliphate throughout the history of Islam until its abolition in 1924.

The only acceptable understanding of caliph, Abd al-Raziq contended, was the notion of human beings as *khalifa*, or God's moral stewards on earth. Abd al-Raziq argued there was a great deal of ambiguity and uncertainty about the claims scholars made about the nature of the caliphate. First, there was an ancient debate as to whether the caliph's authority derived from God or from an electoral college (*ahl al-hall wa 'l-'aqd*) of human beings. In other words, he was skeptical of arguments made by those who claimed that politics had a religious mandate in Islam. Second, he asked why, if the caliphate were a political office, neither the Qur'an nor the Prophet elaborated on the nature of political systems, codes, or ideas. In fact, why did the Prophet not identify a successor or suggest a way in which political succession could be realized? Abd al-Raziq argued that if politics held as important a theological place as the protagonists of the caliphate claimed, then it lacked elaborate foundational teachings to support it. Such teachings were absent precisely because politics was not essential to Islam as a faith. Third, he pointed out that the whole history of the caliphate "was nothing but a catastrophe to Islam and Muslims."[10] Politics, he observed, was based on brute force and authority with hardly any serious effort invested in developing a meaningful political philosophy based on religion.

Among other things, Abd al-Raziq also argued that the office of the caliphate was not part of Muslim doctrine, at least not for Sunni Muslims. Muslims who followed the Shia creed believed the political and spiritual succession after Muhammad was, of course, explicitly designated by the Prophet himself. Shia political theory blamed unscrupulous powermongers among the early Muslims for conspiring against Muhammad's heir apparent, his cousin and son-in-law Ali, and denying him the opportunity to take over the political reins. The debate over succession after Muhammad then became the major point of division between Sunni and Shia Islam. Obviously, as a dyed-in-the wool Sunni, Abd al-Raziq was unconvinced by the Shiite argument over the essential nature of leadership—*imama*—as both political and spiritual.

Muhammad's successors, Abd al-Raziq claimed, wrongly claimed to have succeeded him in his political office when no such political office existed in the first place. If they claimed to rule in the Prophet's name, then they did so only for strategic purposes in order to adopt his religious aura so as to legitimate their political authority. He shows persuasively how the first caliph, Abubakr, was at first called "steward (caliph) of God" but then decried the title as too onerous and arrogant and modestly preferred to be called the "successor to the Messenger/ Prophet of God." The change in titles was meant to show how loyal Abubakr was to the path established by the founder of the community, the Prophet. While Abd al-Raziq did not directly claim Abubakr was acting mala fide, the implict message was clear: the modest Abubakr knowingly or unknowingly subverted the pro-phetic tradition and opened the door for later caliphs to make exaggerated claims of being God's shadows on earth.

Abd al-Raziq's central complaint was that Muslim caliphs, with few exceptions, were absolute and autocratic sovereigns who lacked accountability.[11] Abd al-Raziq may have been implying it was a good thing that the caliphate ended in 1924. Perhaps he was motivated by modernist impulses, or maybe he tried to sooth bruised Muslim feelings over the abolition of the caliphate by showing the redun-dancy of the institution. Whatever Abd al-Raziq's motives, his views did not find appeal among Muslim audiences because his revisionist account lacked persuasion. Whether the founding teachings of the Prophet were misunderstood or distorted by later generations, it was difficult to fault an extensive legacy of constitutional jurisprudence as a grotesque misunderstanding. Abd al-Raziq might have fared better had he explained why the caliphate was no longer functional and proposed an alternative model of governance. He opened the door for secular government in Islam by arguing that as long as the moral elements of justice and fairness were adhered to in any system of governance, such a system met the minimum moral requirements of Islam as a religion. Islam never advocated any kind of theocratic authority, he insisted. Abd al-Raziq attempted to rewrite Islam's political theology, though he did not fully succeed in doing so.

Unreconstructed Political Theology

Despite the absence of the caliphate as a model of governance in the twentieth century, within religious sections of Egyptian civil society and elsewhere the aspi-ration to establish Islamic governance was high. At one stage the idea of the caliphate was conceived as a commonwealth of nations. The Organisation of Islamic Cooperation (OIC), formerly the Organisation of the Islamic Conference, formed in 1969, was supposed to be the vehicle for that aspiration, but it was largely ineffective. However, Islamically inspired social movements such as the Muslim Brotherhood, Salafi networks, the South Asian Jamat-i Islami, and their allies across the world gained increasing visibility. Within these religiously inspired circles of professional men and women a hybrid Islamic political model was conceived. Muslims would adopt the nation-state modeled on Western con-ceptions of the state, but they would infuse it with soundings from Muslim politi-cal theology based on conceptions of the caliphate. In other words a political theology belonging to an imperial caliphal order was promoted under the guise of the modern nation-state.

Features of this caliphal political theology included the authority of the caliph. In traditional political theology obedience to the authority of the caliph was paramount, and dissent was outlawed as sedition. Subjects were organized in a hierarchy of status, a ranking that discriminated between Muslims and those belonging to other faiths. The question of the role and place of the Sharia in governance and legislation remained a vexed issue in many states, especially as the contest intensified between secular-minded ruling elites and the rising tide of Islamist-minded populations.

So while Muslim-majority nation-states announced citizenship and equality for all, they often failed in practice to provide equal treatment to religious and ethnic minorities. While ancient and early modern caliphal regimes awarded non-Islamic faith communities some autonomy and limited self-rule in certain spheres, there never was a pretense of equality of subjects. Yet, in twentieth-century restatements of Islamic governance those antique notions were to be translated into discourses of citizenship. Constitutions of Muslim-majority states were, in theory, adorned with the notion of equality for people of all faiths and genders, but the reality was often different.

Both secularist and Islamist thinkers in Muslim-majority countries were often hard-pressed to show how they would give equal citizenship and share power with religious minorities. Even secular regimes did not fare better in dealing with religious minorities in a substantive and principled sense. Similarly, the status of women in both politics and the law was another challenge. Again, cultural patriarchy discriminated against women, as did patriarchal laws based on custom and religion.

Political theologies from a caliphal-imperial epoch carry within them cultural and institutional memories embodied in real-life experiences over generations. Without transforming the political and theological cultures by way of revisionist and reconstructionist thinking, even the best political models and institutions can become shipwrecked. One legacy of the premodern Muslim political theology that endured into the modern period was its inherent authoritarian nature that both modern secularist and Islamist political actors inherited and imposed with impunity.[12]

Islamism, Authoritarianism, and the Nation

The long-delayed ideal of a caliphate in the twentieth century found its first stage in the making of an Islamic state, which meant retrofitting the nation-state with Islamic accoutrements and rationales. Advocates of Islamism readily promoted the sovereignty of God rather than the sovereignty of the state or the sovereignty of the constitution. The emblem of God's sovereignty was the application of the

Sharia, the *Grundnorm* of the Islamic state. Often Sharia was imported into existing legal systems unrevised, resulting in appalling transgressions and miscarriages of justice. Yet, in the eyes of Islamists, failing to apply this basic norm meant that both the state and the society languished in heresy and unbelief. Islamism enthusiastically introduced an imperial Muslim political theology as an active political ingredient into the womb of debates about the modern nation-state. Contemporary incarnations of Muslim political theology remained crude and unsophisticated and led to catastrophic consequences everywhere. While outwardly or structurally it appeared modern, inwardly its political philosophy and political culture remained wedded to the ethos of another time. But the idea of an Islamic state had so much power and traction that a range of actors from religious traditionalists to monarchical regimes made some kind of Faustian bargain with Islamism. For politically activist Muslims, especially a new generation of intelligentsia, the simplicity, rhetoric, and power of Islamism to resist the West were its most seductive aspects.

Only some Gulf Arab countries followed a large range of Sharia regulations. But in countries such as Egypt, Tunisia, Algeria, Syria, Iran, and Pakistan the postindependence political models were secular. Islamic law was confined to family law and related matters. The secular elite was the best equipped and qualified sector to administer and run these modern Muslim countries, as the religious traditionalists were not skilled to run a modern state. But as the twentieth century progressed, the political contestation increased and Islamism challenged the secular order in many countries.[13]

The Iranian revolution inaugurated a new momentum for the Islamization of the state, and this was followed by military takeovers in Pakistan and then Sudan resulting in the greater Islamization of the legal and political systems in both countries. Islamic parties periodically led governments in Jordan and Morocco under monarchical regimes. However, the discourse of oppositional Islamism was often rhetorically emancipatory but authoritarian in practice. When, in 1992, the military in Algeria aborted democratic elections that Islamist parties were poised to win, a decade-long civil war depleted that country's resources and turned Algeria into a mediocre state.

For nearly a century authoritarianism was a concern voiced by opposition groups in the Muslim world, but when in power neither secularists nor Islamists ever made serious efforts to curb it. Rhetorical lip service to liberty was hardly matched by acts of liberty or demonstrable efforts to uphold the sacrosanct character of individual or community rights. Neither the aftermath of the anticolonial struggles nor the Iranian revolution nor other experiments in Islamism have ended authoritarianism. Instead, the unreconstructed Muslim political theologies of a bygone era raised their ugly head to wreak havoc in emerging nation-states— Turkey, Pakistan, Sudan, Iran, Egypt—from the 1970s to after the Arab Spring of January 2011. In the more successful democratic Muslim experiments, such as, for example, the AK Party in Turkey, there are ominous signs of a return to authoritarianism. Hence, there is a need to explore a Muslim political theology that is antiauthoritarian and reaches grassroots communities as a basis for holding leadership accountable.

At least a century ago the theological and ethical call to resist authoritarianism was made by a conscientious and outstanding Syrian scholar, Abd al-Rahman al-Kawakibi (1848–1902), who wrote a brilliant treatise called *The Nature of Despotism and the Destruction of Subjugation.*[14] As an activist scholar, Kawakibi battled Ottoman despotism and was imprisoned. On his release he became active in the politics of his native city of Aleppo and later joined the reformist movement of Rashid Rida in Cairo. Kawakibi's writings might have greater relevance today than ever before as restless Muslim populations around the world seek theological resources to deepen their resistance to authoritarian rule. In order to give his ideas currency, in 2006 Prince Hasan bin Talal of Jordan established the Al-Kawakibi Democracy Transition Center, which has an active chapter in Tunisia, as Majid's chapter in this book noted.

With an economy of words Kawakibi showed how despotism and subjugation were antithetical to Islamic teachings. Supporting his claims with texts derived from the Qur'an, the prophetic tradition, Muslim political writings, and arguments from reason and common sense, Kawakibi showed how despotism and subjugation were antithetical to Islamic teachings. Despotism succeeded, Kawakibi argued, because despotic regimes took control of knowledge and the education system. He insisted that the most abhorrent form of despotism occurs when learning is replaced by ignorance. This led him to promote the need for a cultural revolution to undo entrenched forms of despotism and authoritarianism, with a view to reconstructing society with freedom at its center.

Religion, Kawakibi pointed out, had a role in advancing the moral and ethical struggle against authoritarianism. He cited a teaching of the Prophet Muhammad, who said, "The moral command (*nasiha*) is the fulcrum of salvation (religion)."[15] Religion in a nutshell, in his view, was all about morality and the pursuit of the ethical. If religion failed to achieve such ends, it turned into the opposite. Kawakibi, in tones reminiscent of Antonio Gramsci, placed the burden of advancing the ethical literacy of society squarely on the shoulders of the intellectuals in order to combat despotism. He disdained those Muslim intellectuals who placed their mastery of language in the service of political sycophancy or focused their energies on the perfection of dogma and matters related to the afterlife while ignoring the material conditions of ordinary people in this world. He reminded his audience that scholars who peddle such ideas are no threat to authoritarian regimes, and he mocked bookish intellectuals "who stored up in their heads vast amounts of information as if they were padlocked libraries."[16] In contrast, he noted, "The despot does indeed tremble at scholars who are the carriers of the *knowledge of life* such as philosophy (theoretical and applied), rights of nations, the nature of society (sociology), governance (politics), history and rhetoric."[17]

Kawakibi would certainly be disappointed by the turn many intellectuals have taken in Arab Spring countries, especially Egypt, where they celebrated the collapse of democratic rule and favored the return of military rule. Here his warnings about the complicity of the clerical establishment with power were not entirely wrong.

The Clerical Establishment

The relationship between the Islamists and the rank-and-file clerical establishment, the ulama, was always a tense one. While the ulama periodically and expediently showed solidarity with the goals of the Islamists in their bid to establish a Sharia-based political order, they often found doctrinal grounds to disagree vehemently with Islamists over theology and the interpretation of Islamic law. In Pakistan the standoff between the ulama groups and the Jamat-i Islami was legendary, with little love was lost between them. The ulama viewed the Islamists as lacking orthodoxy and learned credentials. In a country like Egypt most of the representative ulama groups—foremost among them those affiliated with al-Azhar—supported the ruling government in principle but expressed mild dissatisfaction if the government did not comply with their Islamic interpretations. Independent ulama groups who fostered a more radical political agenda challenged the authority and the legitimacy of the state from time to time.

The 2012 and 2013 Egyptian constitutions, written under the auspices of the Muslim Brotherhood, praised al-Azhar (in the preamble), guaranteed it autonomy, and declared it to be "the main reference in theology and Islamic affairs" (article 7). The ulama at al-Azhar represent a broad range of thinking including orthodox traditionalists who follow the canonical interpretations of law and theology, neotraditionalists, moderate traditionalist-scripturalist reformists, radical scripturalist-foundationalists, those with modernizing tendencies, and many individuals who embody a hybrid of these inclinations.[18]

Establishment and antiestablishment religious scholars in Egypt, it should be noted, do not conduct their debates in the language of the constitutional provisions of modern Egypt. Rather, their main discourse is in the language of traditional Islamic political theology. Teachings and guidelines of Muslim political theology are used to figure out when a ruler (*imam*) is legitimate and the status of a ruler after being unseated. Despite the fact that Egypt has a version of democracy at work, the language of political theology provides built-in presumptions of autocracy.

The political theology shared widely among the religious scholars urges obedience and loyalty to the government in power on the pragmatic argument that stability is preferable to revolution, instability, and lawlessness. When this prag-matic thread of premodern political theology was adopted by contemporary tradi-tional authorities, they rarely gave attention to whether substantive values of justice, equality, the distribution of wealth, the welfare of the society, and the overall quality of life of the citizenry were provided for by the government. Princi-pled premodern versions of political theology did pay attention to questions of justice, but the pragmatist tradition, a reflexive political theology that views power as an exclusive merit, prevailed historically and continues to do so in contemporary times. While this is true for most in theory, the Salafi Call group viewed the Mubarak and Sadat governments as illegitimate because these regimes did not enforce the Sharia. The goal of the Salafi Call group was to "ensure that post-Mubarak Egypt would not be a place where bearded men are arrested and tor-tured, improve the country's deplorable standard of living, and make the Egyptian government Islamically legitimate."[19]

It is not clear what prompted the ulama of al-Azhar to switch their loyalties and support the military in the June 2013 coup. What is important to recognize is that the clerical establishment in Egypt has a long history of patrimonial relation-ships with successive governments, as Malika Zehgal points out.[20] Despite the ideological diversity within al-Azhar, a core thread of its leadership always viewed the Brotherhood with suspicion. This attitude may have moderated over time as sections of the Azhar ulama became enchanted with the brand of political Islam promoted by the Brotherhood. High-visibility Azhar graduates who were also prominent members of the Muslim Brotherhood, such as Muhammad al-Ghazali and Yusuf al-Qaradawi, made the Brotherhood acceptable in the eyes of later Azhar graduates. Yet, the orthodox core of al-Azhar viewed the Brotherhood's process theology as resulting in political activism and so somewhat contrary to the mainstream Sunni tradition that effectively separated governance and religious authority.

Both the clerical establishment and political rulers often preferred the modus operandi of a quietist religious authority. Religious authority would only occasion-ally raise its prophetic voice in order to advise political rulers when they violated the governance norms of Islamic morality, but they hardly contemplated deposing a ruler. In Egypt's new constitution al-Azhar effectively became the equivalent of Egypt's official "church," even though Egypt also had the office of the state mufti, the chief religious jurisconsult, who issued interpretations of Islamic law and signed off on death penalties.

It appears that Morsi's Brotherhood government tried to win over al-Azhar by giving it autonomy and making it a source of religious authority by means of article 7. So the question arises: Why did al-Azhar switch loyalties as soon as Morsi faced democratic resistance?

Al-Azhar seems to have adopted the age-old political-theological pragmatism: In the event of a contest between two contenders, it is prudent to give loyalty to whoever commands overwhelming authority (*shawka*).[21] With the rise of popular sentiment against Morsi in large-scale demonstrations, al-Azhar threw away the constitutional rule book of democratic process and backed the multitude who invited the winning horse—namely, the army—to take power. Therefore, based on this logic, it made perfect sense to see the grand shaykh of al-Azhar, the Salafi leader, and the Coptic pope seated together at the inauguration of General Sisi after the elected president had been deposed. The Coptic pope most likely preferred a secular military government to an overtly Islamist political party ruling Egypt. It is also worth noting that, in the dying days of Mubarak's rule, the leadership of al-Azhar very reluctantly—and only at the eleventh hour—demonstrated their support for the revolutionary uprising against the dictator's rule. This reflects a long-established, pro–status quo, pragmatist Muslim political theology.

Opposition to the deposition of Morsi was evident in another version of Azhar orthodoxy that adopted a more principled approach to political theology and acknowledged the rules of the game defined by democratic and constitutional governance. Spontaneous groups, one calling itself "Ulama against the Coup," claimed the support of several thousand Azhar scholars who signed a petition to proclaim the legitimacy of Morsi's presidency and protested his wrongful removal.

Interestingly, both the pragmatists and those who adopted a principled approach used the same argument either to support the June 30, 2013, coup deposing Morsi or to oppose it. Each side went back to the same event in the Islamic past, the insurrection of the Kharijites against the rule of Ali in the seventh century. The Kharijites' insurrection and rebellion against legitimate rule had given them infamy.

Shaykh Ali Goma, official mufti of Egypt till February 2013, was among the pragmatists who opposed the ousting of Mubarak and later also defended the overthrow of Morsi by the military. Addressing the military high command days after the June 30 coup, Goma equated the Muslim Brotherhood with the Kharijites and urged the armed forces of Egypt to use violence to subdue Morsi's supporters to whom he referred as the "dogs of hell." As a deposed ruler, Goma opined, Morsi had forfeited his claim to legitimacy. The public appeal to the military to intervene on June 30, 2013, effectively made Sisi the legitimate ruler, given his exhibition of overwhelming force (*shawka*) as head of Egypt's armed forces. Yet a few years earlier, in November 2010, Dr. Ali Goma wrote: "Muslims are free to choose whichever system of government they deem most appropriate for them, provided they respect and uphold basic principles of equality, freedom and human dignity. Indeed, these principles for which liberal democracy stands are themselves part of the foundation for the Islamic world view; it is the achievement of this freedom and dignity within a religious context that Islamic law strives for."[22]

It becomes difficult to understand how the Goma, the lover of liberal democracy, could approve military rule and the use of lethal violence to subdue nonviolent protest. One explanation is that Islamic pragmatist norms of early political theology trumped the norms of democratic governance, especially in the absence of a reconciliation of the two.

Mounting a bruising critical attack on the coup was Shaykh Yusuf al-Qaradawi, a leading religious figure based in the Gulf state of Qatar. Qaradawi took refuge in Qatar during the years when the Brotherhood was outlawed in Egypt. Among some Sunni Muslims he enjoys what comes close to a pontifical reputation thanks to his popular weekly show on Al Jazeera television called *Sharia and Life* in which he addresses issues of faith, law, ethics, and politics. In Qaradawi's view, General Sisi and the army resorted to insurrection (in the same manner as the Kharijites) by deposing a legitimately elected ruler. Qaradawi went even further and criticized the grand shaykh of al-Azhar for approving the military coup by endorsing General (now Field Marshal) Sisi's inauguration. Such a frontal attack is rare within the clerical establishment, and the recriminations between supporters and opponents of the two figures—Shaykh al-Azhar Ahmed el-Tayeb and Qaradawi—were ugly. Qaradawi, who was appointed to the Council of Senior Scholars of al-Azhar, resigned in protest from that council in the aftermath of his political disagreement with el-Tayeb, whom he claimed had resorted to political pragmatism in supporting the military leader of the June 30, 2013, coup. Egypt's new 2013 constitution guarantees the independence of al-Azhar, and the Council of Senior Scholars will in the future elect the new shaykh or president of this important institution of learning.

In Syria, too, one of the leading Sunni scholars, Shaykh Said Ramadan al-Buti, resorted to a political theology that supported the Bashar al-Assad regime in the wake of the uprisings in that country. Buti tried to assure the Sunni groups that it was in their best interest to support the Damascus government and engage in dialogue with the regime instead of opposing it. But when Syrian nonviolent protest spiraled into civil war, Buti continued to support the status quo. In the end he met a violent death in 2013 when a suicide bomber detonated an explosive device in the Damascus mosque where he was giving a class. Speculations abound regarding whether Buti was on the verge of defecting and about who really assassinated him—the militarized opposition groups who disagreed with him or the regime that might have gotten wind of his plans to defect. Nevertheless, in the absence of political stability and representative governance, the risk of chaos and the loss of life increases in the Middle East and North Africa.

Conclusion: A Return to the Ethical

The contemporary Tunisian thinker and philosopher Abu Yarub al-Marzuki repeatedly encourages his audiences to profit from the political insights of the legendary North African polymath Abdurrahman Ibn Khaldun (1332–1406). As the earliest protagonist of what we would today call sociology and political science, Ibn Khaldun receives credit for making us understand how societies work. He fully understood the negative impact authoritarianism and injustice had on the morale of society. "Injustice," he wrote, "precipitates the ruin of civilization."[23] When people are disposessed of their property, are overtaxed, and have their rights infringed, then, in Ibn Khaldun's view, they lose all incentive to better themselves and their societies.[24] Authoritarianism and tyranny contribute to the decline of society and the loss of opportunity, development, and well-being.

The Arab Spring has demonstrated that the people are determined to change their destiny through peaceful protests, uprisings, and, if necessary, bloody civil wars. But the revolutions have also been reversed in several places. It appears that while civil society can easily be mobilized, it also lacks the inner and deeper resources to make transformation a lasting process. In my view the real damage of decades of authoritarianism has been the denial of people's opportunity to think and actualize the ethical teachings of their religions. Muslim societies are exposed to an ethical tradition of duty-based ethics (*fiqh*) that imposes some degree of restraint but does not actualize norms of autonomy that are located within self, community, and society. Reliance on a strong authority—the father, the cleric, or the political strongman—only reinforces patriarchal and paternalistic authority to the detriment of the productive values that every vibrant society needs.

In fact Marzuqi, like Kawakibi a century ago, is unique among contemporary Arab philosophers in identifying the ethical and knowledge deficit of Arab-Muslim societies. "We own neither an ethics nor knowledge" to mediate the crisis, he said in a fairly damning but honest assessment of the situation in 2008.[25] "Ethics is not merely to pronounce values," Marzuqi said, "but to act upon them." In a direct attack on authoritarianism he said, "Freedom allows the ethical to develop. . . . Freedom is the foundation of knowledge and ethics."[26] Ibn Khaldun would most likely have agreed with Marzuqi. After authoritarianism has stripped away the purpose of life, it ultimately attacks the moral core of society and denatures it to the extent that the abnormal appears normal. It takes a revolution of another kind to rehabilitate the moral core of nations. But to echo Marzuqi's analysis, any reconstruction begins with freedom and knowledge as the preconditions for the important but difficult journey of refashioning the morality of individuals and groups. Marzuqi might be right: In order for any future Arab Spring to flourish, it must begin with the individual and of necessity internalize an ethics based on freedom.

Notes

1. Rancière, *Dissensus*, 29.
2. Ibid., 30.

3. Salem, "Challenging Authoritarianism, Colonialism, and Disunity."
4. See Akyol, "Turkey's Model Nation."
5. al-Ījī, al-Jurjānī, and ʿUmayra, *Kitāb Al-Mawāqif*, 3:574–84.
6. Lambton, *State and Government in Medieval Islam*, 85.
7. Arendt, *Origins of Totalitarianism*.
8. Ḍāhir, *al-Ṣirāʿ bayna al-tayyāaayn al-dīnī aa-al-ʿalmānī*, 370.
9. al-Ījī, al-Jurjānī, and ʿUmayra, *Mawāqif*.
10. ʿAbd al-Rāziq and Ḥaqqī, *al-Islām wa-uṣūl al-ḥukm*, 76.
11. al-Ījī, al-Jurjānī, and ʿUmayra, *Mawāqif*, 3:574–78.
12. See Balqazīz, *State in Contemporary Islamic Thought*, esp. 37–44.
13. Moustafa, *Struggle for Constitutional Power*.
14. Kawākibī and ʾImara, *Ṭabāʾiʿ al-istibdād wa-maṣāriʿ al-istiʿbād*.
15. Ibid., 82.
16. Ibid., 46.
17. Ibid., 45; emphasis added.
18. See Zaman, *Modern Islamic Thought in a Radical Age*, 86–96.
19. Brown, "Rise and Fall of the Salafi Al-Nour Party in Egypt."
20. Zeghal, "Religion and Politics in Egypt: The Ulema of Al-Azhar, Radical Islam, and the State (1952–94)."
21. al-Azmeh, *Muslim Kingship*, 117.
22. Ali Gomaa, "Islam and Modernity."
23. Khaldūn, *Muqaddimah*, 2:103.
24. Ibid., 2:107.
25. Mūsá, "Munāẓara dārat ishkālīyatuhā al-ra'īsīya ḥawla al-fikr al-dīnī wa al-falsafī fī muwājahat al-taḥaddiyāt al-rāhina."
26. Ibid.

Bibliography

ʿAbd al-Rāziq, ʿAlī, and Mamdūḥ Ḥaqqī. *al-Islām wa-uṣūl al-ḥukm*. Beirut: Dār Maktaba al-Ḥayāt, n.d.

Akyol, Mustafa. "Turkey's Model Nation." *New York Times*, February 16, 2014. www.nytimes.com/2014/02/17/opinion/turkeys-model-nation.html.

Arendt, Hannah. *The Origins of Totalitarianism: New Edition with Added Prefaces*. Orlando: A Harvest Book, Harcourt, 1976.

al-Azmeh, Aziz. *Muslim Kingship: Power and the Sacred in Muslim, Christian and Pagan Politics*. London: I. B. Tauris, 1997.

Balqazīz, ʿAbd al-Ilāh. *The State in Contemporary Islamic Thought: A Historical Survey of the Major Muslim Political Thinkers of the Modern Era*. Contemporary Arab Scholarship in the Social Sciences. London: I. B. Tauris, 2009.

Brown, Jonathan. "The Rise and Fall of the Salafi Al-Nour Party in Egypt." *Jadaliyya*, November 14, 2013.

Ḍāhir, Muḥammad Kāmil. *al-Ṣirāʿ bayna al-tayyārayn al-dīnī wa-al-ʿalmānī : fī al-fikr al-ʿarabī al-ḥadīth wa-al-muʿāṣir*. 2nd ed. Beirut: Dār al-Bīru_nī, 2009.

Gomaa, Ali. "Islam and Modernity." *Contending Modernities* (blog), University of Notre Dame, November 22, 2010. http://blogs.nd.edu/contendingmodernities/2010/11/22/islam-and-modernity/.

al-Ījī, ʿAḍud al-Dīn ʿAbd al-Raḥmān ibn Aḥmad, ʿAlī ibn Muḥammad al-Jurjānī, and ʿAbd al-Raḥmān ʿUmayra, eds. *Kitāb al-Mawāqif*. 3 vols. Beirut: Dār al-Jīl, 1417A.H./1997.

Kawākibī, ʿAbd al-Raḥmān, and Muḥammad ʿImāra, eds. *Ṭabāʾiʿ al-istibdād wa-maṣāriʿ al-istiʿbād*. Cairo: Dar al-Shuruq, 2012.

Khaldūn, Ibn. *The Muqaddimah: An Introduction to History*. Translated by Franz Rosenthal. 3 vols. Bollingen Series 43. Princeton, NJ: Princeton University Press, 1980.

Lambton, Ann K. S. *State and Government in Medieval Islam: An Introduction to the Study of Islamic Political Theory; The Jurists*. London Oriental Series. Oxford: Oxford University Press, 1981.

Moustafa, Tamir. *The Struggle for Constitutional Power: Law, Politics, and Economic Development in Egypt*. New York: Cambridge University Press, 2007.

Mūsá, Āmāl. "Munāẓara dārat ishkālīyatuhā al-raʾīsīya ḥawla al-fikr al-dīnī wa al-falsafī fī muwājahat al-taḥaddiyāt al-rāhina." *Asharq al-awsaṭ*, June 24, 2008. http://classic.aawsat .com/details.asp?section = 17&article = 476095&issueno = 10801#.VC7LaL5rXas.

Rancière, Jacques. *Dissensus: On Politics and Aesthetics*. Translated by Steven Corcoran. London: Continuum, 2010.

Salem, Ahmed Ali. "Challenging Authoritarianism, Colonialism, and Disunity: The Islamic Political Reform Movements of Al-Afghani and Rida." *American Journal of Islamic Social Sciences* 21, no. 2 (Spring 2004): 25–53.

Zaman, Muhammad Qasim. *Modern Islamic Thought in a Radical Age: Religious Authority and Internal Criticism*. Cambridge: Cambridge University Press, 2012.

Zeghal, Malika. "Religion and Politics in Egypt: The Ulema of Al-Azhar, Radical Islam, and the State (1952–94)." *International Journal of Middle East Studies* 31, no. 3 (1999): 371–99.

9

The One and the Many

Religious Coexistence and Belonging in Postapartheid Society

ABDULKADER TAYOB

South Africa has one of the most progressive constitutions in the world, one that includes a rigorous protection of the freedom and equality of all religions. It would seem unthinkable to compare South Africa's liberal and progressive approach with those of North African countries, where religion has played and continues to play a dominant and divisive role in state, nation, public life, and constitution. If anything, religion in general and Islam in particular are major obstacles in the democratization and liberalization of North Africa. In South Africa, it would seem, such issues have been clarified in the South African Constitution and in political practice since 1994.

In reality there is a much more complex relationship between religion, nation, constitution, public life, and values in South Africa. Since the end of apartheid in 1994, South African scholars of religion have written on religion, the nation, the 1996 Constitution, the religious sensibilities of the presidents of the country, the tension generated between parliament and religious groups on abortion and same-sex marriages, conflicts between the constitution and Islamic law over South African Muslim marriages, court decisions and debates on religious symbols and practices in public life, and the competing values and communities generated by the new state and religious traditions. Taken together, these scholarly reflections suggest that the relationship between religion, nation, and state is far from settled in

This chapter is based on research supported by the South African Research Chairs Initiative of the Department of Science and Technology and the National Research Foundation of South Africa. Any opinion, finding, and conclusion or recommendation expressed here is that of the author, and the NRF does not accept any responsibility or liability in this regard.

postapartheid South Africa. To be sure, the situation has improved much since the fall of apartheid. The Dutch Reformed Church (DRC) played a dominant role in the development and promotion of apartheid South Africa. It was often said that the DRC was the apartheid state "at prayer." Then, from the 1960s onward, various churches and religious groups began to oppose the theology of the DRC. Eventually a David-and-Goliath struggle emerged on the streets of South African cities between theologies that supported apartheid and theologies that opposed it.[1] Toward the close of apartheid and the beginning of the transition in the 1990s, many but not all religious groups supported democratic developments and change.[2]

It is not easy to generalize and describe the relationship between religion and state in postapartheid South Africa. In Annie Leatt's dissertation on the secular ambition of the postapartheid state, she says that we do not have enough information yet, noting that the quest for a secular authority faces interesting challenges.[3] In this chapter, therefore, I examine a sample of scholarly literature that reflects on the role and meaning of religion in public life in postapartheid South Africa. I realize that I focus mostly on studies dealing with two religions in particular, Christianity and Islam. The selection was made partly on the basis of my expertise and partly on the bias in the literature itself. There are fewer studies on Judaism, Hinduism, or Buddhism than on Islam, even though they can all be described as minority religions in the country. Nevertheless, I include in the analysis scholars of religion and theologians who advocated, explored, and explicated developments on relations between religions and the state. Based on this sample, I argue that binary models do not adequately reflect the complex relationship between religion and state in South Africa. The relationship between religions and state cannot be reduced to a situation where either religion or the state is dominant, as some of the theoretical literature is proposing. I therefore propose that Michel Foucault's concepts of utopia and heterotopia provide a useful framework for understanding religions in postapartheid South Africa. Using his concepts, I propose that religions reflect the nation but are also very likely to invert, subvert, and ignore it.

Religion and the Nation-State

With the emergence of fundamentalisms in general and then Islamic radicalism, it would seem that modern states and religious traditions were bound to oppose each other. Most critical scholarship focuses on the inevitability of the collision course between religions and states. There are three possible scenarios: religion as sanctioned by the state, or state religion; religious control of the state in some form of theocracy, or religious state; or a pragmatic arrangement between the institutions of religion and state.[4]

Adrian Hastings, Bruce Lawrence, Bruce Lincoln, and Talal Asad have discussed modern religious developments as they were influenced and even determined by the modern state. They propose very different analyses, but their work points to the close relationship between the modern state and religions. Hastings questions the secularized narrative of nation building that has effaced the importance of religion in some theories, such as those proposed by Ernest Gellner and Benedict Anderson. Hastings states that the religious history of Europe also played a very important role in the emergence of modern nationhood and nation-states. More significantly, he argues that key symbols of Christianity were incorporated into the nation.[5] Taking a more familiar and binary approach than Hastings, Lincoln points to the emergence of the modern state in Enlightenment ideas that led inevitably to the limitation of the power of religion. He offers a number of permutations of the relationship between the power and authority of state and religions. Religious conflicts are closely related to and dependent on the strength and stability of the modern state. When the power of the modern state declined in recent times, he argues, the authority of religions increased. This was the root cause of modern conflicts involving religions.[6] Lawrence's book on modern fundamentalisms illustrates this relationship. In his analysis, new fundamentalist movements worldwide are defined by and committed to opposing modernity in general and the modern state in particular.[7]

Asad's work is more closely related to Hastings than to Lincoln or Lawrence, but Asad takes an anthropological approach to the formation of the state in Europe. Working with the project of the secular as the hallmark of the modern state, he points to its cultural production. The state, he argues, should not be taken at face value as merely a rational and effective means of organizing groups and individuals. The formation of the secular in Europe included the reproduction and reconfiguration of pain, human rights, the person, and even religion. The modern state authorized religion through a complex array of cultural mechanisms and brute force. Religion in modern society was one of the products of state politics.[8]

This brief review can be summarized as follows: Lawrence explains fundamentalism as a response to modernity in general and the modern state in particular. Lincoln develops this insight to follow the fortunes of religious authority in a dynamic and dialectical relation with the state on a global scale. Focusing on Europe, Asad shows how modern religious developments were a product of the secular. So influenced, the modern state determined the course of religion. With the exception of Hastings, these authors emphasize, then, the agency of the modern state. The modern state was the direct cause of religious mobilization and impact. Only Hastings points to the important role played by religion in the production of the modern nation-state. As Hastings argues, these theoretical frameworks and variations leave very little space for the agency of religious groups and individuals.

I want to follow Hastings in my analysis of the relationship between state, nation, and religions in South Africa. I will show that religious discourse, as represented by religious groups and individuals, is not always at the mercy of state machinations, nor is it totally preoccupied with its impact. Often, religious discourse enjoys a longer history and also a deeper engagement with individuals and groups. In my view the theoretical frameworks of Lawrence, Lincoln, and Asad play down the intense engagements of religious groups and individuals in modern societies as part of their longer histories. I propose that Foucault's concept of heterotopia provides a more apt language to reflect on the complex agency of religion within a modern state.

In an article published in 1967, Foucault examined the production of space in modern societies and nations. He suggests that space in Europe was more resistant to secularization than time was. While time was open to the regimentation of the secular, space was resilient to authorization: "Now, despite all the techniques for appropriating space, despite the whole network of knowledge that enables us to delimit or to formalize it, contemporary space is perhaps still not entirely desanctified."[9]

Foucault identifies the spaces that elude rationalization and control, allowing the subjective, the cultural, and the religious to invade or persist amid the secular: "And perhaps our life is still governed by a certain number of oppositions that remain inviolable, that our institutions and practices have not yet dared to break down. These are oppositions that we regard as simple givens: for example between private space and public space, between family space and social space, between cultural space and useful space, between the space of leisure and that of work. All these are still nurtured by the hidden presence of the sacred."[10] The sacred, for Foucault then, represents the spaces that elude the state and its agents. There is an implicit definition of the sacred here: in-between spaces and their many subjective relations that the modern state has not actually authorized or taken control of.

Foucault describes various attempts by the modern nation-state to inscribe a new space that replaces the cosmologically defined space of the ancien regime. Such a new space is infused with new ideals and values. Foucault calls this space utopia and insists that by definition it does not exist. Foucault suggests that apart from this imaginary category of nonexistent space, there are other real spaces set apart in a society. Such spaces are "real places—places that do exist and that are formed in the very founding of society—which are something like counter-sites, a kind of effectively enacted utopia in which the real sites, all the other real sites that can be found within the culture, are simultaneously *represented, contested, and inverted*."[11] As examples, he submits that brothels, cemeteries, stadiums, and even boats are heterotopias. Unreal utopias reflect the imaginary places of the new nation, but heterotopias are real spaces that emerge in their shadows, "formed in the very founding of society." The heterotopic spaces are not pure representations of utopias but cannot be detached from them. Sometimes they reflect the new nation, but they could just as easily contest and invert it.

Foucault's concepts of utopia and heterotopia provide a language for thinking about the complex relation between religion, nation, and state. The South African postapartheid state has established an elaborate framework for a new utopia. Beginning with the constitution, this imaginary utopia was reflected in the office of the president, the houses of parliament, its bills and acts, its array of courts, commissions set up to uphold the values of the constitution, schools, and public festivals and gatherings. If we were to follow Foucault closely, it is perhaps too early to know if the heterotopia of the South African nation will turn out to be shopping malls or street protests, national sport events or gatherings around *braai* (barbecue) fires. Each of these may already have begun to take shape as the unstable heterotopias of the new nation. But I would like to suggest that Foucault's concepts may be employed to understand the discursive spaces occupied by religions in South Africa. Religious discourses are best described as heterotopic; they cannot be extricated from the utopias they reflect. But they also go beyond the utopia of the new nation, which they "simultaneously *represented, contested, and inverted.*"

Imagining the South African Nation

Since the fall of the apartheid state, scholars of religion and theology in South Africa have reflected on the challenges faced by the nascent postapartheid state. They have proposed how the state should be related to religion and religious values but have also reflected on the religious and symbolic practices of the nation and state. The prescriptive and descriptive reflections are imaginative in their own ways. The prescriptions offer ideas about how religion should relate to the new nation, while the descriptions capture important trends in the short history of the postapartheid state. I want to illustrate the heterotopic nature of these discursive spaces. They sometimes reflect the new utopia but more generally invert, go beyond, and subvert it.

Religious Inclusivity

I begin with a persistent tradition in the South African religious field that pays homage to the constitution. It is a discourse in South Africa that *reflects* the nation. In the years leading up to the first democratic elections and constitution in South Africa, religious individuals and organizations engaged in an intense debate on the future of religions in South Africa. Albie Sachs, an African National Congress (ANC) leader who would later become a Constitutional Court judge, may have initiated this discussion in an article published in 1990.[12] In the article, he proposes the idea of a constructive cooperation between religion and state—that South Africans should stay clear of both a religious state and a highly secularized state that keeps religion and state in strict separation. The idea was to turn away from the religious nationalism of the apartheid state but not to follow some Western models of complete separation. In the next few years, the South African chapter of the World Conference on Religion and Peace adopted this framework and promoted it among religious communities, particularly those who were most clearly identified with the struggle against apartheid. In November 1992, religious leaders working in the council produced a document titled *Declaration on Religious Rights and Responsibilities*, which was signed by some of the major religious groups and individuals in the country. It rejected the establishment of a religious state but advocated a vigorous freedom of religion for all groups in which religious communities could and should contribute to a future South Africa.[13] The publication of the document reflected the dominant sentiment among prominent religious leaders. It navigated the opportunities and challenges of holding in balance freedom, responsibility, and activism in relation to the nation and the state. In Foucault's sense the declaration represented or imagined a utopia of the diversity of religious belonging and engagement in one country.

Among the early reflections on the new South Africa, there were two articles, one written by Charles Villa-Vicencio and the other by John de Gruchy, that went beyond the rights, responsibilities, and obligations of religions toward the nation. These two articles imagined an engagement with the new democracy and pointed to another side of South African religious discourse. Both essays were presented in a Festschrift to one of the great anti-apartheid theologians of the country, Beyers Naudé. De Gruchy's essay evaluated the contrasting claims made by religion and the nation-state. Working with the idea of patriotism, de Gruchy said that its real origins may be found in Christianity. He accepted that both Christianity and the new democracy demanded commitment and loyalty but noted a qualitative difference between the two: "Thus a patriotism shaped by the gospel has at least two components: the prophetic, or critical solidarity, and the pastoral, or redemptive service and sacrifice. A true prophet is one who speaks the truth and stands for justice while identifying fully with the follies and the fate of his or her people irrespective of the way in which they respond."[14]

According to de Gruchy, a nation not founded on prophetic patriotism would potentially and inevitably lead to folly. In contrast, prophetic patriotism stood for critical solidarity with a nation and its follies. Christians should embrace both forms of patriotism but never lose sight of their difference. In this short essay de Gruchy set out the conditions of critical engagement with the new South Africa. He asserted a clear ontological hierarchy between commitment to religion and to nation. His was a patriotism that merged with the nation but also departed from it. Since 1994 a number of theological voices, inside and outside Christianity, have taken on this critical relation with the state.[15] In contrast with the *Declaration on*

Religious Rights and Responsibilities, this view did not fully reflect the nation but took a critical stand from the inside.

Villa-Vicencio's essay in the same Festschrift proposed a different approach to the nation. Patriotism, in his view, would have to be a product of hermeneutics and dialogue. Villa-Vicencio saw the new nation emerging from multiple stories that had not yet been told and heard in the country. South Africans entered the nation with different narratives and different memories. The main task of nation building was a hermeneutical process of telling and listening to these narratives so that South Africans recognized that they "see, hear and understand in a different way."[16] In a later publication, Villa-Vicencio collected one such set of stories from leading activists, both religious and nonreligious, in the anti-apartheid struggle. He regarded their stories as a "foretaste" of a new theology for South Africa. He argued optimistically that "bound into a common ethical vision, without the identity of any of the constituent parts being lost in the greater whole, [they can provide] a new national soul [from which] . . . a new nation [can] be born."[17]

This kind of theology was, he said, an example of "the history-making influence of people (created, says the Psalmist, to be just a little inferior to God)."[18] In this last remark the vision of Villa-Vicencio merged with de Gruchy's as he paid homage to transcendentalism. However, it is clear that Villa-Vicencio presented a more immanent approach to the creation of higher values than de Gruchy did. In the latter's work the narrative and symbols of Christianity remained dominant, while Villa-Vicencio's theology was open to the future and to other impulses, both religious and nonreligious, in which Christianity loses its central place.

De Gruchy and Villa-Vicencio provided significant and leading examples of the relationship between the nation and religion. Different from each other, they both mapped the new nation through theological discourse. De Gruchy's approach showed the deep roots of the nation in a Christian perspective. In this theology, however, there was much that lay inside and much that lay outside both the nation and the state. Villa-Vicencio supported an imminent process of thinking and narrating the nation. Dialogue and hermeneutics were also fundamental methodological tools from theology, but there were no guaranteed results from the past. Villa-Vicencio's vision took a step away from Christianity and a step closer to the utopia of a new nation. De Gruchy's vision held a critical distance and maintained separation between nation and church.

A careful reading of de Gruchy points to another dimension of Christian discourse in South Africa. He claimed a higher authority and place for critical patriotism, but one rooted in the symbolism of Christianity. This latter dimension, the symbols and language of Christianity read into the new nation, was present in South African religious discourse and merits attention. This narrative of Christianity merging with the nation can be seen in many statements of the former archbishop of the Church of the Province of Southern Africa, Desmond Tutu. On the occasion of the first election, for example, Archbishop Tutu conveyed a powerful configuration of the nation in the following:

> We are brothers and sisters, we are one. With his Cross God has effected reconciliation among us all. Jesus, so says the Epistle to the Ephesians, is our peace. He has broken down the middle wall of partition. And the Epistle to the Galatians says: "In this Jesus now, there is neither Jew nor Greek, slave nor free, male nor female." Through the Cross God has said "No" to racism and its injustice and oppression. For racism is a sin and that is why we call on all of our people not to vote for parties which exploit fears and prejudices.[19]

Unlike de Gruchy, the archbishop did not maintain a careful line between true and false patriotism. The nation was embraced in the symbolism of Christ. The archbishop's formulation was utopian in the sense that it pointed to a united nation merging with a Christological event, but it was also deeply sectarian in the use of the symbols of Christ and Jesus. And yet Archbishop Tutu's Christology also pointed beyond sectarianism: "In this Jesus now, there is neither Jew nor Greek, slave nor free, male nor female." His Christological vision potentially displaced Christianity. There was a fine balance between a utopia infused by Christianity and one that pointed beyond it.

The symbolism of the new nation to be born came together in the Truth and Reconciliation Commission (TRC) instituted by parliament in 1995. The commission listened to the testimonies of victims and perpetrators of violence and then presented its report to the president in 1998. The TRC was a momentous process in the first years of the postapartheid state and attempted to start the process of reconciliation after years of apartheid and colonial rule. Ebrahim Moosa and Piet Meiring authored reflective pieces on the TRC process that are relevant to this article and reinforce the reflections presented by de Gruchy, Villa-Vicencio, and Tutu. Moosa discussed the proceedings of the hearings as a simulacrum of justice, arguing that the hearings recalled the Eucharist. The TRC hearings brought victims and perpetrators face to face with each other to search and hope for reconciliation. Moosa argued, however, that the hearings neither offered Abrahamic justice nor real reconciliation. It was the Eucharist brought on the national stage to simulate reconciliation.[20] Moosa's reflections echo the intricate relation between the nation and Christian symbolism: derived from the symbolic language of Christianity, the hearings were not quite the real thing. The hearings were a simulacrum, neither quite a Eucharist nor reconciliation. His characterization of the TRC as simulacrum drew on the postmodern discourse of doubt and deconstruction. In the context of this article, however, he achieved the same goal as Villa-Vicencio and de Gruchy. The TRC was not a Eucharist, but only a simulation thereof.

We can appreciate Moosa's reflections by turning to Meiring's discussion of the Christian character of the TRC. He recalled in his article that the chairperson of the TRC, Archbishop Tutu, was very consciously adopting Christian prayer, liturgy, and values against the feeble resistance of the lawyers. Meiring made no apology for the TRC's dominant Christian symbolism, however, and stressed that the same values and practices were present in other religions. He also said, however, that the Christian character of the rituals was justified because most people of South Africa were Christian. Meiring's reflections also reveal the presence and absence of Christianity in the national hearings—a privilege that was not enjoyed by other religions. He seems to say that the ritual symbols were not really Christian because the values were shared by all, but he also seems to believe that the symbols had to be Christian to represent the people of South Africa.

These reflections from de Gruchy, Villa-Vicencio, Moosa, and Meiring suggest the uneasy relationship between Christianity and the nation. This theological discourse claims the nation but also immediately withdraws or includes the voices of other religious traditions in this Christian framework. The dialogue contrasts with the apartheid theology that reflected the dominant ideology of the time. This fully sectarian theology is still present, but highly dissimulated in public life. The new discourse infused the nation with Christian symbolism, but a symbolism that immediately distanced Christianity from the act of Christianization. These examples show that the utopia of the nation did not exhaust religious discourse. In fact, one can contrast these reflections with the above-mentioned *Declaration on Religious Rights and Responsibilities* that defined the limits and roles of religions in the nation-state. The declaration was aligned to the utopia of the new nation in an uncomplicated way while these reflections point to the unsettled and dialectical relationship between the nation and religions with Christianity in the center.

Islamic Inclusivity

One could turn to many more examples of heterotopia inscribed by Christian discourse as described above. I want rather to present a case from the South African experience of Islam to show heterotopia in a different form. Muslim Personal Law (MPL) has become a topic of intense debate and acrimony among Muslims in South Africa since 1994 and has defined the relation between Muslims and postapartheid democracy like few other issues. The Constitution of South Africa (article 15 of chapter 2) recognizes "marriages concluded under any tradition, or a system of religious, personal or family law." The particular application of this principle to Islam has been highly controversial among Muslims since the adoption of the Interim Constitution in 1994. Human rights activists have argued that Islamic law is a product of human history, subject to continued interpretation and adjustment. In their view the South African Constitution represents shared universal values in the light of which Muslim marriage norms may be reinterpreted.[21] This discourse, I submit, is utopian with regard to the new nation.

The majority of Muslims believed, however, that a compromise with the constitution was inherently impossible. They argued that MPL, in contrast with the human construction of the constitution, was divine in origin and intent. Its provisions should not be subject to compromise and historical conditioning.[22] It would appear that this discourse was antithetical to the nation and thus subversive in its heterotopia. There are certainly such elements present in Muslim discourse in the country with respect to the constitution and Islamic law. However, a closer examination reveals a different heterotopic nature. One position, radically opposed to the state's intervention, illustrates this. The *Majlis*, a newspaper published in Port Elizabeth in the Eastern Cape with wide coverage and an Internet site, has consistently rejected attempts to formulate a law that would balance and mediate Islamic law and the constitution. It associated the various bills presented for public debate with *kufr* (disbelief), suggesting that any Muslim associated with the bills was a heretic. Interestingly, it also advised Muslims on how to deal with the supreme law of the land: "There is ample room to work within and round the country's Constitution to ensure that Muslims regulate their lives in accordance with the Shariah while this is not possible with MPL legislation because such legislation is *kufr* legislation presented in the name of Islam."[23]

The author of the article in *Majlis* rejects the reinterpretation proposed by Moosa and others to reinterpret MPL in line with the constitution but recognizes a space created by the constitution for the practice of religion. He argues that the relevant clause (chapter 2, clause 15) does not compel Muslims to approach the state to recognize their marriages. It only provides the *possibility* for the state to recognize MPL. Muslims in South Africa should comfortably get along without the intervention and interference of the constitution in the practice of the Sharia. I submit that this one example illustrates *indifference* in heterotopia. A clever reading was followed by indifference, an attitude of "we will carry on as we did in the past." Like the Christian discourses cited above, this one claims a religious prerogative beyond the constitution. It does not, however, claim a hypernarrative of the nation but accommodates itself alongside the nation by producing an attitude of indifference.

Diversity

I would like to move to other real and potentially disruptive religious discourses in the new nation. The discourse of Islamic radicalism, which surfaced in the vigilante movement of People Against Gangsterism and Drugs (PAGAD), is an equally good and complex example. PAGAD emerged in 1996, stating its intent to rid the working-class Cape Flats of the scourge of gangsters and drugs. PAGAD leaders and spokespersons employed very explicit and strong religious symbols and ritual in their campaigns, which have led to intense public debate on the organization's true nature. Security specialists in the country saw PAGAD as an exemplary model of Islamic fundamentalism's rejection of democracy.[24] They read only subversion of the new utopia. Others saw PAGAD as giving expression to underlying socioeconomic concerns that were being overlooked in mainstream religious thinking at the time.[25] In the context of this article PAGAD sometimes represented ambivalence and sometimes rejection among Muslims of the new democratic state.

The popularity of Pentecostal churches and new Islamic reform movements has had a deep impact on religious groups in South Africa, as elsewhere in Africa. Pentecostal churches have mushroomed throughout the country and across the various classes in society. Analysts in South Africa are only beginning to turn attention to their meaning and impact. Riann Ingram found that for those experiencing urbanization for the first time Pentecostal churches act as a bridge between African traditional religious worldviews and modernity.[26] Anthony Balcomb looked at their politics generally and divided Pentecostals along the political spectrum from liberationists on the one side to those opposed to the liberal constitution on the other side.[27] In a more recent article Balcomb sums up their complex relation: "The advent in South Africa of one of the most liberal constitutions in the world has brought the Pentecostals, and their Evangelical brothers and sisters, out of the closet and into the public arena with a vengeance."[28]

Balcomb notes their rejection of landmark legislation on rape, abortion, and other liberal policies of the new democratic state. They take very seriously the imminent advent of the kingdom of God, which they see as emerging sometimes in the family and sometimes in the political order. While they might be seen as the antithesis of the new democratic order, they also promote the consumerism and individualism that are the hallmarks of the new liberal society.[29] Balcomb summarizes their theology: "Their message to the people is clear and simple. God loves them, God wants to affirm them, and God wants them to be successful."[30] This theology is fully in accordance with the new society, even while it rejects some of the society's historic legislative achievements.

A similar discourse might be traced in new Islamic reform groups flourishing in the country. There are a number of studies that have examined the continuing strength of the transnational Tablighi Jama'at that was rooted in South Africa in the 1960s.[31] This puritan revivalist group eschews politics and calls on Muslims to focus on their personal salvation and responsibility to God. It has been joined by other recent reformist groups who draw their inspiration from the Middle East. The latter are not as mobile as the Tablighi Jama'at but have begun to change the religious landscape of South African Muslims. There is currently an intense debate between the established groups and the new groups in Cape Town.[32] To these may be added a multitude of mystical groups that have joined the mosaic of Muslims in the country. Replicating the model of the Pentecostal churches, new Islamic reform movements use a unique symbol system to root themselves in the consumerist culture of the new South Africa.[33] The upshot of these new movements is increased devotion, higher attendance for religious rituals, and a burgeoning religious economy. However, as Goolam Vahed and Shamil Jeppie remind us, these discourses do not escape the realities and histories of race and class in South Africa.[34] Turning to Foucault's language, Islamic reformist visions certainly do not reflect the utopia but neither do they unequivocally subvert nor invert the nation. It might be best to describe them as ignoring the utopia while benefiting from the constitutional democracy of the country.

Religion in the Public Sphere

I would like to move now to religious symbols employed in the political and public spheres. David Chidester and Gerald West have pointed out that religious symbols are not the monopoly of religious groups and institutions. They are invoked in a unique way in public life. West has examined the discourses of Presidents Mbeki and Zuma in their employment of biblical and theological tropes, and Chidester has followed with a broad sweep of the public invocation of religion.

In his oft-quoted speeches, Mbeki regularly invoked the Exodus as a key motif of liberation and development for the new nation. He was continuing a trend established by liberation theologians in the struggle against apartheid. President Zuma, according to West, equated South Africa more enthusiastically with the Promised Land. South Africa had become the New Jerusalem.[35] West sees Zuma favoring not liberation theology but rather evangelical Christianity with its particular morality, "narrowly construed as personal morality."[36] In contrast with de Gruchy, Villa-Vicencio, Moosa, and Meiring, the presidents of the country were blurring the lines between nation and struggle, and between nation and the kingdom of God. Using the terms of Foucault, the discourses of Presidents Mbeki and Zuma reflected and mirrored the nation in utopias.

Chidester questions whether this analysis exhausts religious symbols in the public and political spheres. The presidents, he says, were not only employing Christian symbols but also turning to a multitude of symbols that Chidester collectively calls "wild religion." Chidester's unique approach takes "religion as an open set of resources and strategies for negotiating a human identity, which is poised between the more than human and the less than human, in the struggles to work out the terms and conditions for living in a human place oriented in sacred space and sacred time."[37] Chidester tracks religious symbols and tropes throughout the public life of the nation, focusing not on the traditions and communities that owned and controlled religious symbols but on the symbols' "wild" and untamed nature. Chidester is particularly interested in the invention and reinvention of African religious symbols and rituals, which enjoyed tenuous links with religious communities. While the influence of African religions was curtailed through colonialism and mission, they were reinvoked in South Africa's public sphere. Whereas previously such African religions were considered wild and subject to domestication, they were now celebrated as authentic for the new South Africa. African symbols, emblematic of wild religion, were ushered into the public sphere in celebration of the new nation. Examples include African symbols and religions used in President Zuma's invocations, the sacrifice of a bull at the inauguration of the 2010 World Cup in South Africa, the production of heritage space, and the invocation of fundamentalism in the media.[38] Wild religion did not produce a nation through careful balancing of the religious and secular sensibilities or of the particular and general discourse of religious visions. Rather, wild religion in the public sphere broke "the mold of . . . [a] redemptive narrative by enabling the emergence of different stories about religion in South Africa."[39] Across the landscape of the country, new sacred signs and their profanities were invoked to imagine a complex nation.

Chidester's framework includes the work of West but places it in a different context. His reflections on postapartheid public life alert us to the intense negotiation and contestation between the sacred and profane in the public sphere. Chidester is clearly articulating the emergence of a radical view of civil religion in South Africa. In Foucault's terms, the employment of religious symbols by presidents, journalists, and public figures turns all utopian visions into heterotopias.

Conclusion

I have shown that South Africa after apartheid does not present a simple relationship between religion and nation-state. While relations between nation, state, and religion in South Africa are very different from those in North Africa, their complexity is not easily captured in the usual theories of separation or authorization. Using a sample of reflections and discourses in postapartheid South Africa, I have shown that a careful application of Foucault's concepts of utopia and heterotopia offers a better analysis of the relation between religion and nation-state since 1994. Religious discourses in South Africa cover a wide range of topics from a regular commitment to the constitutional order, on the one hand, to a potential and real inversion of the same constitutional order, on the other. I have also pointed to the intricate ways in which some Christian readings embrace and occupy the nation and simultaneously distance themselves from a theocratic state or religious nationalism.

There is one element in Foucault's theory that does not seem to work with discursive spaces occupied by religions in South Africa. Foucault suggested that both utopia and heterotopia were "formed in the very founding of society." He was referring to these spaces formed at the foundation of modern states. In applying this conceptual apparatus to religions, I have had to take note that patterns of religious discourse and the nation predate 1994. This is very clear in the Pentecostal churches whose idea of the kingdom of God has a long and illustrious history. Similarly, the relatively smaller Islamic groups also bring to the new nation their ideas of polity rooted in the past. Limiting oneself to the construction and production of such discourse after the founding of the new nation in 1994 excludes these longer histories from our analysis. Working with heterotopias, therefore, should not exclude the possibility and challenges of developments beyond and before the nation.

Utopia and heterotopia provide a dynamic model for the relationship between religion, state, and nation. In South Africa the particular relationship between religion and state discussed by religious groups and leaders in the years leading to the first democratic election was eventually written into the constitution. This by itself guaranteed a dynamic, though often unstable, relationship, much to the chagrin of both nation builders and theological gatekeepers. That model relationship was utopian, but it has spawned a profusion of heterotopic spaces in the country.

Notes

1. Klaaren, "Creation and Apartheid," 370–80; Walshe, "Christianity and the Anti-Apartheid Struggle," 383–99.
2. Lubbe, "Christians, Muslims and Liberation in South Africa," 24–33.
3. Leatt, "State of Secularism."
4. Salvatore, *Public Sphere.*
5. Hastings, *Construction of Nationhood.*
6. Lincoln, "Conflict," 269–83.
7. Lawrence, *Defenders of God.*
8. Asad, *Formations of the Secular.*
9. Foucault, "Of Other Spaces, Heterotopias."
10. Ibid.
11. Ibid., emphasis added.
12. Sachs, *Protecting Human Rights in a New South Africa.*
13. Kritzinger, *Believers in the Future.*
14. De Gruchy, "Patriotism, True and False," 60.
15. Leatt, Jeannerat, and Erklank, "Public Faith and the Politics of Faith," 5–16; De Gruchy, Koopman and Strijbos, "Introduction: From Our Side," 1–8.
16. Villa-Vicencio, "Telling One Another Stories," 110–11.
17. Villa-Vicencio, *Spirit of Hope,* xiii.
18. Ibid., xiii.
19. Tutu, *Rainbow People of God,* 256.
20. Moosa, "Truth and Reconciliation as Performance," 113–22.
21. Moosa, "Muslim Family Law in South Africa," 331–54.

22. Toffar, "Quranic Constitution and Its Expression in Law," 1–20.
23. The *Majlis*, "Miscellaneous *fatwas.*"
24. Botha, "PAGAD: A Case Study of Radical Islam in South Africa."
25. Pillay, "Problematising the Making of Good and Evil," 38–75.
26. Ingram, "Similarities in Pentecostal and Traditional African Culture,"339–60.
27. Balcomb, "From Apartheid to the New Dispensation," 5–38.
28. Balcomb, "Well Healed and Well-Heeled," 30–42.
29. Ibid.
30. Ibid., 31.
31. Moosa, "Worlds 'Apart,'" 206–21.
32. Dumbe and Tayob, "Salafis in Cape Town in Search of Purity, Certainty and Social Impact," 188–209.
33. Tayob, "Consuming, Producing, Defining Halal."
34. Vahed and Jeppie, "Multiple Communities," 252–86; Vahed, "Changing Islamic Traditions and Emerging Identities in South Africa," 45–73.
35. West, "Jesus, Jacob Zuma, and the New Jerusalem," 44.
36. Ibid., 47.
37. Chidester, *Wild Religion*, ix.
38. Chidester, *Wild Religion*.
39. Ibid., x.

Bibliography

Anderson, Benedict. *Imagined Communities: Reflections on the Origin and Spread of Nationalism.* London: Verso, 2006.

Asad, Talal. *Formations of the Secular: Christianity, Islam, Modernity.* Stanford, CA: Stanford University Press. 2003.

Balcomb, Anthony. "From Apartheid to the New Dispensation: Evangelicals and the Democratization of South Africa." *Journal of Religion in Africa* 34, nos. 1–2 (2004): 5–38.

———. "Well Healed and Well-Heeled: Pentecostals in the New South Africa—Their Message, Structures and Modes of Socio-Political Intervention." *Missionalia* 35, no. 3 (2007): 30–42.

Botha, Anneli. "PAGAD: A Case Study of Radical Islam in South Africa. 2005." *Terrorism Monitor* 3, no. 17 (September 2005). www.jamestown.org/single/?tx_ttnews[tt_news]=561.

Chidester, David. *Wild Religion: Tracking the Sacred in South Africa.* Berkeley: University of California Press, 2012.

Clasquin, Michel. "Religion, Ethics and Communal Interaction in the New South Africa: The Case of the Declaration on Religious Rights and Responsibilities." *Missionalia* 22, no. 1 (1993): 13–35.

de Gruchy, John. "Patriotism, True and False: Reflections on Bonhoeffer, Oom Bey and the Flag." In *Many Cultures, One Nation: A Festschrift for Beyers Naudé*, edited by Charles Villa-Vicencio and Carl Niehaus, 55–68. Cape Town: Human and Rosseau, 1995.

de Gruchy, Steve, Nico Koopman, and Sytse Strijbos. "Introduction: From Our Side." In *From Our Side: Emerging Perspectives on Development and Ethics*, edited by Steve de Gruchy, Nico Koopman, and Sytse Strijbo, 1–8. Pretoria: UNISA, 2008.

Dumbe, Yunus, and Tayob, Abdulkader. "Salafis in Cape Town in Search of Purity, Certainty and Social Impact." *Die Welt des Islams* 51, no. 2 (2011): 188–209. www.ingentaconnect.com/content/brill/dwi/2011/00000051/00000002/art00002.

Foucault, Michel. "Of Other Spaces, Heterotopias." *Architecture, Mouvement, Continuité* 5 (1984): 46–49. http://foucault.info/documents/heteroTopia/foucault.hetcroTopia.en.html.

Gellner, Ernest, and John Breuller. *Nations and Nationalism.* 2nd ed. London: Oxford University Press, 2007.

Hastings, Adrian. *The Construction of Nationhood: Ethnicity, Religion and Nationalism.* Cambridge: Cambridge University Press, 1997.

Ingram, Riann. "Similarities in Pentecostal and Traditional African Culture: A Positive Potential in a Context of Urbanization and Modernization." *Verbum et Ecclesia* 27, no. 1 (2006): 339–60.

Klaaren, Eugene M. "Creation and Apartheid: South African Theology since 1948." In *Christianity in South Africa: A Political, Social, and Cultural History,* edited by Richard Elphick and T. R. H. Davenport, 370–80. Berkeley: University of California Press, 1997.

Kritzinger, Johannes Nicolaas Jacobus, ed. *Believers in the Future: Proceedings of the National Inter-Faith Conference on Religion-State Relations: December 2–4 1990, Johannesburg.* Cape Town: World Conference on Religion and Peace, South African Chapter, 1991.

Lawrence, Bruce B. *Defenders of God: The Fundamentalist Revolt against the Modern Age.* New York: Harper and Row, 1989.

Leatt, Annie M. J. "The State of Secularism: Constituting Religion and Tradition towards a Post-Apartheid South Africa." PhD diss., University of the Witwatersrand, Johannesburg, 2011.

Leatt, Annie M. J., Caroline Jeannerat, and Natasha Erlank. "Public Faith and the Politics of Faith: A Review Essay." *Journal for the Study of Religion* 23, nos. 1–2 (2010): 5–16.

Lincoln, Bruce. "Conflict." In *Critical Terms for Religious Studies,* edited by Mark C. Taylor, 269–83. Chicago: University of Chicago Press, 1998.

Lubbe, Gerrie. "Christians, Muslims and Liberation in South Africa." *Journal of Theology for Southern Africa* 56, no. 2 (1986): 24–33.

The *Majlis.* "Miscellaneous *fatwas.*" www.themajlis.net/QA-index-myqa-yes-id_cat-30.html #433.

Piet Meiring. *Chronicle of the Truth Commission: A Journey through the Past and Present.* Washington, DC: Carpe Diem Books, 1999.

Moosa, Ebrahim. "Muslim Family Law in South Africa: Paradoxes and Ironies." In *Muslim Family Law in Sub-Saharan Africa: Colonial Legacies and Post-colonial Challenges,* edited by Shamil Jeppie, Ebrahim Moosa, and Richard Roberts, 331–54. Amsterdam: Amsterdam University Press, 2010.

———. "Truth and Reconciliation as Performance: Spectres of Eucharistic Redemption." In *Looking Back, Reaching Forward: Reflections on the Truth and Reconciliation Commission of South Africa,* edited by Charles Villa-Vicencio and Wilhelm Verwoerd, 113–22. Cape Town: University of Cape Town Press; London: Zed, 2000.

———. "Worlds 'Apart': Tablighi Jama'at in South Africa Under Apartheid, 1963–1993." In *Travellers in Faith: Studies of the Tablighi Jama'at as a Transnational Islamic Movement for Faith Renewal,* edited by Muhammad Khalid Masud, 206–21. Leiden: Brill, 2000.

Pillay, Suren. "Problematising the Making of Good and Evil: Gangs and PAGAD (People against Gangsterism and Drugs)." *Critical Arts* 16, no. 2 (2002): 38–75.

Sachs, Albie. *Protecting Human Rights in a New South Africa.* Cape Town: Oxford University Press, 1990.

Salvatore, Armando. *The Public Sphere: Liberal Modernity, Catholicism, Islam.* New York: Palgrave Macmillan, 2007.

Tayob, Shaheed. "Consuming, Producing, Defining Halal: Halal Authorities and Muslim Consumers in South Africa." MA thesis, University of Cape Town, 2012.

Toffar, Abdul Kariem. "The Quranic Constitution and Its Expression in Law: A Legal Dilemma in a Non-Muslim State." *Occasional Journal of ICOSA* 2 (2001): 1–20.

Tutu, Desmond. *The Rainbow People of God: A Spiritual Journey from Apartheid to Freedom*, edited by John Allen. Cape Town: Double Storey, 2006.

Vahed, Goolam. "Changing Islamic Traditions and Emerging Identities in South Africa." *Journal of Muslim Minority Affairs* 20, no. 1 (2000): 45–73.

Vahed, Goolam, and Shamil Jeppie. "Multiple Communities: Muslims in Post-Apartheid South Africa." In *State of the Nation: South Africa 2004–2005*, edited by John Daniel, Roger Southall, and Jessica Lutchman, 252–86. Pretoria: HSRC, 2005.

Villa-Vicencio, Charles. *The Spirit of Hope: Conversations on Religion, Politics and Values.* Berkeley: University of California Press, 1996.

———. "Telling One Another Stories: Towards a Theology of Reconciliation." In *Many Cultures, One Nation: A Festschrift for Beyers Naudé*, edited by Charles Villa-Vicencio and Carl Niehaus, 105–21. Cape Town: Human and Rosseau, 1995.

Walshe, Peter. "Christianity and the Anti-Apartheid Struggle: The Prophetic Voice within Divided Churches." In *Christianity in South Africa: A Political, Social, and Cultural History*, edited by Richard Elphick and T. R. H. Davenport, 383–99. Berkeley: University of California Press, 1997.

West, Gerald. "Jesus, Jacob Zuma, and the New Jerusalem: Religion in the Public Realm between Polokwane and the Presidency." *Journal for the Study of Religion* 23, nos. 1–2 (2010): 43–70.

10

A Popular Revolution?

Gender Inequality and Political Change in North Africa

KATHERINE MARSHALL

A World Bank report on gender equality in the Middle East and North Africa (MENA) region focused on what it termed the "MENA puzzle."[1] Since 1970 the MENA countries, on average, have made remarkable progress in narrowing gaps in education and health between women and men, although they continue to lag far behind with regard to income levels, political life, and women's economic engagement. Girls and boys are almost equally enrolled in primary and secondary school, fertility rates have declined rapidly, and health indicators such as maternal and child mortality show great improvement. At the tertiary education level women outnumber men in several countries. Yet critical indicators that affect economic performance, family welfare, and moves toward political equality—women's labor force participation and share in elected political office—are far behind world averages. The region's cultural and religious heritage goes a long way toward explaining the puzzle and points to various reforms that are the topic of debate. The underlying issues involved have great significance for the region's future prospects.

This chapter focuses on the complex gender dynamics in North Africa at play in the ongoing political and social change. The euphoria of the early 2011 Arab Spring has given way to a far more complex and uncertain picture. Unfolding events have increasingly highlighted women's rights, though how and how far this has been achieved has varied from place to place and over time. The chapter begins with a brief reflection on gender roles and how issues tended to be framed

Azza Karam made especially useful comments on a draft. Thanks to Nava Friedman and Chris Riley for support with data.

139

before the Arab Spring. It explores women's roles during the 2011 Arab Spring events and then reviews specific issues around gender that have arisen during the ongoing uprisings and in the transition, focusing especially on constitutional and legal issues. It concludes with some reflections on where matters stand and on challenges for the future.

North Africa and the Sahel: Women and Gender

The distinctive gender gaps that mark the Arab nations are the subject of various analyses and commentary (including the World Bank report cited above). A landmark document was the 2004 United Nations Development Programme (UNDP) Arab Human Development Report: *Towards the Rise of Women in the Arab World*.[2] Its significance lay in its bold analysis and the fact that it was very much a product of actors from the region. It linked prospects for the region's progress unequivocally to human rights and equality for women: "In terms of human development, the rise of women entails: (a) Complete equality of opportunity between women and men in the acquisition and employment of human capabilities; (b) Guaranteed rights of citizenship for all women on an equal footing with men; and (c) Acknowledgement of, and respect for, differences between the sexes. Women are different from men, but that in no way implies they are deficient. Under no conditions is it acceptable to use gender differences to support theories of inequality between the sexes or any form of sexual discrimination."[3]

The real situation on the ground is far removed from this ideal. World Values Surveys have underscored that, in several regional countries, perceptions of women's roles in the home, education, employment, and politics are distinctly more traditional than the global average. The World Economic Forum's annual reports on gender gaps paint a mixed picture of rapid progress on some fronts and lagging relative indicators on others.[4] The following graph and table summarize the situation.[5]

In short, the Arab nations of the Middle East and North Africa have distinctive features marking gender roles. At a technical level, there is a widespread appreciation that gender roles are linked to broader social and economic (as well as political) progress. In addition, relevant policies and indicators vary quite significantly by country.

The World Bank report highlights the importance of legal frameworks and cultural and social norms (which are obviously linked) in explaining the puzzle. Both laws and norms give rise, first, to restrictions on mobility and choice and, second, to family and community approaches that influence the choices open to girls and boys. In some places there has long been formal acceptance of principles of equality in constitutions and in adherence to international covenants. In practice, however, law, implementation of law, and custom have shaped different outcomes. For example, women tend to be seen by employers as more costly and less

FIGURE 10.1.
Gender Gap Index for Select North African and Middle East Countries

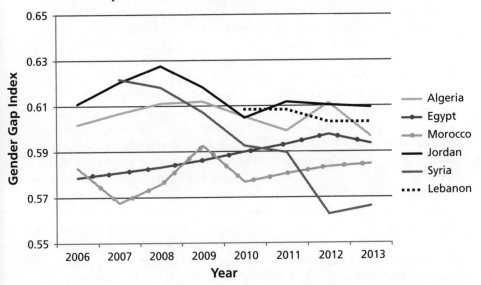

productive, and traditions of "guardianship," embodied in laws as well as custom, restrict women's work outside the home. Women's labor force participation, at 25 percent, is the lowest in the world. These attitudes and rules affect and are shaped by personal relations and family life. A striking illustration is the persistence, especially in Egypt, of the practice of female genital cutting. Despite decades of advocacy by powerful leaders, legal interdiction, fatwas by distinguished religious leaders, and mountains of evidence on its harmful effects, the practice has remained alarmingly common, even in urban areas.

Debates about gender norms in the region (and in Muslim societies more broadly) have long tended to be fraught, subject to many stated and unstated

TABLE 10.1
Gender Gap Index Rankings for Select Countries in North Africa, 2013

Country	Global	Economic Participation and Opportunity	Educational Attainment	Health and Survival	Political Empowerment
Algeria	124	133	106	108	62
Egypt	125	125	108	51	128
Morocco	129	129	109	88	111

limitations. They raise fundamental issues of universal rights and norms versus cultural rights, religious beliefs, and practices and of the religious dimensions of geopolitics. The debates are also colored by mixed attitudes toward what are described as feminist agendas. There are deep skeptics in many quarters, whether they articulate their views openly or not; some question human rights approaches grounded in full equality between men and women while others are skeptical of the validity of cultural, religious, and regional justifications for different treatment of women and men. To summarize briefly, Western feminism can be interpreted as dehumanizing and disrespectful of religious and cultural heritage, generating perceptions that Western approaches have a whiff of orientalism and vestiges of colonial attitudes. Global women's advocates can be perceived as patronizing bulldozers, painting Muslim women simplistically as victims in need of liberation from patriarchal domination. A common response from the women in question is that Muslim women will deal with their equality in their own ways. Some of the topics that have generated contentious debates have been (and remain) whether women's equality necessarily entails fully equal treatment under the law, how global human rights norms apply in different societies taking into account their distinctive cultures and histories, and how different kinds of advocates work together in partnership. These tensions tend to be framed (rather facilely) as a tension between secular and religious approaches, but the realities are far more complex and nuanced. Egyptian novelist Ahdaf Soueif reflects such a view in her comment: "We are really tired of people outside telling us how to live our lives and how to organize our society and what is best for us as women."[6]

Gender equality, at least on the surface and in formal policy statements and constitutions, has long been officially accepted as a norm across the region. Countries endorsed the Convention on the Elimination of All Forms of Discrimination against Women (CEDAW). However, in some respects the formal acceptance is effectively negated by significant reservations that a number of countries in the region have lodged, as well as by realities on the ground.[7] There has been action as well as advocacy to change discriminatory laws, and women's political participation has advanced, albeit slowly. However, many changes have been rather cosmetic, and many observers have concluded that little has been done to change the deeply patriarchal nature of Arab politics and society.

The ambiguities and divided views about gender roles surface in various settings, such as in debates about the role of religion in educational curricula or about women's dress. However, real change is not easy to measure: How does one weigh various trends? Women's voices are increasingly heard. Rising numbers of women wear the *hijab*. Stories abound about lavish external funding of conservative mosques and religious media where, inter alia, so-called liberated women who spoke and dressed in ways perceived as feminist were portrayed as undermining core social values. One pitfall is too sharp a focus on the divides between secular and religious approaches and actors. The ideals of a secular society have held significant sway in formal institutions, notably in Egypt and Tunisia, complicating the debates about how religion and culture affect gender norms.

These tensions underlie the long-standing and central debate as to how far religion accounts for the puzzle. The CEDAW reservations make clear that Islamic teachings on gender have been contested, to say the least. To a degree, the debates were framed as secular versus religious and, to some extent, men versus women. However, the situation is far more complex. Of particular importance is the fact that significant groups of women, in different countries, react strongly against the characterization of Islam as oppressive.

Various commentators have long warned of a gulf separating elite feminists and the majority of women across the region. Isobel Coleman of the Council on Foreign Relations highlights how far women's roles are contested in all countries. Even though the region's distinctive roles for women go a long way to account for disappointing economic performance, this appreciation is often confined to a small elite.[8] Most advocates for reforms of law and practice have come from the social and political elite, imbued with consciously secular values. Activists and scholars such as Fatima Mernissi, Leila Ahmed, and Azza Karam highlight the dangers inherent in elite women's alienation from the Islamic values that are so important to most of the populations.[9] This separation has generated a backlash. The divide obscures the important emerging Islamic feminism, a brand of feminism that sets out to reclaim and reinterpret religious texts and teachings. It includes efforts to revisit Quranic texts and Muslim history to highlight the richness of traditions and Prophet Mohammed's relatively advanced teachings on male and female roles in the seventh-century context. Sadly, more radical Islamic ideas, with perceived and sometimes real links to terrorism, also color attitudes and politics in different ways across the region. These can lead to hesitation in accepting narratives that portray religious actors and traditions positively or even in engaging constructively and seriously with religious ideas and actors. At issue are questions about the extent to which women's rights, as seen from a universal, global perspective, can be compatible with Muslim social values. These issues remain to a large extent unresolved.

Thus the situation before the spring of 2011 was complex, with mixed narratives about gender. Circumstances varied by country, colored by history and distinctive cultures. Tunisia prided itself on a strongly egalitarian ethos, even as economic inequalities within the society became more pronounced. Women's rights tended to be subsumed within broader debates about civil liberties in Egypt. Morocco earned wide respect in international circles for its carefully negotiated reforms of the family law statute (the Mudawana) in 2004 through a process that engaged both Islamic intellectuals and political and social leaders, including a wide range of women's groups, both secular and religious in their focus. In contrast, Saudi Arabia has become renowned for deliberate conservatism vis-à-vis women's roles. International development programs provided support for a wide range of women's civil society groups, addressing issues ranging from girls' education to legal reforms to action to stop domestic violence.

Women in the Arab Spring

When in December 2010 and early 2011 eyes turned to Tunisia and then Egypt, the uprisings taking place were striking for their egalitarian, open, modern flavor. This image was conveyed perhaps first and foremost by the language and stated goals of the protests, but also by the much commented on use of social media and technology by the leaders of the uprising to communicate and as an aid to organization. Youth and modern vigor were integral to the ethos of the Arab Spring. Women, it was clear, were very much part of the events, although gender agendas were not central in any way. Women were blogging, organizing, demonstrating, writing articles, being interviewed in the press, being arrested, and supporting the protests from start to finish. Some of the most visible and vocal leaders were women, especially in Egypt and Yemen. In Libya, women from diaspora communities worked with local women to organize and to provide logistic support. Many commentaries remarked on the egalitarian feel of the events and the rather universal calls for change and good governance. In a less modern way the fervor recalled historical revolutionary movements in which the shared commitment, danger, and goals at the barricades helped break down barriers that had separated class and gender. Hope was in the air, including hope that the barriers that accounted for the puzzling lack of progress on women's rights were crumbling.

Early outside interpretations of the events highlighted their nonreligious—that is, non-Islamic—flavor, even as many demonstrations included prayers and religious leaders took part. The secular character was described as a portent of a new secularism that, it was assumed, would include gender equality and full women's rights. Subsequent events brought home vividly how far those early interpretations underestimated the political strength of Islamist groups and the divides that separated elite groups from a generally more conservative majority.

There were some early sour notes, especially reports of violence against women in the seemingly peaceful crowds. Some of the violence—notably the iconic "blue bra" brutality in which a woman in an *abaya* in Cairo was beaten and dragged, her underwear visible, all captured on videos—was inflicted on the protesters by government troops and elicited greater sympathy and solidarity. There was horror at reports of enforced virginity tests on protesters. But then stories emerged of harassment and violent attacks on women by the protesters themselves. Some horrendous examples of rape in full daylight and in crowds were reported. At first these were described as isolated incidents, but over time the violence against women came to be seen either as reflecting social currents or as backlash against the egalitarian spirit.

In short, euphoric and proud images of women at the barricades, leaders at last, liberated from traditional constraints to mark their own paths, gave way to a less clear understanding of what women were doing and how far they were respected by their male colleagues. Quotations from women leaders stressed the sense of common purpose, often downplaying any gender agenda. The protests were about the common good and about accountable democracy. But the political and social realities were as complex as they had been before 2011. And, indeed, as the social and political constraints were lifted the challenges to women's rights in many instances increased.

Constitutions and Challenges

The story of the post-protest transitions is still unfolding and has followed very different paths in each country—and sometimes several different paths within a country. Among other factors, political Islam has taken on increasingly important and visible roles, to some extent filling a void left by absent or poorly organized political parties. Islamic political parties have been an important part of the region's fabric since the 1920s, and, given their strong political structures, they were able to mobilize the populace. Their agendas owed much to the long legacy of autocratic rule in which political expression and debate was discouraged or prohibited.[10]

Muslim-inspired political parties do not have a single position on gender and women's rights. Their common call for an Islamic state has, however, resulted in a generally traditional understanding of Sharia regarding the place of women. As a result, even in places where women's equality was long enshrined in constitutions and essentially taken for granted (as in Tunisia), new questions about the meaning of equality are being raised. This egalitarian stance on women's rights has, however, often been rejected by conservative groups in Islam who call for a return to more traditional, religious approaches. Unexpectedly (at least to many observers), simmering contests about women's rights came forcefully into the open, often at the center of debates on constitutional, legal, and social reforms.

Another phenomenon, all too familiar to students of revolution, was that the acceptance of women's active roles during the tumult of protest gave way to calls for women to return to more "normal" roles. The specifics varied by country, but one Egyptian activist was quoted as lamenting: "Men are telling women, 'Go back home, it's not your time now, we want to build democracy, you should be home.' . . . It's not proper that the people who led the revolution are now completely out of the scene."[11]

Some calls by women activists for progress in the wake of uprisings and revamped constitutions and legal structures have been met with the response that women's rights and complex legal reforms involving women and family are not the highest priority and should be dealt with later. Some women activists have voiced such views. Master Mimz, a protest rapper in the UK, reflects something of this tone in the lyrics to her song "Back Down Mubarak," in which she states: "First give me a job—then let's talk about my *hijab*." Omaima Kamel, former Freedom and Justice Party (FJP) presidential advisor in Egypt, commented that the socioeconomic issues facing women in Egypt were the ones that demanded highest priority.[12] She, and others who hold similar views, do not argue directly that women's rights are a priority. Rather, they argue that socioeconomic issues—which include family and legal reforms—are important in the context of a transition but need to be elaborated and understood as a concern for the whole of society and not for women only.

Women's rights have featured centrally in the politics of constitutional reform across the North African countries. In Egypt women's rights have been sharply contested from 2011 on. As one Egyptian activist remarked, "The utopia of Tahrir is now facing the harsh test of reality." A range of symbolic and real questions and proposals have surfaced and been sharply contested. Early in the transition period a committee appointed to draft constitutional amendments included experts in law and politics and members of minority groups, such as a Coptic Christian and a member of the Muslim Brotherhood, but not a single woman. Women led no political parties and were generally absent from negotiations over the transitional process.[13] Whether or not a woman could be president was an issue for the Muslim Brotherhood and Salafist parties in early constitutional discussions. The Muslim Brotherhood tended to take a position for ensuring women's access to all their rights, consistent with the values of Islamic law and maintaining the balance between their duties and rights; it became clear that Muslim Brotherhood leaders did not see women's rights as natural and inalienable but regarded them as restricted by Sharia and women's duties in society.

The full extent of questions raised is reflected in the troubling and revealing statement issued by the Muslim Brotherhood during a 2013 United Nations meeting (see appendix 1). It called into question many generally accepted understandings of women's rights, highlighting deep concerns about the social changes under discussion. Note, for example, this statement: "A closer look at these articles reveals what decadence awaits our world, if we sign this document." The articles of concern include "granting girls full sexual freedom, as well as the freedom to decide their own gender and the gender of their partners (i.e., choose to have normal or homosexual relationships), while raising the age of marriage," and "replacing guardianship with partnership, and full sharing of roles within the family between men and women such as: spending, child care and home chores." The Egyptian government, under the Muslim Brotherhood–led FJP, did ultimately sign the statement of the UN Commission on the Status of Women, but the Muslim Brotherhood statement is illustrative of the underlying concerns and debates, which have also surfaced during successive constitutional discussions.

Appendix 2 shows how the most recent constitution (approved on January 14, 2014) compares to the earlier version of 2012. Both show a cautious strengthening of women's rights.

In Tunisia, women's rights have become a crucial concern in negotiations about what the new Tunisia should look like.[14] The spirit of loyalty and unity between men and women experienced during the Jasmine Revolution seemed to dissipate, and women were harassed in the streets for their dress, smoking, or walking without a male relative.[15] In 2012, a young woman was raped by police officers and, when she took the officers to trial, was charged by the justice system for public indecency. Tunisia's personal status code (enacted first after independence in 1956) is famous within the Muslim world and beyond for its abolition (or reinterpretation) of classical Islamic precepts. Tunisia is the only Arab Muslim country that prohibits polygamy and provides equal divorce rights for men and women. Tunisia has stood as a model of law and implementation for wide-ranging issues affecting women, including divorce and custody, family planning, and labor force participation. During the transition, however, a catch became clear: The measures were at times described as imposed from above ("state feminism") and were not well rooted in the society. Tunisian feminists feared, rightly, from shortly after the power transition in 2011, that the progressive legislation would come under challenge as Ennahda, an Islamist movement, held power and the influence of Salafist organizations became clear. A tug-of-war ensued. Various efforts, for example to define women as "complementary" to men and to change the regime applicable to single mothers, were beaten back. An active civil society is credited with keeping the issues in view and defeating the various proposals.[16] One change that did take hold, however, was the right for public servants and students to wear the *hijab* (prohibited before the revolution). In January 2014 a revised constitution that enshrines women's rights was on the verge of approval.[17]

Morocco also saw a surge of civil society engagement beginning early in 2011, focused on government accountability and more democratic governance. As in other countries, women's rights and their role in political decision making have been constant issues. A new constitution passed in July 2011 guarantees equality between women and men. With the king's political support for reform (and long-standing evidence of support for women's rights specifically) and the momentum created by the Arab Spring, civil society organizations sought to strengthen women's rights and to increase women's representation in elected offices. Thirty leading women's rights associations formed an alliance, the Feminist Spring for Equality and Democracy, to lobby the constitutional drafting committee and to present them with detailed recommendations. The new constitution included most of their recommendations and a number of important provisions that protected the political, social, cultural, and economic rights of women. The constitution's preamble commits the state to "ban and combat discrimination against anyone based on sex." But, while female representation in Moroccan governments has never been high, the 2014 Islamist-led coalition had only a single female minister. The government issued the *Government Plan for Gender Equality 2012–2016* with the objective of institutional anchoring for gender equality, equal access for girls to education and health, the fight against violence and all forms of discrimination against women, women's equal access to positions of responsibility and decision making in government, and the fight against the vulnerabilities faced by rural women and girls.

In Libya, a similar roller coaster of shifting debates and emotional intensity has surrounded questions of women's rights and roles. Libyan women played active and significant roles during the turbulent period of uprisings that led to changes in government. As Manal Omar of the US Institute of Peace observed: "There is one part of the narrative that everyone seems to agree on: women were a crucial motivating factor in the midst of the struggle for freedom. Whether it was the hundreds of Libyan women who traveled with the men to the frontlines to form makeshift kitchens or the women positioned inside Qaddafi strongholds who smuggled guns and information, women carved out a space for their participation. Women across Libya nursed the injured, while Libyan women in the diaspora returned to provide technical assistance to the newly formed NTC."[18] And, Omar underscores, Libyan women have a long history of organizing, dating back to a women's group established in Benghazi in 1955. "As in most dictatorships in the region, citizens were not discriminated against by gender, but rather, by loyalty to the party."[19]

Yet in the ensuing period a range of challenges have emerged, not least to well-established legal rights and cultural norms.[20] These extend to changes in law and participation in governance processes. Even during a period where the focus was on the Libyan national reconciliation process, Mustafa Abdul-Jalil, chairman of the Libyan National Transitional Council (NTC), sought to loosen Qaddafi-era restrictions on the practice of polygamy. Indeed, the Constitutional Chamber of the Supreme Court in Libya abolished all restrictions on the practice of polygamy in February 2013.[21] Religious leaders also sought to limit women's rights outright: Grand Mufti Sheikh Sadeq al-Ghariani called for a separation of sexes in law and society and urged the government to restrict women's freedom of marriage.[22]

Violence against women is an issue across the region, and legal recourse for women is very limited. Data on trends is difficult to obtain, but surveys indicate a perception that women's security is less than it was and that violence, both public and domestic, is on the rise. Perhaps more importantly, there is a widespread perception that posttransition governments have been slow and ineffective in addressing the problem of violence directed against women.

An underlying issue has been, and remains, public attitudes and support for women's rights. The lack of full societal commitment to equality, even where women had made strides, has become more evident as new energies and freer expression have followed the 2011 uprisings. It is clear that public opinion on rights remains divided. A recent Pew survey illustrates the ambivalence (Table 10.2).

In several countries at least half of the respondents say men make better political leaders. On economic issues most respondents say women should be able to work outside the home, but most also believe that when jobs are scarce, jobs for men should be the first priority. And in the personal realm, many of those surveyed believe a woman's family should help choose her husband, rather than the woman herself choosing. There is a way to go before equality is accepted as more than a word.

Reflections and Paths Ahead

"Women may have sustained the Arab spring, but it remains to be seen if the Arab spring will sustain women."[23]

The history of revolution and reform in North Africa is still unfolding, and the outcomes, even the directions, as far as women's rights and roles are concerned remain unclear. Principles like women's rights to education and (at least nominally) opposition to gender-based violence are accepted as givens, which are encouraging signs. However, many other topics are less certain. These include an appreciation of the need for and benefits of women's political leadership and the need for equality within a family setting. The key question in many debates is the extent to which a women's rights agenda is compatible with the "peculiarities" of Arab culture as defined by Islamists.[24]

TABLE 10.2
Gender Gaps on Views about Gender Equality

	% Saying women should have equal rights as men			
	Total	Men	Women	Gap
	%	%	%	
Jordan	63	44	82	−38
Pakistan	76	65	87	−22
Tunisia	74	65	84	−19
Egypt	58	53	63	−10
Lebanon	93	88	98	−10
Turkey	84	83	85	−2

PEW RESEARCH CENTER Q85.

Source: Pew Research Center, Global Attitudes Project, *Most Muslims Want Democracy, Personal Freedoms, and Islam in Political Life*, July 10, 2012, www.pewglobal.org/2012/07/10/most-muslims-want-democracy-personal-freedoms-and-islam-in-political-life/.

Women's economic equality has rarely figured as a central issue. However, given the need to advance socioeconomic development in the region, socioeconomic issues have critical importance for the region's future. Women's labor force participation was a critical issue before the Arab Spring, as described above, and it remains so, taking on increasing importance in light of the economic challenges facing the region, including women's low participation in formal labor markets and their roles in the more fragile, poorly documented, but important informal economy.

Addressing security and violence, including state-sponsored violence and domestic violence, is also a priority.

With women's rights sharply contested, debates and tensions are likely to continue. Activists see a need to remain vigilant in the face of conservative religious interpretations of women's roles. In this context the pre-crisis divisions between secular and Islamic feminists could undermine the common efforts needed to keep women's rights on the agenda and to work for their application. This suggests two sets of actions. First, there is a need to bridge the divide between religious and secular and to find areas of common ground. Potential actions include the development of specific policy responses that are subject to robust debate and submission to the test of evidence. The role of outside partners and advocates can be significant, and there is an urgent need to build better knowledge about what is happening on the ground. Second, there is a need to develop the capacity to engage more actively and effectively with Muslim leaders and institutions on gender issues, using a common language and working with organizations like Al-Azhar and local groups. Given the high religiosity of the societies, it is critical that religious institutions and beliefs be taken into account.

Recent events in Muslim communities south of the Sahara highlight the importance of engaging the deep divides within Islam and the dynamic political and social forces at work. The brutal violence that has shaken the Central African Republic in 2013 and 2014 is unmistakably, on the surface, linked to conflict between Muslim and Christian identities, though divisions within the Islamic communities are also significant. The kidnapping of almost three hundred Christian Nigerian schoolgirls by the extremist Muslim group Boko Haram in Nigeria at first passed almost unnoticed in Nigeria (as had kidnappings of thousands of Muslim girls). In the worldwide media the Chibok kidnapping provoked a firestorm of commentary and energetic response: It fed the starkest stereotypes of a religion irrevocably set against women's rights and the most important path to those rights—education. These two iconic events obviously have their roots in specific societies and countries, but they underscore the point that religious perspectives on both stability and good governance are often linked, even if implicitly or indirectly, to the respective roles of men and women. They also reinforce negative images of Islam that go well beyond the specifics of the country and region.

It is time to delve deeper into the forces that encourage extremist movements and especially their focus on delineating and limiting women's equal rights.

The bottom line is mixed: With the widespread changes taking place, there is an unprecedented opportunity for constructive reforms and the kind of dialogue that can reshape attitudes in positive directions. However, events make it unmistakably clear that there are real risks of backlash and backsliding that set women back in society, politics, and the economy. Women's rights are playing central roles in the complex political and social development of the region, and they are critical for building resilient, just, and prosperous societies in the future. Women's rights thus need to be addressed thoughtfully and with care through a variety of prisms—tribal, regional and ethnic, political, social and economic, and secular as well as religious. Keeping up the momentum for women's equality and grounding reforms in the distinctive and positive cultural and religious heritage of the region calls for determination, creativity, and wisdom.

Appendix 1. Muslim Brotherhood Statement on the Fifty-Seventh Session of the UN Commission on the Status of Women (CSW), March 4 to 15, 2013, at UN Headquarters

[The CSW] seeks to ratify a declaration euphemistically entitled "End Violence against Women."

That title, however, is misleading and deceptive. The document includes articles that contradict established principles of Islam, undermine Islamic ethics and destroy the family, the basic building block of society, according to the Egyptian Constitution.

This declaration, if ratified, would lead to complete disintegration of society, and would certainly be the final step in the intellectual and cultural invasion of Muslim countries, eliminating the moral specificity that helps preserve cohesion of Islamic societies.

A closer look at these articles reveals what decadence awaits our world, if we sign this document:

1. Granting girls full sexual freedom, as well as the freedom to decide their own gender and the gender of their partners (i.e., choose to have normal or homosexual relationships), while raising the age of marriage.

2. Providing contraceptives for adolescent girls and training them to use those, while legalizing abortion to get rid of unwanted pregnancies, in the name of sexual and reproductive rights.

3. Granting equal rights to adulterous wives and illegitimate sons resulting from adulterous relationships.

4. Granting equal rights to homosexuals, and providing protection and respect for prostitutes.

5. Giving wives full rights to file legal complaints against husbands accusing them of rape or sexual harassment, obliging competent authorities to deal husbands punishments similar to those prescribed for raping or sexually harassing a stranger.

6. Equal inheritance (between men and women).

7. Replacing guardianship with partnership, and full sharing of roles within the family between men and women such as: spending, child care and home chores.

8. Full equality in marriage legislation such as: allowing Muslim women to marry non-Muslim men, and abolition of polygamy, dowry, men taking charge of family spending, etc.

9. Removing the authority of divorce from husbands and placing it in the hands of judges, and sharing all property after divorce.

10. Cancelling the need for a husband's consent in matters like: travel, work, or use of contraception.

These are destructive tools meant to undermine the family as an important institution; they would subvert the entire society, and drag it to pre-Islamic ignorance.

The Muslim Brotherhood urges the leaders of Muslim countries and their UN representatives to reject and condemn this document, and to call upon this organization to rise to the high morals and principles of family relations prescribed by Islam.

The Muslim Brotherhood also calls on Al-Azhar (the highest seat of learning for Muslims) to take the lead, condemn this declaration, and state clearly the Islamic viewpoint with regard to all details of this document.

Further, we urge all Islamic groups and associations to take a decisive stand on this document and similar declarations.

In conclusion, we call on women's organizations to commit to their religion and morals of their communities and the foundations of good social life and not be deceived with misleading calls to decadent modernization and paths of subversive immorality.

God Almighty says: "God wants to forgive you, but those who follow whims and desires want you to deviate far away from the Path). {Quran 4 : 27}

The Muslim Brotherhood

Cairo: March 13, 2013

Appendix 2. Egyptian Constitutions of 2012 and 2013, Comparison of Clauses Involving Women

2013	2012
Article 11	*Preamble*
The state shall ensure the achievement of equality between women and men in all civil, political, economic, social and cultural rights in accordance with the provisions of the constitution.	Further, there is no dignity for a country in which women are not honored. Women are the sisters of men and hold the fort of motherhood; they are half of society and partners in all national gains and responsibilities.
The state shall endeavor to take measures ensuring the adequate representation of women in parliament, as prescribed by law, and to ensure women's right to hold public office and senior management positions in the state and to be recruited by judicial institutions without discrimination.	Article 10 The state shall ensure maternal and child health services free of charge, and enable a balance between a woman's duties toward her family and her work.
The state is committed to the protection of women against all forms of violence, and to empower women to balance their family and work duties.	The state shall provide special care and protection to female breadwinners, divorced women and widows.
It is also committed to providing care and protection to mothers, children, women-headed households, elderly and the neediest women.	

Source: Rizk and Sharnoubi, "Egypt's Constitution 2013 vs. 2012."

Notes

1. World Bank, *Opening Doors*.
2. United Nations Development Programme, *Arab Human Development Report 2005: Towards the Rise of Women in the Arab World*.
3. Ibid.
4. World Economic Forum, *Global Gender Gap Report 2013*.
5. Data from the World Economic Forum's *Gender Gap Report 2013*. All the available data from North Africa is included, with Jordan, Syria, and Lebanon included in the graph for comparison. (Data is unavailable for Libya or Tunisia.) The index "benchmarks national gender gaps on economic, political, education and health criteria, and provides country rankings that allow for effective comparisons across regions and income groups, and over time" (*Global Gender Gap Report 2013*, 3). The graph tracks the index itself in six countries over time. The table displays the overall and subcategory rankings of North African countries relative to all countries from which data was collected. The index was calculated for 133 countries in 2013.
6. Cited in Naber, "Women and the Arab Spring."
7. For reservations by country see UN Women, "Declarations, Reservations and Objections to CEDAW." An example is a reservation for Egypt: "Reservation to the text of article 16

concerning the equality of men and women in all matters relating to marriage and family relations during the marriage and upon its dissolution, without prejudice to the Islamic *Sharia's* provisions whereby women are accorded rights equivalent to those of their spouses so as to ensure a just balance between them. This is out of respect for the sacrosanct nature of the firm religious beliefs which govern marital relations in Egypt and which may not be called in question and in view of the fact that one of the most important bases of these relations is an equivalency of rights and duties so as to ensure complementarity which guarantees true equality between the spouses. The provisions of the *Sharia* lay down that the husband shall pay bridal money to the wife and maintain her fully and shall also make a payment to her upon divorce, whereas the wife retains full rights over her property and is not obliged to spend anything on her keep. The *Sharia* therefore restricts the wife's rights to divorce by making it contingent on a judge's ruling, whereas no such restriction is laid down in the case of the husband."

8. Coleman, *Paradise beneath her Feet*.

9. For example, see Mernissi, *Beyond the Veil*; Ahmed, *Women and Gender in Islam*; and Karam, *Woman's Place*.

10. See, for example, Karam, *Transnational Political Islam*.

11. Eckel, "Egypt's Leading Female Voice for Change Warns That Revolution Is Backsliding."

12. CARE International, *Arab Spring or Arab Autumn?*

13. Mohammed, "Women and the Arab Spring."

14. Voorhoeve, "Legacy of an Authoritarian Regime."

15. Johansson-Nogues, "Gendering the Arab Spring?"

16. Ibid.

17. For a thoughtful analysis see Stepan, "Tunisia's Transition and the Twin Tolerations," 94–97.

18. Omar, "Women in Libya and the Arab Spring."

19. Ibid.

20. See an informative Human Rights Watch report on gender rights published in May 2013: *Revolution for All: Women's Rights in the New Libya*.

21. Mohammed, "Women and the Arab Spring."

22. Ibid.

23. Rice et al., "Women Have Emerged as Key Players in the Arab Spring."

24. Framed in CARE International, *Arab Spring or Arab Autumn?*, 13.

Bibliography

Ahmed, Leila. *Women and Gender in Islam: Historical Roots of a Modern Debate*. New Haven, CT: Yale University Press, 1992.

CARE International. *Arab Spring or Arab Autumn? Women's Political Participation in the Uprisings and Beyond*. London: CARE International, 2013. www.care-international.org/upload document/news/publications/reports%20and%20issue%20briefs/english/report_women-arab -spring_english%202013.pdf.

Coleman, Isabel. *Paradise beneath Her Feet: How Women Are Transforming the Middle East*. New York: Council on Foreign Relations, 2010.

Eckel, Mike. "Egypt's Leading Female Voice for Change Warns That Revolution Is Backsliding." *Christian Science Monitor*, October 5, 2012. www.csmonitor.com/World/Global

-News/2012/1005/Egypt-s-leading-female-voice-for-change-warns-that-revolution-is-back sliding.

Human Rights Watch. *A Revolution for All: Women's Rights in the New Libya.* Human Rights Watch, May 27, 2013. www.hrw.org/sites/default/files/reports/libya0513_brochure_LOW RES_0.pdf.

Johansson-Nogues, Elisabeth. "Gendering the Arab Spring? Rights and (In)security of Tunisian, Egyptian and Libyan Women." *Security Dialogue* 44, nos. 5–6 (2013): 393–409. http://sdi.sagepub.com/content/44/5-6/393.full.pdf+html.

Karam, Azza M. *Transnational Political Islam: Religion, Ideology and Power.* London: Pluto, 2004.

———. *A Woman's Place: Religious Women as Public Actors.* New York: World Conference on Religion and Peace Women's Program, 2001.

Mernissi, Fatima. *Beyond the Veil: Male-Female Dynamics in Modern Muslim Society.* Rev. ed. Bloomington: Indiana University Press, 1985.

Mohammed, Reem. "Women and the Arab Spring: Tough Choices to Make." OpenDemocracy, October 25, 2013. www.opendemocracy.net/arab-awakening/reem-mohamed/women-and -arab-spring-tough-choices-to-make.

Naber, Nadine. "Women and the Arab Spring: Human Rights from the Ground Up." *International Institute Journal* 1, no. 1 (Fall 2011): 11–13. http://hdl.handle.net/2027/spo.11645653 .0001.104.

Omar, Manal. "Women in Libya and the Arab Spring." *World Post*, November 4, 2011. www.huffingtonpost.com/manal-omar/arab-spring-libya-women_b_1076873.html.

Pew Research Global Attitudes Project. "Most Muslims Want Democracy, Personal Freedoms, and Islam in Political Life." Pew Research Center, July 10, 2012. www.pewglobal.org/2012 /07/10/most-muslims-want-democracy-personal-freedoms-and-islam-in-political-life/.

Rice, Xan, Katherine Marsh, Tom Finn, Harriet Sherwood, Angelique Chrisafis, and Robert Booth. "Women Have Emerged as Key Players in the Arab Spring." *Guardian*, April 22, 2011. www.theguardian.com/world/2011/apr/22/women-arab-spring.

Rizk, Mariam, and Osman El Sharnoubi. "Egypt's Constitution 2013 vs. 2012: A Comparison." *Ahram Online*, December 12, 2013. http://english.ahram.org.eg/News/88644.aspx.

Stepan, Alfred. "Tunisia's Transition and the Twin Tolerations." *Journal of Democracy* 23, no. 2 (April 2012): 94–97.

United Nations Development Programme. *The Arab Human Development Report 2005: Towards the Rise of Women in the Arab World.* New York: Regional Bureau for Arab States, 2006. www.arab-hdr.org/contents/index.aspx?rid=4.

UN Women. "Declarations, Reservations and Objections to CEDAW." http://www.un.org /womenwatch/daw/cedaw/reservations-country.htm.

Voorhoeve, Maaike. "Legacy of an Authoritarian Regime: The Future of Tunisia's State Feminism." Consultancy Africa Intelligence, January 16, 2013. www.consultancyafrica.com/in dex.php?option=com_content&view=article&id=1193:legacy-of-an-authoritarian-regime -the-future-of-tunisias-state-feminism&catid=59:gender-issues-discussion-papers&Itemid =267.

World Bank. *Opening Doors: Gender Equality and Development in the Middle East and North Africa.* MENA Development Report. Washington, DC: World Bank, 2013. http://documents .worldbank.org/curated/en/2013/02/17235637/opening-doors-gender-equality-development -middle-east-north-africa.

World Economic Forum. *The Global Gender Gap Report 2013.* Geneva: World Economic Forum, 2013. www3.weforum.org/docs/WEF_GenderGap_Report_2013.pdf.

11

A "New" Pan-Africanism

Future Challenges

CHRIS LANDSBERG

Fifty years after the establishment of the Organization of African Unity (OAU) in 1963 and just more than a decade after the founding of its successor, the African Union (AU), in 2003, the achievements and setbacks of Africa need to be assessed and responded to, both on the continent and in Africa's donor countries. Has the AU delivered on the promises made at the time of its inception, to "enable Africa to meet challenges of the 21st century and strengthening the position of Africa vis-à-vis the global economy and international community"?[1] Specifically, is it enhancing peace and security, stability and governance, democracy, development, and cooperation? More importantly, what is required to transcend the gap between AU policy and implementation?

The early hopes of the Arab Spring and the African Renaissance simply cannot be realized without AU promises being implemented by member states across Africa, from north to south. Indeed, a realistic hope of success in Africa is dependent on at least the modest execution of AU policy. This chapter seeks to describe a new wave of Pan-Africanism, which I have elsewhere described as the new "Afro-continentalism."[2] It involves the creation of common institutions and the promotion of the cosmopolitan values and principles captured in the founding documents of the AU.

The AU has declared 2013 and 2014 the years of "Pan-Africanism and African Renaissance," with Kay Mathews arguing that we are witnessing the "re-emergence of Pan-Africanism under the general rubric of the African Renaissance."[3] John Stremlau, in turn, identifies the key objectives of the renaissance as economic recovery, the promotion of democracy, the termination of neocolonial relations between Africa and the world's economic powers, the mobilization of African countries to counter the geopolitical and strategic interests of the world's most powerful countries, and the development of people-centered economic growth and development.[4]

Stremlau stresses the centrality of democracy in the pursuit of these ends, arguing that "for an African Renaissance to prevail, governments must be held accountable for constructing credible political guarantees for the rights of individuals and ethnic minorities, while minority governments must be pressed to become more inclusive."[5]

In order to assess the state of Pan-Africanism it is necessary to understand the origins and current state of AU institutions, whose task it is to monitor and promote democratic governance in Africa.

Pan-Africanism since the Birth of the AU

Committed to the value of "African solutions for African problems," the continent's leading state actors have clearly negotiated a new, progressive Pan-Africanism that makes a fundamental break with the past as characterized by the period of the OAU. Whereas the OAU placed a huge emphasis on unity, political liberation, and noninterference in the domestic affairs of African states, the AU has placed issues of development, governance, democratization, economic growth, and peace and security on the continental agenda.

During 2000 and 2001, the process of restructuring Africa's governance architecture crystallized when four leading African states—South Africa, Nigeria, Senegal, and Algeria—and their continental partners undertook the following eight initiatives that were at the time regarded by some African leaders as "radical policy directives":[6]

- the creation of an Africa Renaissance
- the establishment of the Conference on Security, Stability, Development, and Cooperation in Africa (CSSDCA) and its formal incorporation into the OAU's conflict prevention, management, and resolution machinery (established in 1993)
- the decision taken in Lomé in 1999 by the OAU to transform itself into the African Union
- the acceleration of the OAU-mandated drafting of the Millennium Africa Recovery Plan (MAP) under the leadership of South African president Thabo Mbeki, Nigerian president Olusegun Obasanjo, and Algerian leader Abdelaziz Bouteflika
- the merger of the MAP and the Omega Plan (the initiative spearheaded by Senegalese president Abdoulaye Wade) to create the New Africa Initiative
- the launch of the New Partnership for Africa's Development (NEPAD)
- the development of the African Peer Review Mechanism (APRM)

- The formation of a partnership with the industrialized world through strategic relations with the G8 and other actors

In 2000 the AU adopted the Constitutive Act of the Union, and this became the constitutional foundation of the new union.[7] It spelled out key objectives aimed at navigating the transition from the OAU to the AU. These objectives included the following:[8]

- achievement of greater unity and solidarity between African peoples and organizations
- defense of the territorial integrity and independence of its member states
- acceleration of the political and socioeconomic integration of the continent
- the promotion of international cooperation, taking due account of the Charter of the United Nations and the Universal Declaration of Human Rights
- the furtherance of peace, stability, and security on the continent
- the implementation of democratic principles and institutions, popular participation, and good governance
- the protection of human and people's rights and other relevant human rights instruments
- the establishment of the necessary conditions that enable the continent to play its rightful role in the global economy and in international negotiations; promote sustainable development at the economic, social, and cultural levels; and help with the integration of African economies
- cooperation in the field of human activities to raise the living standards of African peoples
- coordination between existing and future regional economies
- the development of the continent by promoting research, especially in science and technology
- working with relevant international partners on the eradication of international diseases and the promotion of health on the continent

These plans clearly represent a major paradigm shift in which politics, economics, social reform, culture, and interstate cooperation are paramount. They spell out a comprehensive set of aims geared toward addressing Africa's challenges. The design and construction of these eight policy initiatives form the crux of the new African architecture that constitutes a major break with the past.

Ten years after the establishment of the AU, it is clear that the new continental architecture depends heavily on political will, human and financial resources, the strengthening of new institutions, intra-African cooperation, the forging of new strategic partnerships between Africa and the outside world (notably the industrialized powers), and respect for new norms, values, and principles. In the words of the chairperson of the AU Commission, Alpha Konare, in 2003, the AU faced "operational constraints" as well as "inadequacy of material and financial resources which did not make it possible for these mechanisms to function as one would have expected."[9] In the words of an assessment of the work of the AU a year later, the AU Commission declared: "The resources that we need for the integrated Africa to become a force to be reckoned with, a force that we can all rely upon, include among other things, the political will to achieve integration, the leadership and commitment of the Commission, the accession of the people to the integration endeavour, the optimal use of all our assets (namely our population, culture, languages, dialogue, economies, and human and financial resources)."[10]

In 2013, ten years after Alpha Konare and the AU Commission published the "Vision and Mission" document, South Africa's Nkosazana Dlamini-Zuma, the newly elected chair of the AU Commission, oversaw the publication of the AU's *Vision 2063*, an ambitious fifty-year vision for the AU and for the continent—in continuity with the principles of democratic practice and human rights contained in the Konare document.

The 2013 paper released by the African Union, the United Nations Economic Commission for Africa (UNECA), and the United Nations Development Programme (UNDP), titled "Democratisation and Peace-Building in Africa: Policy Reflections," stated: "There is no gainsaying that the optimum achievement of the noble goals set out for Agenda 2063 will be highly dependent upon firm and solid foundations, especially the nurturing and consolidation of democratic governance, sustainable peace and political stability. In essence democracy and peace should form the key anchors of AU Agenda 2063."[11]

The problem is that many of these fundamentals are in short supply on the continent, and this inadequacy will negatively affect the chances of successful implementation. What is, however, clear is that the once-sacrosanct legal principle of the sovereignty of states and noninterference in their domestic affairs has ended, being counterbalanced by a greater emphasis on the rights of peoples and the responsibility of governments toward their citizens.

Organs and Structures of the AU

The OAU functioned with a "single source of authority," the Assembly of Heads of State and Government, which made noninterference in the internal affairs of these states a near-sacred principle. It did not even allow the questioning in public of government actions, and it certainly did not envisage the "pooling" of sovereignty. The prime objective of the OAU was the collective struggle for national liberation from colonialism, the fight against minority domination, and the defense of national sovereignty.

The AU has a more democratized approach, in recognition of a need through-out the continent to put in place institutions that would deepen democracy. Article 5.1 of the Constitutive Act of the Union spells out what is required to establish these bodies, aimed at establishing "multiple sources of authority."[12] These include the Assembly of Heads of State and Government (as the highest decision-making body), judicial structures (courts), and democracy-enhancing institutions (the Pan-African Parliament). The assembly of the union, composed of heads of state and government or their duly accredited representatives, meets at least once annually and has the responsibility to promote the AU's policies, including bolstering democracy.

These leaders are supported by various institutions to promote democracy, peace, and security. Since its inception, the AU has sought to respect national sovereignty while affirming the right to intervene where circumstances deem it necessary—and in fulfilment of this decision, it has suspended the membership of governments coming to power unconstitutionally, as indicated below.

Central to AU governance policy is the establishment of NEPAD and the APRM under NEPAD's auspices; NEPAD provides management oversight, and the organizations are sometimes in tension. Edwin Ijeoma reminds us that NEPAD espoused "principles which underpin objectives [such as] African owner-ship and responsibility, promotion of self-reliance, democratic principles, human rights, the rule of law and good governance, promotion of gender equality, respect for sanctity of human life, promotion of social justice and fostering a new relation-ship with developed countries that would be based on mutual respect and respon-sibility and accountability."[13] This again shows that the new Pan-Africanists committed themselves to cosmopolitan values such as democracy, the rule of law, and good governance, which is testimony to the realization that, after the attain-ment of political liberation, the emphasis needs to be on the democratic right of Africans to decide how they wish to be governed.

In 2012 a key architect of the new Pan-Africanism, former South African president Thabo Mbeki, argued: "This [NEPAD] Programme creates a new para-digm of development in Africa. It integrates various central objectives such as ending poverty and underdevelopment, deepening democracy, enhancing the capacity of our governments, and defining a new relationship with the developed world." He stressed that NEPAD is "not a set of projects but a new and coherent paradigm."[14] Regarding the Arab Spring rebellions, Mbeki argued that "in order to avoid popular rebellions, such as those which happened more recently in North Africa, this elite [political leaders] needs to create the necessary political space through a process of democratisation." He called for a radical repositioning of "the African state as a vital and powerful social institution dedicated to serve the people," and this would be done through "the building of democratic develop-mental states."[15]

The APRM is the most innovative instrument for promoting good governance to emerge in Africa since the earliest days of independence. It makes provision for public monitoring of delivery under the Conference on Security, Stability, Development and Cooperation in Africa. The CSSDCA and NEPAD seek to establish common positions for AU member states and to coordinate the work of African countries during international negotiations. These organs and programs also allow for a more active role in policy formation and governance by civil society.

The principles of the AU are clear; the implementation, however, is often lacking. This highlights the urgent need to endow the Commission of the AU, as defined below, with the requisite autonomy and powers as well as the financial and human resources needed for it to become an effective and efficient arm of the African Union. To this end, it is important to identify the structures and institutions through which the implementation can realistically occur.

The Commission of the African Union is the secretariat of the AU. It is composed of the chairperson, his or her deputy, and commissioners. It represents the union and defends its interests under the direction of the assembly and the Executive Council. It can initiate proposals for submission to the other organs of the union and executes decisions taken by them.

The Executive Council, composed of the foreign ministers or such other ministers or representatives as are designated by the governments of member states, is responsible for coordinating and taking decisions on policies in areas of common interest to member states. Work needs to be done to ensure that the Executive Council becomes an organ that can translate decisions of the assembly into operational guidelines that can be implemented.

The Permanent Representatives' Committee, composed of permanent representatives or other plenipotentiaries of member states, is responsible for preparing the work of the Executive Council and acting on the latter's instructions.

The Peace and Security Council (PSC), composed of fifteen member states, is responsible for the promotion of peace, security, and stability in Africa as well as for preventive diplomacy and restoration of peace. In discharging its responsibilities with respect to the deployment of peace support missions and interventions in the event of genocide, war crimes, or crimes against humanity, the PSC may consult a Panel of the Wise composed of five African personalities and mobilize a standby force to facilitate its intervention strategies.

The African Court of Justice is established to adjudicate civil cases related to the protection of human rights and the monitoring of human rights violations. The intent is to upgrade it into a criminal court through which to adjudicate gross violations of human rights in accordance with the African Charter on Human and People's Rights.[16]

The Economic, Social and Cultural Council is an advisory organ composed of different social and professional groups—particularly youth organizations, women's associations, and civil society groups—from member states of the union.

The African Court of Human and People's Rights established at the Ouagadougou Summit in 1998 has jurisdiction in cases of human rights violation by any member state, the African Commission on Human and People's Rights, and African intergovernmental organizations. The court can hear cases filed by individuals and nongovernmental organizations with observer status in the union when the member state concerned makes a declaration to this effect. The court is composed of eleven judges elected by the assembly for six-year terms that are renewable only once.

Many of the AU's provisions are at the lofty level of policy while the institutions put in place to implement policy continue to be weak. The NEPAD Democracy and Political Governance Initiative states that there is a need "to promote political representivity, thus providing opportunities for all citizens to participate in the political process in a free and fair political environment."[17] The initiative further highlights the need to ensure "the effective participation of women, minorities and disadvantaged groups in political and economic processes."[18] The legitimacy and integrity of the AU, NEPAD, and other structures, institutions, and programs need to be continually tested on the basis of their impact on the lives of ordinary African citizens.

Civil society organs are poorly organized. This is reflected in the CSSDCA unit, which is grossly understaffed and underfunded. Indeed, at times the unit comprised three officials who were expected to service the entire continent. NEPAD's civil society structures also remain weak, and its operatives seem more interested in inviting civil society participation during implementation processes than in actual policymaking, design, and construction processes. There are also tensions between NEPAD and other structures of the AU. To help overcome and prevent the kind of fissures that opened up so extensively in Arab Spring countries, the participation of civil society stakeholders is required during all stages of AU affairs, from policy initiation and agenda-setting processes, to implementation, to monitoring and evaluation phases. For this to happen the AU will have to be less "state-centric" and more "people-centric," demonstrating a clearer commitment to "human security," as proclaimed by the Constitutive Act of the Union.

A decade after the establishment of these instruments, many of the structures remain weak and many are yet to be properly established. In fact there is now a recognition that the continent's institutions are generally weak and in need of overhaul. In line with the Constitutive Act, especially article 33, there is need to establish realistic time frames for operationalizing the institutions of the union and to address concerns about inadequate financial and human resources.

Closing the Policy-Implementation Gap

Whereas the OAU was earlier concerned with issues of freedom, political emancipation, and the termination of colonialism and white-minority domination, the new Pan-Africanism is concerned to redress poverty, underdevelopment, and massive socioeconomic challenges.

Economic Challenges

Poor Africans today continue to find themselves marginalized and excluded from decision-making and governance processes related to the economy. The economies of the continent have seriously underperformed. Africa's share of world trade has, for example, fallen from 6 percent in 1980 to less than 2 percent in 2002. Yet analysts predict the possibility of unprecedented growth in the African economy. Africa's economy is today relatively more robust than in the past, yet it continues to be fragile because of the downturn in the global economy.

Current growth has happened partly because of cooperation and economic integration processes at regional and subregional levels, which have resulted in Regional Economic Communities (RECs) such as the Southern African Development Community (SADC), the Southern African Customs Union (SACU), and the Common Market for East and Southern Africa (COMESA) that have emerged as important building blocks in continental growth. Tensions have at the same time emerged between some of the stronger regional economies—the SADC and the Economic Community of West African States (ECOWAS) among them—that have sought to protect their economic autonomy and growth. There are at the same time weaker and less well-organized RECs that resent what they see as the interference in their affairs by NEPAD and other AU structures, accusing them of favoring the stronger economies in the Union.

Political Reform

Regional integration had been placed on the agenda long before the AU was created. This impulse toward creating a common African economy, bolstered by appropriate continent-wide institutions, social services, and democracy, has challenged other African states that resist this level of coordination and control. The pertinent question is how to maximize overall continental growth without undermining the level of cohesion that exists between regional neighbors. Good neighborliness has over the years given way to overt conflict between states sharing common borders, resulting in regional wars and coup d'états. This has led to a dominant principle in AU policy that allows for intervention in the affairs of member states in order to counter these developments. African leaders such as South Africa's Thabo Mbeki, Nigeria's Olusegun Obasanjo, Algeria's Abdelaziz Bouteflika, Mozambique's Joaquim Chissano, and Senegal's Abdoulaye Wade were at the center of this policy development, which supersedes the OAU principle of noninterference in the domestic affairs of states.[19] Article 4 of the Constitutive Act of the AU also recognizes the right of member states to "request intervention by the Union in order to restore peace and security."[20] While the OAU prevented the military regimes of Côte d'Ivoire and Comoros from attending its summit in Lomé in 2000, during the period when the notion of "sovereignty as responsibility" was beginning to take root in African diplomacy, this policy was not systematically enforced until after the establishment of the AU in 2002, when it was routinely implemented. Since then the memberships of Mauritania, Guinea, Niger, Madagascar, Côte d'Ivoire, Mali, Guinea-Bissau, and the Central African Republic have been suspended.[21]

Democratization

An important 2013 report by the South Africa–based Centre for Conflict Resolution (CCR) reminds us that "between 1960 and 1990, no single party in Africa lost power."[22] That report goes further to argue that substantial progress was made after the end of the Cold War: "Between 1989 and 1998, the number of multi-party political systems in Africa increased from five to 35 [and] after 2002, ruling parties were voted out of power in Benin, the Central African Republic (CAR), Ghana, Kenya, Lesotho, Mali, Mauritius, Sao Tome and Principe, Senegal, Sierra Leone, and Zambia."[23]

In 2002 NEPAD adopted the Declaration on Democracy, Political, Economic and Corporate Governance. This declaration proclaimed that "Africa faces challenges and the most urgent of these are the eradication of poverty and the fostering of socio-economic development, particularly through democracy and good governance."[24] In 2007 the AU stresses the need to inculcate and promote shared values of governance and democratic principles, reminding African governments, ruling elites, and opposition parties that they were expected to promote democratic political systems in their respective countries. The Shared Values project emphasized good governance (including combating corruption), promoting the independence of the judiciary, strengthening relations with civil society organizations, and the promotion of a free media. Although most African states ratified these principles, the implementation was again often lacking. The APRM, in turn, requires member states to "ensure that the policies and practices of the participating states conform to the agreed political, economic and corporate governance values, codes and standards contained in the Declaration on Democracy, Political, Economic and Corporate Governance."[25]

The essential problem is that a culture has developed over the decades in which African states have refrained from implementing their professed commitments to agreed continental values and norms. The gap between policy and implementation is clearest in regard to the African Charter on Democracy, Elections, and Governance. The CCR reminds us that "Africa's governance framework relies on voluntary compliance. If the co-operation of member states is withheld, the system is undermined. The *African Charter on Democracy, Elections and Governance* of 2007 only reached its threshold of 15 signatories in January 2012."[26] African states have a poor record in ensuring that continental initiatives filter down to the domestic level.

The AU Charter speaks of the need to promote and enforce democracy, good governance, and free and fair elections. Article 17, for instance, declares that "state parties should establish and strengthen independent and impartial national election bodies." Governments have a responsibility to "establish independent electoral bodies," and article 18 states that the AU Commission may "in consultation" with the state party concerned, send special advisory missions to strengthen election processes.[27] Article 23 indicates that "illegal means of assessing or maintaining power constitutes an unconstitutional change of government," and article 25 establishes steps to be taken by the Peace and Security Council when such an "unconstitutional change of government" is judged by the AU to have occurred. The AU would thus have authority to impose sanctions on the perpetrators of unconstitutional actions and their collaborators. Sadly, even the threat of punitive measures is proving insufficient to ensure that all African states implement these requirements of the charter.

Challenges of Institution-Building

The AU faces an institutional crisis. It boasts a host of institutions but struggles to make these institutions effective structures of implementation. In discussing the need for a politics of democratization, the AU Commission stated as early as 2003 that the AU must become better at the following:[28]

- playing the role of catalyzer in the democratization process in Africa
- harmonizing electoral systems across the continent
- observing elections, both upstream in the election of national governing structures and downstream to ensure that these structures implement the will of the electorate
- combating the reemergence of autocratic tendencies
- ensuring that constitutions developed consensually are, where necessary, modified on the same basis to promote a democratic culture in African society
- developing governance indexes that are regularly disseminated in member states
- encouraging media coverage of democratic and electoral processes
- involving parliaments in the consolidation of democracy, peace, and security

This is an ambitious agenda that requires strong institutions and sound relations between the continent's various structures and organs, most notably the AU and NEPAD. Indeed, the relationships between the AU and NEPAD and between NEPAD and the RECs have not been constructive. African leaders, together with officials within the AU Commission, need to take the lead in ensuring that new institutions are empowered to implement the decisions of the AU. In so doing, the AU Commission is likely to be torn, for the foreseeable future, between the need to initiate its own institutional reform and demands by member states to have the reforms cater to their specific national preferences.

Human and Financial Resources

Notwithstanding the fundamental overhaul of the policy landscape in Africa over the past decade, which has seen Africa called a "new frontier" and "new growth point," the transition from the OAU to the AU remains a complex and challenging process, especially with regard to human and financial resources and in terms of setting policy priorities. The financial situation is in fact dire. According to "Democratisation and Peace-Building in Africa," a report produced by the AU, UNECA, and UNDP, five of the fifty-four AU member states—South Africa, Nigeria, Libya, Egypt, and Algeria—each pay US$16 million per annum, which amounts to more than 66 percent of the AU budget. The other forty-eight countries are expected to pay only a third, and even then they struggle to meet their commitments.[29] By mid-2012 only eleven African states were up-to-date with their contributions, and a massive forty-three states were behind.[30] Many member states do not pay their dues in full and/or on time, and this creates huge financial problems for the AU. While some cash-strapped states are incapable of paying, many others, who continue to contribute their dues to the UN and other international organizations, lack the political will or interest to pay their AU dues.

The AU faces the challenge of increasing, professionalizing, and equipping its staff with the necessary skills while simultaneously making its structures effective and efficient. Moreover, there are tensions between the AU and NEPAD over integrating the latter into the former. These tensions have ensured that NEPAD, like the AU, also has staffing and human resources problems. NEPAD has put all such policy and procedural matters, such as appointing staff and creating necessary structures, on hold because of uncertainty deriving from the tensions between the two groups. Limited financial resources, both for the AU and for subregional organizations, remain a major problem affecting all facets of these institutions' operations.

The AU and subregional organizations must convince member states that it is worth their while to pay their dues to the AU. The members must recognize the value they receive for their money; this means that the AU will have to begin to move its lofty protocols, agendas, and ideals from the realm of promises and vision to that of reality on the ground.

The Way Forward

Writing in 2012, I suggested that "the African challenge is essentially a challenge of development, and the African crisis is primarily a crisis of the state."[31] I opined that Africans have to respond simultaneously to a two-pronged problem—namely, governance and development—brought about by decades of misrule and externally driven exploitation.

During the course of the past decade, Africans have certainly put the question of democratic governance firmly on the continental agenda, but this agenda has not taken root and African leaders have in many instances not taken the lead in ensuring the consolidation of democracy. The AU cannot meet the challenges unfolding in countries facing the impact of the Arab Spring or those related to the African Renaissance without ensuring that democracy is entrenched across the continent.

African states need to own the stated continental agenda and to internalize and domesticate its policies and programs with regard to democratization, governance, peace, and security. The foundation has been laid in the charter of the AU. It now needs to be implemented.

The high-level panel that looked at the audit of the AU and its organs in 2007 made the point that there is an urgent requirement for "institutional revamping" of the AU and its organs to ensure that the charter is implemented.[32] It recommended that mechanisms be put in place to strengthen and improve coordination between these organs and member states. The panel further suggested that governments and nongovernmental organizations act in tandem to promote a "new Pan-African consciousness" that takes the values enshrined in the Constitutive Act of the AU as its point of departure.

I end where we started. The declaration of the years 2013 and 2014 as the years of Pan-Africanism and African Renaissance is insufficient in itself. African states that jealously protect their sovereignty—even where their governing practices undermine the well-being of their citizens and the development of the continent as a whole—are a major stumbling block to realizing the goals of the African Union. Although these member states have ratified the Constitutive Act of the AU, the leaders of these governments cling desperately to power. The AU has limited corrective power, short of supporting military interventions designed to promote democratic government. The AU, like the United Nations, the European Union, and regional African organizations, see such intervention as a last resort. The reality is that the AU recognizes the need for compliance with the democratic principles ratified by member states through its support for peacekeeping and other initiatives in several African countries. Political transition and nation building on the African continent and elsewhere in the world is a slow and uneven process. This said, the effort of the AU in the implementation of a "new" Pan-Africanism is something that African national states and global powers must support. The long-term alternatives are not worthy of consideration.

Notes

1. Landsberg, "Emerging African Continental Union and the Drive for Political Development," 51.
2. For an explanation of the concept "continentalism," see Landsberg, "Afro-Continentalism?," 436–48.
3. Mathews, "Renaissance of Pan-Africanism," 25.
4. Stremlau, "African Renaissance and International Relations," 62–63.
5. Ibid., 67.
6. Landsberg, "Fifth Wave of Pan-Africanism," 125.
7. Cited in African Union, United Nations Economic Commission for Africa (UNECA), and the United Nations Development Programme (UNDP), *Democratisation and Peace-Building in Africa*, 18.
8. Ibid.
9. African Union, "Summary of the Deliberation of the Brainstorming Session," 2.
10. African Union, "Strategic Framework of the African Union Commission, 2004–2007," 1.
11. African Union, UNECA, and UNDP, *Democratisation and Peace-Building in Africa*, 35.
12. African Union, "Study on an African Union Government, Towards the United States of Africa," 14.
13. Ijeoma, "Strengthening Public Sector Skills in Africa," 78.
14. Ibid.
15. Ibid.
16. New Partnership for African Development, Democracy and Political Governance Initiative, Midrand, 2002.
17. Ibid.
18. Ibid.
19. For an analysis of the doctrine of non-indifference, see Mwanasali, "From Non-Interference to Non-Indifference."
20. Cited in Landsberg, "Emerging African Continental Union and the Drive for Political Development," 52.
21. Centre for Conflict Resolution (CCR), "African Union at Ten," 3.
22. Ibid.
23. Ibid.
24. African Union, UNECA, and UNDP, *Democratisation and Peace-Building in Africa*, 34.
25. Sulemean, Uys, and Reid, "African Peer Review Mechanism," 36.
26. Centre for Conflict Resolution (CCR), "African Union at Ten," 3.
27. For a summary of the charter regarding elections, see McMahon, "African Charter on Democracy, Elections and Governance," 58.
28. African Union, "Summary of the Deliberation of the Brainstorming Session," 17.
29. African Union, UNECA, and UNDP, *Democratisation and Peace-Building in Africa*, 54.
30. Ibid.
31. Landsberg, "Peace-Building as Governance," 121.
32. Department of Foreign Affairs, "African Union Audit Workshop," 25.

Bibliography

African Union. "Strategic Framework of the African Union Commission, 2004–2007," Final Draft, March 4, 2004, Addis Ababa.

————. "Study on an African Union Government, Towards the United States of Africa." Addis Ababa, November 2006.

————. "Summary of the Deliberation of the Brainstorming Session of the Commission of the African Union and Eminent Personalities, Building the African Union in the 21st Century," Addis Ababa, October 25–28, 2003.

African Union, United Nations Economic Commission for Africa (UNECA), and United Nations Development Programme (UNDP). *Democratisation and Peace-Building in Africa: Policy Reflections and Prospects.* Contribution to the OAU/AU Golden Jubilee and the draft AU Agenda 2063, background paper, Addis Ababa, 2013.

Centre for Conflict Resolution (CCR). "The African Union at Ten: Problems, Progress and Prospects." International Colloquium Report, Berlin, Germany, August 30–31, 2012. www.fes.de/afrika/content/downloads/AU_Report_FINAL.pdf

Department of Foreign Affairs. "The African Union Audit Workshop." Pretoria, South Africa, April 23, 2003.

Ijeoma, Edwin Okey. "Strengthening Public Sector Skills in Africa: The Role of NEPAD." *Africa Insight* 38, no. 2 (September 2008): 77–90.

Landsberg, Chris. "Afro-Continentalism? Pan-Africanism in Post-Settlement South Africa's Foreign Policy." *Journal of Asian and African Studies* 47, no. 43 (2012): 436–48.

————. "The Emerging African Continental Union and the Drive for Political Development." *Open Space* 2, no. 1 (November 2007): 51–57.

————. "The Fifth Wave of Pan-Africanism." In *West Africa's Security Challenges, Building Peace in a Troubled Region,* edited by Adekeye Adebajo and Ismail Rashid. Boulder, CO: Lynne Rienner, 2004.

————. "Peace-Building as Governance: The Case of the Pan-African Ministers Conference for Public and Civil Service." In *Peace-Building, Power and Politics in Africa,* edited by Devon Curtis and Gwinyayi A. Dzinesa. Johannesburg: Wits University Press, 2013.

Mathews, Kay. "Renaissance of Pan-Africanism: The AU and the New Pan-Africanists." In *The African Union and its Institutions,* edited by John Akokpari, Angela Ndinga-Muvumba, and Tim Murithi. Johannesburg: Fanele (Jacana), 2008.

McMahon, Edward R. "The African Charter on Democracy, Elections and Governance: A Positive Step on a Long Path." *Open Space* 2, no. 1 (November 2007): 35.

Mwanasali, Musifiky. "From Non-Interference to Non-Indifference: The Emerging Doctrine of Conflict Prevention in Africa." In *The African Union and Its Institutions,* edited by John Akokpari, Angela Ndinga-Muvumba, and Tim Murithi. Johannesburg: Fanele (Jacana), 2008.

New Partnership for African Development. Democracy and Political Governance Initiative, Midrand, 2002. www.un.org/africa/osaa/nepad.html.

Stremlau, John. "African Renaissance and International Relations." *South African Journal of International Affairs* 6, no. 2 (Winter 1999): 23–33.

Sulemean, Fatima, Leanna R. Uys, and Steve Reid. "The African Peer Review Mechanism: The South African Experience of Health Academics." *Africa Insight* 38, no. 2 (September 2008): 36–49.

12

The Potential of an African Assertion—Once More, in the Name of a Renaissance

ERIK DOXTADER

t is difficult to hear. The sounding call of a renaissance echoes, again and again, but does not fully resonate. It remains in the air in a way that never quite reaches the ear, or never quite provokes a desire to lend an ear. The call slips away, all too quickly, into an imperative to act—every other gesture is idle if not a distraction or a luxury—whose cost is nothing less than aural blindness, an inability and unwillingness to see what appears in the midst of the word's expression. Without time to listen, the call's question, a calling to a question, goes unheard. And this call is a question, a defining question that may not have a definitive answer.

Set out in the name of Africa (whence this name?), the call of a renaissance is a question of discovering words that open a way to beginning again—in words. It is a question of recalling an expression whose inexplicable origin opens space to ask after the originating power of language, a creative power that may define the human condition and defy human control. Such inquiry is not a theological wager, although it has proven rather easy to forget that the currency of a renaissance is a promise of being born again. Nor is it impractical, despite all the protestations to the contrary. Unspeakable violence. So many voices silenced. So much expression distorted, deterred, and denied. In confronting the damage wrought by colonial exploitation, it is astonishing to hear a widely expressed and deep lament over the loss of language being used as a pretense for action that discounts and evades the question of (its) language. Thus a renaissance founders, unable to offer a hearing to that which holds and expresses the potential for becoming new.

Ambivalent Inspirations

The only ailment that has no cure is the spawn of a curse.

THABO MBEKI

African—Renaissance. These two terms touch, tentatively, as if they have yet to form a concept, let alone the conception that portends rebirth. They touch in ways that provoke an image of capture—again—and which capture the imagination—again. Surely, there is no viable claim here, no ethical assertion, as to how Africa's future rests on one of Europe's decisive turns, a moment in which a young humanism turned its light on "dark ages" in a way that laid a foundation for the colonialism that excluded the African from the fold and fortune of history. And yet, this tentative and incongruous constellation may equally assert Africa's capacity to recall that which has for so long functioned as a curse and to do so in a way that recollects the deeper promise of a renaissance, a spirit of discovery that renders the human condition anew. As these terms begin to touch in the name of a beginning, African—Renaissance requires a light touch. The idea cannot be forced into the form of an ideal or rendered subservient to the demands of practical policy. To do so is to forget the tensions that sit beneath its inspiration to make history.

The African Renaissance has inspired much talk. Much of what has been articulated in its name has been said before. Looking across the twentieth and early twenty-first centuries, the idea has been cast variously and repeatedly as a unifying symbol, development model, policy initiative, critical diagnosis, hopeful prediction, disingenuous ruse, and call to struggle.[1] What provokes all of these diverse and divergent assertions? What gathers and then sets them under the banner of an African Renaissance? As they are said again and again, what prevents them from being heard as little more than disingenuous and distracting chatter, naïve to the possibility that there might be a limit to the number of times Africa can be reborn? Individually and together, these are questions of inspiration. Asking after the grounds that inspire all the words that have been dedicated to the African Renaissance, they recall a very old expression that speaks to its cause, an idea that sheds light on the roots of its development and the aim it serves.

Semper aliquid novi Africam adferre—Africa always brings forth something new.[2] These words have inspired—for better and for worse. To more than a few, including former South African president Thabo Mbeki, these ancient words deserve to be spoken in the name of an African Renaissance.[3] Attributed to Pliny the Elder, the expression contains an implicit reference to Aristotle's earlier claim in *The History of Animals* that "Libya always produces something new." Read in context, Aristotle's was a zoological speculation about crossbreeding among large cats (lions, panthers, etc.). The new was the emergence of an unprecedented animal, a unique beast. Soon enough, however, Aristotle's wonder was taken as a sign of Africa's capacity to produce the strange, the dangerous, or the monstrous.

Whether by design or typographical error—the Greeks words for "new" and "evil" bear a close resemblance—Aristotle's dictum was recast by Zenobius as "Africa always brings some new strange evil." In rather short order, as Italo Ronca puts it, Aristotle's position was turned "from an African ethology to anti-African ethics."[4]

Africa always brings forth something new. Perhaps the history of this dictum does not have the *last* word. Perhaps the discourse that has grown around and from it amounts ultimately to dicta, a pronouncement that lacks the power to dictate the fate of its object and to strip its subject of the potential to become otherwise. If so, the appeal of Pliny's words may be less that they sound a timeless promise than that their recollection and utterance performs something of the rebirth that defines and enacts a renaissance. How? What can happen when this ancient phrase is spoken in the name of an African Renaissance?

While it featured diverse and uneven forms of development, the European Renaissance is widely thought to have hinged on a turn back to the ancients. It took form, as Paul Johnson puts it, with the "rediscovery and utilization of ancient virtues, skills, knowledge and culture, which had been lost in the barbarous centuries following the Roman Empire in the West, usually dated from the fifth century AD."[5] Much more and much less than an attempt to overcome a "dark age" by way of a golden age, the work of renaissance began in a confrontation with barbarism, a form of violence that attacks speech, that endeavors to deny human beings the standing and capacity for meaningful expression. Against such dehumanization, a silence that it may well have caused and then reproduced in a different form, renaissance culture aimed to discover lost words in the name of inventing modes of interaction and forms of exchange that could redefine and reweave the political, economic, and ethical threads of culture.

Embodied in its call to set the liberal arts above the dry strictures of Scholasticism and pursued by figures such as Petrarch, Valla, and Agricola, the Renaissance (re)turned to original words in the name of making a definitive turn with(in) language, a turn that requires not the mimicry of what has been said but a recollection of the fundamental relationship between saying and creating, the ways in which *logos* constitutes action that makes a difference.[6] Seen this way, the invocation of Pliny in the name of an African Renaissance is a speech act that endeavors to remake the ground of sense and meaning. In the (re)turn to old words, to original words that speak to the possibility of origination, there is a calling to the question of the word itself, a question of how to discover and create (within) the power of language that has been severed from experience and lost in history's labyrinth. Put differently, it is a short step from the invocation of Pliny to Dani Nabudere's claim that an African Renaissance will unfold only within a recognition of how "the predominance of orality and verbality in the African world-view presents humanity with the possibility of tracing back the origin of concepts of things and world-views."[7]

Soon enough it will be important to ask how the recollection of language opens into the question of "the origin of concepts." For the moment, however, the more pressing idea is that there are old words which inspire talk of rebirth. As Pliny's legacy demonstrates, these words are not free. They hold and express a history of violence, an impulse to colonial conquest that may be perpetuated by their very utterance. So too, Pliny's dictum is ultimately only an example, an instance that represents the larger question of how to find and recall those words that afford inspiration. Only in a politics of authenticity does the ancient word arrive pure and unscarred, which is precisely why the recurring invocation of Pliny is important. To utter Pliny's words in the name of a renaissance is to undertake and perform a definitive element of the work that defines a renaissance, a recollection of those words that are not one's own and whose utterance opens a space in which to begin again in one's own terms.

Reclaiming Potential

Is language a possession, ever a possessing or possessed possession? Possessed or possessing in exclusive possession, like a piece of personal property? What of this being-at-home in language toward which we never cease returning?

JACQUES DERRIDA

A return to a definitive old word inspires and underwrites the call for a defining turn, a moment of rebirth. It is an appealing logic, evidenced not least by the way in which the African Union declared 2013 to be the year of "Pan-Africanism and African Renaissance" by invoking Kwame Nkrumah's claim at the 1963 Conference of African Independent States: "Africa must unite or perish."[8] Are these the words that inspire a renaissance? Are they the right words? How many have perished in the name of unity since 1963? Since 1994?

The old words come loaded. When mobilized in the name of a renaissance, Pliny's adage does not readily disclose how it served a colonial impulse any more than Nkrumah's explains the ways in which unity can coalesce into horrific violence. The defining turn back to old words comes loaded with a problem of how to define the form of its content and the content of its form. On the one hand, this is a question of how to define the occasion, elements, and value of a renaissance that may *be* a renaissance only insofar as it upsets its own ground, troubles its own properties, and refuses the values with which it is justified. On the other, it is a question of whether there can or will *be* a renaissance if its generative operations and aims are simply left to float, to become whatever and however they might become. If prefigured necessity and abstract possibility inspire little more than myth, the power of old words may turn on how they hold the potential to define a renaissance—as a potential.

The African Renaissance has been defined in myriad ways. Looking broadly, it has been set out as an expression of democratization's third wave; the mobilization of an identity politics; a campaign to alter the local, national, and global principles of political governance, social interchange, and economic exchange; a defense of humanism; an appeal to reimagine education; and a rallying cry to develop indigenous thought, public culture, and new forms of (post)national political discourse.[9] While it is important to consider what, if anything, gathers these interpretations, it is equally important to resist the distraction that comes with piling idea upon idea and consider what can be gleaned within just a few select accounts of what the African Renaissance *is*:

Malegapuru Makgoba:

> The African Renaissance is a unique opportunity for Africans to define ourselves and our agenda according to our own realities and taking into account the realities of the world around us. It is about Africans being agents of our own history and masters of our own destiny.[10]

Ademola Araoye:

> The African Renaissance, a black-centered counterpoise to the dominant structure of ideas and the norms and institutions that govern relations in the global system, seeks a radical repudiation of the structure of relationship between these powerful forces. Its Africanist worldview contrasts sharply with established negative understandings and interpretations of the African cosmology by the African who has been redesigned by the travails of history to repudiate self and his own. The African Renaissance therefore seeks to retrench the principal euro-centric and other external ideational structures that constitute the foundations of the dominant order that has always defined the peripheral locus and irrelevance of the black world in the universe.[11]

Pitika Ntuli:

> The African Renaissance, as a counter-hegemonic vehicle growing out of our awareness of the need for meaningful change, offers us an opportunity to reinvent ourselves in line with our new insights as we pass through a transition period in which our perceptions and values, the way we look at our new society and our relationship with each other, must be restructured to meet new realities.[12]

Thaninga Shope:

> The renaissance of our Africanness is not about rediscovering, but about reiterating who we are and what we as Africans are all about.[13]

Offered over a range of fifteen years, these definitions blur the lines between diagnosis, aspiration, and valuation. Each asserts the importance of the real, a reality in which the experience of subjection calls for an interplay of reflection and action. Both ongoing and yet to come, this movement involves moments of opposition, appropriation, differentiation, and expression, all of which are deemed to underwrite the work of individual and collective self-definition. In slightly different ways, each of these definitions is thus a claim about the nature and value of definition, the way the act of definition is imposed, refused, and returned. The new abides in the power to name an experience of historical subjugation, the terms of principled resistance, and the meaning of living in (self) relation.

It is difficult to define a renaissance, let alone proclaim one.[14] Returning to a broad view and looking across the variety of its definitions, the African Renaissance appears as an ontological question, an epistemic project, a political agenda, and an ethical commitment. Where does one begin? Does a renaissance emerge from the recollection and institutionalization of that which has already been accomplished, or does it turn on a struggle for creativity whereby it is possible to remember that institutions take power only by forgetting the contingency of their foundation? This question is fundamental, a problem of what is to be made of "Africa"—the very subject and object of a renaissance—and what "Africa" can say about itself in light of its history.[15] Save for those who have little time for ontological puzzles, the policy prophets who come armed with "practical" arguments about what Africa *must* do, most commentators recognize that the appeals to history, experience, and culture which drive many accounts of the renaissance are themselves open theoretical questions, each of which demands reflection on the precise operation and the constitutive action through which a renaissance unfolds.[16]

Such reflection amounts to difficult work, all the more so when it is short-circuited by a tempting terminological play that turns reflection on the creative quality of a renaissance into a game of bait and switch. Evident in more than a few accounts, the problem looks something like this: in the name of a "rebirth," an emerging or already unfolding renaissance is cast as a moment of "renewal" or "reform" or "discovery" that "restores" or "transforms" or "reappropriates" in ways that "regenerate" or "revive" or "reawaken" or "rehumanize."[17]

The permutations are nearly endless—as the meaning of one term is called into question, it is simply explained by the substitution of another, and so on. The result is a near babble, one that admittedly exposes the expansive depth and breadth of the problems to which renaissance is called, but in a way that equivocates a number of different operators, all of which have very different implications for the generative conditions, movements, and ends of a renaissance. The conflation of "revival" and "rebirth," for instance, makes it difficult to discern whether a renaissance simply lends energy to already existing goods or if its promise rests on the appearance of something new. Going a bit deeper, the confusion of "creativity" and "reform" obscures the question of whether renaissance is a promise of emergence ex nihilo, an event with identifiable grounds, or a moment that inevitably blurs the difference between what it presupposes and what it is called to instantiate. Deeper still, the difference between "discovery" and "restoration," two terms that anchor many accounts of renaissance, is a theoretical question if not *the* question that founds theory itself—what are the conditions under which one is willing and able to take leave of the city in the name of an encounter that exceeds experience, discloses the limits of self-certainty, and alters the norms that guide human interaction?[18]

There is a thin divide between those forms of ambiguity that provoke theoretical action and those that sow confusion in the name of deterring change.[19] With respect to the African Renaissance, the hodgepodge deployment of an increasing host of concepts both hampers and deters inquiry into the affinities and differences between the creativity of a renaissance, the generative quality of revolution, and the incremental change brokered by political and cultural institutions. And while theory does not promise a conclusive answer, the practical cost of the terminological-conceptual jig in many accounts of the African Renaissance is a consideration of whether the work of renaissance is conditioned by Africa or if renaissance is a condition for the emergence of the African. It also obscures the ways in which the characteristic qualities of a renaissance are inextricably linked to questions of violence and death. How does the human desire to create appear in the face of mortality? What forms and magnitudes of destruction create the need for rebirth—as opposed to restoration? Who must consent to the act of (re)conception? What violence does it perform? What sacrifice is justified in the name of making the new?[20]

Natality, as Hannah Arendt well understood, is not only complicated but Janus-faced. It is both an engine of history and its compensation, a claim of uniqueness that defines the human condition and a redress of the violence that comes with the act of inserting ourselves into the world and making history. To grasp for one without the other may be a very good working definition of tragedy. If so, if the moment of a renaissance has arrived, if Africa is poised for a turn, the likes of which underwrote the European voyages of discovery that inaugurated colonialism, the question that follows is how to discern and define the conditions of (its) emergence in relation to the risk of its assertion. For many, however, this is not an appealing question. At a moment not long beyond the colonial, it is far more attractive to define and justify the African Renaissance as the last phase of the struggle for independence and recognition. But, an independence for whom? A standing in relation to whom? A standing on what?

These definitional questions haunt, a reminder that making history is a double-sided problem. In the name of an *African* Renaissance and an African *Renaissance*, the issue is far less whether colonialism was a crime against humanity—it was—than how to assess the extent and methods of its destructive power and the ways in which it dehumanized those caught in its net. Yesterday and tomorrow are other countries. Today, the question is not only what remains, what can be recollected and remembered out of colonial domination. It is also the deeply discomforting question of *how* it remains and *how* it can be brought forward. In the name of renaissance, the valence of appeals to culture, tradition, experience, and knowledge changes depending on whether these grounds were misrepresented, distorted, deformed, or negated by the forces of colonialism. The latter imply a need for reincarnation—or mourning—while the former suggest an untouched reserve, an available thread with which to stitch past and future into a meaningful present. In between, as Biko put it, the colonial falsification of tradition and its ripping of consciousness requires walking a fine line, an authoritative assertion of normality that neither devolves to the endlessly therapeutic nor replicates the logic of colonial sovereignty.[21]

It is a fine line, so fine that the question of how to define an African Renaissance appears undecidable. Think first on the level of inspiration. To appeal to Pliny is to herald an abstract possibility, a promise of the new that may arrive at some point in future. To invoke Nkrumah is to announce a course of necessity, an imperative grounded solely in the threat of death. Moving forward, the difficulty is not simply that these gestures prefigure and then underwrite various definitions of the African Renaissance such that its rebirth is either a (re)production that demands infinite patience or a totalizing struggle dedicated to preventing the negation of conception. It is also that definitional claims about the generative work of the African Renaissance tack between various formulations of these renderings such that it is difficult to see how each may unravel the other. This is to say that the claimed *necessity* of a renaissance sits in a deep tension with its announced *possibility*; the possible presupposes the existence and integrity of interests, capacities, and resources, all of which are thought to be co-opted, stolen, or destroyed in the case from necessity.[22]

The fine line blurs further. And yet it may prove to be a false distinction. There may remain something between raw possibility and necessity. Think back to the various definitions of the African Renaissance. In a way that is easy to overlook, these renderings are linked by a concern for opportunity, a *kairos*, a moment and an opening given to the work of becoming. As it appears and runs between its possibility and necessity, this opportunity suggests that the African Renaissance may be a potential. It hints that there may be a potential for an African Renaissance. It speaks to how the African Renaissance may be that which expresses potential.

This may say a lot, although not in a definitive way—to say that the renaissance is a mode of potentiality is also to say that it is an impotentiality. As an (in)capacity for becoming new, this means, first and foremost, that the work of renaissance is *(un)necessary*. The promise of rebirth is an opening more than a pregiven form of development, an opening in which it is necessary to ask after and redefine the grounds, meaning, and force of necessity. What must become must come without being pregiven, without a model that forecloses the question of how to read and interpret history's force. If so, a renaissance arrives through a series of *(in)direct* movements, a deliberate departure without destination, a taking leave in a way that moves within and without the given word, that takes the preconceived words of conception handed down by culture, politics, and law and asks after the basis of their power. In other words and for other words, a renaissance is thus *(ex)claimed.* With greater or less urgency, it is an event that shuttles between the intransitive claim of a call and the transitive call of a claim. In one moment, the potential for a renaissance appears in a cry, a unique and involuntary exclamation of surprise, rage, joy, or pain that interrupts the logic and flow of normal conversation—*What?!*—and does so in a way that demonstrates how voice remains in the face of something—we cannot readily say *what* it is for sure—which demands response even as it has rendered being at a loss for words. In another moment, the potential of a renaissance cries for speech, a timely word, a claim that asserts a movement, a way to move from here in the light of what has been and what might become. These spontaneous and deliberate gestures are linked if not indissociable. In the midst of potential, there is no time for given words without which there would be no hope of reconceiving the times.[23]

Becoming Words

What does it mean that the voiceless are suddenly given voice, that the invisible suddenly take form, voice, and numbers but above all seek to reintegrate themselves into certain values, a recourse of which they remain uncertain, beyond the fact that the world has systematically denied, degraded, or suppressed those values.

WOLE SOYINKA

Potential flickers. On again, off again. Back and forth, an unsteady and moving light, a beacon that discloses the landscape without delineating the path, that illuminates a way without revealing which way is forward and which way is back. It's awkward, standing in an uncertain light, endeavoring to discern where one is in relation to what has been and what might be, turning round and round in an attempt to discern which is which and thus what direction marks the way to becoming new. There is something unbecoming about it all—one hopes that no one is watching. While the African Renaissance may be wrapped in the pathos of celebration, this cover does not hide the humiliation that may attend the appearance of its potential, the concession that there is a need to be born again.

The potential of an African Renaissance speaks to the difficult conditions of its beginning, a rebirth that cannot be induced by fate, derived through a method, or carried out solely in deliberation. Between possibility and necessity, this potential is an extended moment and contingent movement of becoming, the gathering of a capacity to come into being that retains its incapacity, a capacity not to be. It is a defining event, a definitional event that questions the ground of definition on which becoming depends. The beginning held in a potential is thus neither an emergence ex nihilo nor the mobilization of fixed topoi. It is a beginning that begins with a question of (its) origin—the *question* of origin: How is the possibility of a renaissance (ex)claimed as an opportunity, an (un)necessary opening in which to ask after the (in)direction of a discourse that conceives the subject and object of a renaissance at the same time that it holds open the question of how it recollects, articulates, and performs principles of (its) conception?[24]

It is more than interesting to find precisely this question at the very start of an essay on the African Renaissance that is widely held up as a seminal expression of its potential. Beneath an altogether underappreciated title—"When Can We Talk of an African Renaissance?"—Cheikh Anta Diop began in 1948 by recognizing that the dilemma of defining an African Renaissance cannot be severed from the question of origination:

> A close look at the African reality reveals that there is on the one hand, a part of tradition that has remained intact and continues to survive despite the modern influence and on the other hand, a tradition that has been altered by contamination from Europe. Is it possible in the two cases to talk of a renaissance? Certainly not in the first case. As for the second, let us examine the situation closely in order to see if one can legitimately use the term renaissance for it. This second case is often merely a form of literary imitation, often bordering on lyricism.[25]

Today, this argument does not have much truck. Ironically, Diop receives credit for raising the question of the African Renaissance but not for grasping the implications of his question: "The development of our indigenous languages is the prerequisite for a real African renaissance."[26] Here, the meaning of invoking Pliny becomes clear. The defining and generative ground of an African Renaissance rests on the recollection and cultivation of original words, the languages with which Africa began.

Diop builds the case with evident care. Lamenting what he sees as the tragic evacuation of "African literature," a flight to foreign tongues in which African authors are motivated by all the wrong reasons and perhaps at the cost of reason itself, he reflects on how the inside has been turned outside (itself). The desire to write in a European language and for a European public sets the African author in a profound double bind: The hope of recognition from foreign audiences requires entering into a form of expression that abandons the experience and knowledge that flows from and through one's own language such that the praise garnered for a work is little more than a feint, a thinly veiled accusation of hypocrisy—the "African" writer can be read but not trusted to the degree that her work appeals in a way that "proves" that she is no longer really African. An author's repudiation of her own tongue forecloses the possibility of an equal exchange. It is also self-defeating. The turn from one's own language divests authorship of genius, the breath of spirit that abides in language, at the same time that it folds the author into the "insatiable zeal for action" that defines modernism, a logic in which there is no permissible time to think about how ideas are created and why creative reflection matters.[27]

For Diop, this form of colonization requires turning back and asking how the inside might yet appear and then resist the outside that purports to speak for it. In his terms, the breath that enlivens culture, the breath that heralds birth and gives full voice to experience, appears in the forms of "oral tradition" that hold space to *ask* the question of language: "The study of our languages is even of greater historical importance for us who, to date, have no ancient writings. By studying how this language gave birth to another and how this happened, we would succeed in building a sort of linguistic chain going from the earliest to the latest and thus get to know about a very important period of our history."[28] Diop is clear in saying that the configuration of this linguistic chain does not rest in a desire for linguistic unity—either literally across cultures or across time. The chain is a question, an opening of the open question of origin. Without seeking to locate and explain genesis, the definitive moment of first existence, it asks after the movements of becoming, the ways in which a language gathers form in a way that gives way to another, a chain of becoming and becoming otherwise.

Looking across literature, music, architecture, and the arts, Diop (ex)claims that the defining question of the African Renaissance is a call to the (un)necessary and (in)direct assumption of language, the myriad ways in which African culture came to develop and deploy its words. In one way, this is precisely what is at stake in Diop's oft-repeated call for Africans to recollect "the black origin of Pharaonic Egyptian civilization in order to determine from there the Black man's contributions to human progress."[29] Without the force of fate, this (re)turn to origins is a pivot, a movement that both sets "the sordid beliefs that have been methodically dished out" to Africa into relief and begins a "period of confused searchings," a protracted moment in which "Africa rediscovers herself" in a language that does not "impede her ability to attain her full potential."[30]

Diop's call to the question of language has not been entirely forgotten. Indeed, one hears its echo in Ngũgĩ wa Thiong'o's recent claim that while the African Renaissance "means, first and foremost, the economic and political recovery of the continent's power," this turn "can be brought about effectively only through a collective self-confidence enabled by the resurrection of African memory, which in turn calls for a fundamental change in attitude towards African languages on the part of the African bourgeoisie, the African governments, and the African intellectual community."[31] The question of language is bedrock. Before they are set in stone and held out as the key to change, norms of political (inter)action and economic (ex)change are proposed, debated, negotiated, and articulated. Such rhetorical work—in the actual sense of the term, where speech is a mode of theoretical and practical action—is easily and often discounted. Sensing this tendency, Ngũgĩ sounds his keynote, a call to "re-member" language such that it is possible to both recall the colonial dismemberment of the word and discover its abiding potential: "Acting as if their native means of memory were dead, or at least unavailable, the continental African chose to use the languages that buried theirs so as to connect with their own memory—a choice that has hobbled their re-membering literary visions and practices."[32] In the wake of the devastation wrought by "colonial education factories," the machines that starved the very body of language and left it immobile, the continent's diverse languages and vernaculars must be nourished and recuperated.[33]

This may not be enough. Both Diop and Ngũgĩ advocate for the recollection and repossession of *particular* languages, the mother tongues that colonial powers compromised, abandoned, and distorted. Beyond this, there is also a multifaceted problem of language as such. If it means anything, a renaissance asks language—it *asks* language—to expose and overcome a colonial discourse that secured something of its power by attributing barbarism to its subjects, a dehumanizing attribution of incomprehensibility that, according to Ngũgĩ, created a desire to go "hiding in another language" and produced a perverse "death wish for African languages by African intellectuals."[34] As an internalized desire to escape *into* the cage, this dynamic is not easily overcome, let alone reversed. It requires picking up (a) language in pieces and creating incentives to relinquish forms of expression that are valued as conduits for recognition. And if such incentives appear, the work at hand still requires using the language at hand to reveal its limits in a way that recalls not just a forsaken language but one's sense of place within it. Thus, there are two things at stake when Ngũgĩ invokes Walter Benjamin to claim that language functions as "medium of memory"—the recovery of a language through which to remember the terms of experience, tradition, and culture *and* the recollection of a relationship to language itself that does not simply replicate the logic of colonial discourse.[35] Having a language of one's own is crucial, but it is only a part of the struggle. The other part is how to *have* language in a manner that does not reduce it to an instrument, a possessed and taken-for-granted tool that conforms fully to the wishes of its operator. The value of having the original cannot overwrite the value of what it means to grasp a sense of its fragile origination.

The potential of an African Renaissance does flicker. Deeply felt even at a distance, this potential appears on the horizon of language, a threshold on which to recollect a power that defies possession. While perhaps a source of frustration, its appearance is not intangible. The work of language underwrites the associations that coalesce into politics and the agreements that enable economics. It thus lacks political capital and provokes disinterest precisely because its unquestioned stability is taken to be a necessary condition for doing "real" things and making "actual" change. This same attribution of stability also indemnifies our sense of self—having words is basic to the conception of what it means to be human. Yet, when Diop asks, "When can we talk of an African renaissance?" he is both conceding that talk occurs—there is language at work in the world—and claiming that language has been lost, distorted, and abandoned. The former is heard as obvious and not particularly interesting. The latter, if it is heard at all, appears incoherent or even hypocritical—on what grounds can one *say* that language is broken to the point that there remains only self-confounding chatter or dehumanizing silence? Very few care to hear that they are expressing themselves poorly or that they lack the capacity to do so. And yet, this is precisely the legacy of colonialism, the attribution and internalization of an inability to speak with meaning, let alone to speak in ways that enact "proper" forms of reason and "legitimate" modes of power. For Diop and Ngũgĩ, the African Renaissance begins here. It begins with a call to discover, a call to discover the potential for creativity that appears when the necessity of language is interrupted by a recollection of its origin, an origin that is not a blueprint but a question of how to create a relationship with *and* within that which makes *and* remakes the relationships that hold the potential to give birth.

Beginning Language

One epoch with its historic tasks has come to an end. Surely another must commence with its own challenges. Africa cries out for a new birth. Carthage awaits the restoration of its glory.

NELSON MANDELA, 1994

The beginning begins with an assertion of potential, a claim that recalls, announces, and enacts the fragile power of an original and originating language. Has such an assertion actually appeared? In June 1994, weeks after delivering his inaugural address on the steps of the Union Buildings in Pretoria and in the very midst of the Rwandan genocide, Nelson Mandela hesitated in his address to the OAU heads of state gathered in Tunis: "We must, in action, say that there is no obstacle big enough to stop us from bringing about a new African renaissance."[36] With Carthage yet in ruins, the renaissance remained an event to anticipate. Twenty-three months later, the times appeared to turn as Thabo Mbeki stood before South Africa's Constitutional Assembly and delivered an address that is now widely known as the "I Am an African" speech.[37]

Very subtly and in a very important way, the first three lines of this address offer more than a clue about the opening turn of the African Renaissance:

On an occasion such as this, we should, perhaps start from the beginning.
So, let me begin.
I am an African.

These lines have provoked. In the preface to their groundbreaking collection on the African Renaissance, Makgoba, Shope, and Mazwai collectively observe how "very few of us understood the foresight, the richness, the depth, the challenges encapsulated in these four words"—I am an African—and they then contend that the words amount to a world-changing formulation.[38] Eddie Maloka maintains that Mbeki's address marked the moment when the idea of an African Renaissance "entered the public discourse," this despite the fact that the concept does not appear as such in the speech.[39] Nabudere cites, with approval, Chris Landsberg and Francis Kornegay's claim that the speech should "be considered as the intellectual foundation for the articulation of the African Renaissance," a view that is echoed by Rok Ajulu's claim that the speech initiated a discourse of renaissance.[40]

Read together, this praise hints that Mbeki's address is best understood as an idiosyncratic preface. Typically written upon the completion of that which it introduces, a preface "announces the path and the semantic production of a concept" and does so in a way that the larger work itself cannot.[41] Addressed to that which is yet to come, it expresses what cannot be said within the lines that it opens, delays, and complicates. Mbeki's speech does all of this, except that it was composed *before* he opened his explicit and well-known campaign to define and promote an African Renaissance. The influential terms of this effort, some of which have been documented, only underscore the significance of his 1996 address.[42] More than just a referent for current debates—although it is certainly that— Mbeki's speech is nothing less than iconic; it is an assertion that both represents and performs its unspoken object: the beginning of the African Renaissance.

What is the secret of this beginning, the secret that always shrouds the moment of birth? Mbeki's position is frequently cast as a more or less problematic argument about the formation, deformation, and reformation of identity. On this reading, the first two lines of the address are taken to be far less important than the third—"I am an African." With this declaration, Mbeki is heard to undertake a lengthy and complex reflection on what it means to be an African, a case that moves from the continent's soil to the warmth of its sun to the dignity of its animal life to the diversity of its peoples—lost, scattered, and still very much present. Across the continent and across history, Mbeki asserts that these peoples have "seen concrete expression of the denial of the dignity of a human being emanating from the conscious, systemic and systematic oppressive and repressive activities of other human beings." In the terms of colonial power, they have been cast as barbaric and have seen "the corruption of minds and souls as a result of the ignoble effort to perpetrate a veritable crime against humanity." And yet, as Mbeki puts it, this crime testifies to what it means to be "born of a people who would not tolerate oppression." It testifies to a struggle against those who would "defend the indefensible," a struggle in which Africans have demonstrated that, "whatever the circumstances they have lived through and because of that experience, they are determined to define for themselves who they are and who they should be."

There is perhaps—perhaps—no tragedy here, not in the proper sense. The wounds of the past are not self-inflicted, self-negating, or self-defining. For Mbeki, to say "I am an African" is to make "an assertion that none dare contest" precisely because it asserts a unity in difference, an identity that gathers itself beyond itself.[43] From the midst of imposed division and fragmentation and with a pan-African, national, communal, and individual perspective, it gathers the part into the whole and whole into the part. Identity is less the product or outcome of this movement than the movement itself, a mode of expression that opens the opportunity to decide what it means to say "I am an African." It is crucial to see (and hear) how Mbeki derives this moment of choice:

> We are assembled here today to mark their ["the great masses who are our mother and father"] victory in acquiring and exercising their right to formulate their own definition of what it means to be African.
>
> The constitution whose adoption we celebrate constitutes an unequivocal statement that we refuse to accept that our Africanness shall be defined by our race, colour, gender or historical origins. . . .
>
> Our sense of elevation at this moment also derives from the fact that this magnificent product is the unique creation of African hands and African minds.
>
> But it also constitutes a tribute to our loss of vanity that we could, despite the temptation to treat ourselves as an exceptional fragment of humanity, draw on the accumulated experience and wisdom of all humankind, to define for ourselves what we want to be.

Several things are happening here, each a kind of demonstration. Standing before the Constitutional Assembly, the architects of South Africa's full and first democratic constitution, Mbeki is refusing the last word, the defining word. The question of what it means to say "I am an African" is not his to answer. This seems curious in light of all that has been said in the run-up to this moment in the speech. In fact, the larger speech risks confirming the popular perception that Mbeki is conceited: *I* am an African . . . this way and that way, and through this over there and through those over there . . . *I* am an African . . . *I* am African.

If it seems too much, the risk is well worth it, precisely because the repetition of the claim serves to gather and present an interlocking set of conceits, a set of metaphors whose transpositions, equivocations, and assertions of resemblance all serve to demonstrate the contingent work of metaphor and raise the question of the conditions under which a metaphor actually works—that is, whether and how it defines one thing through another. Then, in a crucial twist, these conceits coalesce into hyperbole, a form of expression that over-throws (with) words, that sets the word to move along an arc that misses its mark. Moving between and gathering the land and the sky and the animals and the peoples and the cultures and the struggles of a continent, Mbeki's conceits demonstrate the ways in which he is an African in a manner that overwhelms far more than it exaggerates. They push metaphor to its limit and then overthrow it.

This, then, is the genius of Mbeki's speech. It names the qualities that define what it means to be an African at the same time that it stages a remarkably fine-tuned indictment of metaphor, an account of how Africans have long been defined by way of something or someone else. This indictment does not negate metaphor's power but hands its potential back to those who have been subjugated by its work. It overwhelms the range and capacity for metaphor and then throws identity over it, into an open question, a space in which to begin, to take up the question and then the work of individual and collective self-constitution. Now, in this light, recall the first two lines of Mbeki's speech:

> On an occasion such as this, we should, perhaps start from the beginning.
> So, let me begin.

These brief lines matter a great deal. The constitution's words both enact *and* call for words that begin from a beginning and begin a beginning, all in the name of gathering the contingent power of self-definition. And in this moment, it is contingent—perhaps more than at any other time, the appearance of the constitution is understood to be a function of struggle and not the result of fate. And so too Mbeki's speech, as it echoes—so precisely—the constitution to which it is addressed.[44] To move between the two, listening back and forth, is to hear how each asserts words that create the potential for words which call forth the question of self-assertion, the potential for self-definition that is enabled by and yet never fully controlled by the moment of constitution—or the moment of conception, the moment of (re)birth.[45] As beginning and origin thus begin to blur, the secret of Mbeki's speech appears. The African Renaissance begins as the work of hyperbole yields allegory. An overthrow reveals undermeaning, where the latter is not a foundation but a demonstration that invites the recollection of the ways in which definitive words remain open to question, an inquiry that expresses the movement of creativity, an (in)direct and (un)necessary movement whereby and wherein Mbeki can (ex)claim that in the name of a beginning, "nothing can stop us now!"

In light of the arc thrown by Mbeki's speech, where are we now? If there is no doubt that the African Renaissance is now an important commonplace, it is equally certain that this topos has generated heated controversy over precisely how it fits and what it starts. This is understandable and good—a renaissance likely fails as it takes on the quality of a machine. Yet it is also the case that policy debates have worked to ghettoize the question of language that sits at the very heart of Mbeki's position. While few are willing to overtly deny the significance of language in the renaissance project, its question is frequently reduced to (1) an instrumental means of policymaking, (2) a matter of deciding which particular languages should be taught in schools and which languages should be used as the medium of instruction, and (3) a concern for ministers of culture whose portfolios are often predicated on the need to keep the intelligentsia and civil society both happy and out of shouting distance from government.

Individually and together, these tendencies inscribe and enforce a disinterest in language as such. As language is collapsed to a utility function, a distribution-allocation scheme, and an object of institutionally supported aesthetics, there are fewer and fewer incentives to ask how language is (not a) given. There is less and less room to step back from the problem of how humans use language to form relationships with one another and ask how being human comes with a responsibility, a response-ability, to reflect on how one relates to language itself. What is my relation with the language that I take to be mine? Is language a gift? Is it mine to take? How might its power exceed my control in ways that call me to recognize it, to concede my dependence on it such that it comes to entail far less an object to appropriate than an opening in which to extend hospitality?

Are we hospitable to language? Do we hold open the door for *its* creativity? The question may seem curious, perhaps even threatening. It is the very question on which the renaissance may turn. The potential to conceive the new rests not simply on grasping the fundamentally rhetorical grounds of policy—and how these might be reconceived—but also on an attentiveness to the ways in which human beings are constituted through and in the word, the ways in which the work of constitution discloses the potential of a rebirth in the question of *how* humans assume *and* relinquish the power of definition. This potential surely comes with risk, not least when it functions as a call to wait (endlessly) for change and when it is used to defer reflection about the stakes of renaissance itself—as it conceives, misconceives, and fails to conceive. And beneath this, there is more than a little risk in the question of language itself. The passivity that seems to follow from giving away control of the word in the name of reconceiving its defining gift may count as an undue sacrifice, a relinquishment that must be balanced with the self-defeating costs of perpetual, self-certain action, what Diop saw as a dogmatic commitment to the practical that remains blind to its theoretical debts.

In the balance may hang the question of ethical life—the problem of coming to the terms of becoming, the response-ability that inheres in that conception given to the (re)creation of one's relations with self and others, the generative assertion that recollects the fragility of language and struggles to recall the constitutive conditions of its expression. The work of African—Renaissance is not a game, not a language game. It is the assertion of a beginning made in the name of a continent whose origins appear in the shimmer of its becoming words, a potential for expression's renewal and a renewing expression.

Notes

1. On one register, such critical mass can be measured by the voluminous and growing literature dedicated to the possibility of an African Renaissance. Among others, see Makgoba, *African Renaissance*; Fantu Cheru, *African Renaissance*; Udogu, *African Renaissance in the Millennium*. Although a bit dated, a very useful bibliography on the African Renaissance can be found online in the 2001 issue of *Quest: A Journal of African Philosophy*.

2. Ronca, "Ex Africa." Ronca provides a useful survey of the various ways in which Pliny's words have been translated over the course of the centuries. In his estimation, there are some eight different versions of the expression, with the most popular being *Ex Africa semper aliquid novi*.

3. In fact, Mbeki's widely recognized campaign for the African Renaissance includes a detailed reflection on the importance of this expression. See Mbeki, "Address of Thabo Mbeki at the European Parliament."

4. Ronca, "Ex Africa," 574. There is work to be done on whether these particular texts pronounce an indictment of character or if they go a step further and make an explicitly racist claim against those who emerge from Africa.

5. Johnson, *Renaissance*, 4. Also see Nauert, *Humanism and the Cultural Renaissance of Europe*.

6. See Nauert, *Humanism and the Cultural Renaissance*, 14–25; Conley, *Rhetoric in the European Tradition*, 109–28.

7. Nabudere, "Toward an Afrokology of Knowledge Production and African Regeneration," 22.

8. See African Union, "Celebrating Pan-Africanism and African Resistance."

9. The list can be carried on. See Bongmba, "Reflections on Thabo Mbeki's African Renaissance"; and Vale and Maseko, "South Africa and the African Renaissance."

10. Makgoba, *African Renaissance*, xii.

11. Araoye, "African Peer Review Mechanism in the Context of the African Renaissance," 27.

12. Pitika Ntuli, quoted in Dunton, "Pixley Kaisaka Seme and the African Renaissance Debate," 556.

13. Thaninga Shope, quoted in Makgoba, *African Renaissance*, xii.

14. Vale and Maseko thus aver the African Renaissance is an "empty policy vehicle" (277). For one of the first iterations of the contemporary call for an African Renaissance, one that prefigured Mbeki's position, see Mavimbela, "African Renaissance." More recently, see the African Union's 2006 "Charter for African Cultural Renaissance."

15. A substantial amount of the literature on the African Renaissance starts by asking "What is Africa?" and "Who are the Africans?" For instance, see Prah, "African Renaissance or Warlordism?"

16. See Mamdani, "There Can Be No African Renaissance without an Africa-Focused Intelligentsia," 125–34.

17. To this, one can add the shifting conditions and stakes of a renaissance, including critique, belonging, revolt, struggle, redistribution, development, and independence. And to this one can add attempts to differentiate the process and product of renaissance, a distinction that may well be a remnant of rather unproductive debates about the nature of reconciliation.

18. Of course, this raises the questions of whether and how a Western account of theory may load the dice and how a reflective apparatus that levels the playing field could be developed.

19. But perhaps the demand to discern the conditions and plot the arc of a renaissance is completely unreasonable or, worse, a less-than-subtle attempt to foreclose an open-ended and unpredictable invention with the vestiges of colonial reason. Or perhaps the demand marks an attempt to stall or hijack change, an effort to drain the energy of renaissance with a thousand procedural paper cuts, all of which are rationalized as a way of eliminating ambiguity and minimizing risk. On the other side of the coin, it is troubling when theory is confused with method and then reduced to a set of pragmatic strictures in which theory is evacuated from the "real" terms of "everyday life" (consider what's involved in bartering with a storekeeper or flirting in a bar) and then sanctioned as specious, exclusive, and an impediment to action.

20. Two points follow, each a concern that merits consideration beyond what's possible here. First, the renaissance promise of rebirth readily opens to questions of resurrection and what it means to be born again—rather quickly, the work of renaissance can be removed from the hands of those that inhabit this world. Second, the promise of (re)conception ties the renaissance to the problem of rape and raises broader questions about the degree to which feminism has played a tangible role in the contemporary debates over the African Renaissance.

21. Biko, *I Write What I Like*, 49.

22. The dynamic runs in both directions or as a feedback loop. As policy-based definitions of the African Renaissance announce an obligation to overcome colonial domination, the question of whether such violence undermines the feasibility of the proposed initiative can be covered with abstract appeals to tradition and history, the alleged well-springs of value that are then deemed productive only insofar as they are bound into the form of policy. At the same time and from other quarters, experience and memory are presented as the ground of a renaissance, a basis for so-called authentic expression that fends off the question of how the work of renaissance may sweep away the terms of such expression with claims about how the illegitimacy of political decision making warrants the institutionalization of culture.

23. The failure to grasp the fundamental importance of this impropriety, the interruption of the exclamation, well explains the accusation that the African Renaissance is merely and dangerously rhetorical. The charge appears with some regularity. See inter alia Bongmba, "Reflections on Thabo Mbeki's African Renaissance," 303; Jonas, "Quest to Achieve African Renaissance," 95; Vale and Maseko, "South Africa and the African Renaissance," 277. For a useful compensatory reply, see Dunton, "Pixley Kaisaka Seme and the African Renaissance Debate."

24. To be clear, the issue here is not existence, the alleged and likely unknowable moment of genesis. It is rather, as Walter Benjamin put it, a question of the emergence of becoming, the appearance of a claim to necessity that recognizes its own provisionality at the same time that it asserts a way forward. See Benjamin, *Origin of German Tragic Drama*, 45. Also see Derrida, *Voice and Phenomenon*.

25. Diop, "When Can We Talk of an African Renaissance?," 33. First published in French, in a 1948 issue of *Le Musée Vivant*, it ripples across and informs the contemporary literature on the African Renaissance, not least for the way in which it is credited as being a first formulation, a guiding precedent for current debates. Whether accurate or not, this formulation is a precise indication of how little appreciation is given to Diop's explicit concern for the question of language and its potential.

26. Diop, "When Can We Talk," 35. Perhaps the widespread neglect of this claim owes to a presumption that such development has already occurred. Among others, Neville Alexander's important work suggests the contrary, that the political economy of language remains bound to a European idiom. See Alexander, *Ordinary Country*.

27. Diop, "Alarm in the Tropics," 81.

28. Diop, "When Can We Talk," 36.

29. Diop, "Cultural Contributions and Perspectives for Africa," 111.

30. Diop, "When Can We Talk," 44–45.

31. Thiong'o, *Something Torn and New*, 89–90.

32. Ibid., 41.

33. Ibid., 27.

34. Ibid., 62–63.

35. Ibid., 40. For an important reflection on this problem, see Mbembe, "African Modes of Self-Writing," 239–73. What Ngũgĩ has perhaps not fully taken into account is the fuller if not double meaning of Benjamin's claim in his theses on history: "There is no document of culture which is not at the same time a document of barbarism" (Benjamin, "On the Concept of History," 392).

36. Mandela, "Statement by President Nelson Mandela at the OAU Meeting of Heads of State and Government."

37. Here, I am using the ANC's transcript of the speech. Among other places, the speech can also be found in Mbeki, *Africa: The Time Has Come*, 31–36.

38. Makgoba, *African Renaissance*, iv.

39. Maloka, "South African 'African Renaissance' Debate," 2.

40. Nabudere, "African Renaissance in the Age of Globalization," 16. There is a bit of ambiguity here given that Nabudere's attribution to Landsberg and Kornegay cannot be readily confirmed. Nabudere cites an essay by Landsberg and Kornegay in which the quotation does not appear: Landsberg and Kornegay, "African Renaissance." This noted, Kronegay and Landsberg do observe how Mbeki's campaign has left him with the aura of a "true African prophet" (17). Ajulu, "Thabo Mbeki's African Renaissance in a Globalising World Economy," 33. Among many others, see Thiong'o, *Something Torn and New*, 120; Vale and Maseko, "South Africa," 271; Bongmba, "Reflections," 291–96; and Jonas, "Quest," 86.

41. See Derrida, *Dissemination*, 15.

42. Although the idea of an African Renaissance appears explicitly in at least one of Mbeki's 1995 speeches, the larger campaign begins in a 1997 address given in the United States. See Mbeki, "Address by Executive President Thabo Mbeki to Corporate Council of Africa's 'Attracting Capital to Africa' Summit." The need for a second essay thus presents itself, one that traces the announced terms of Mbeki's position and how the defined arc of his vision changes over time.

43. In the South African context, this is altogether evident when Mbeki claims in the opening moments of the speech that "I am the grandchild who lays fresh flowers on the Boer graves at St. Helena and the Bahamas, who sees in the mind's eye and suffers the suffering of a simple peasant folk, death, concentration camps, destroyed homesteads, a dream in ruins."

44. If so, it might then be asked whether the constitution itself depends on any sort of hyperbolic expression. The doubt vanishes when one considers its preamble, a text adapted from the 1993 interim constitution's postamble and the latter's contention that the constitution itself rests on reconciliation, an event that discovers words that turn violence toward productive opposition. I have developed this argument elsewhere. See Doxtader, *With Faith in the Works of Words*.

45. This would be one way of grasping why constitutions are understood as living documents. For a larger account of how a constitution opens a language project that exceeds its own terms, see Habermas, "Constitutional Democracy: A Paradoxical Combination of Contradictory Principles."

Bibliography

African Union. "Celebrating Pan-Africanism and African Resistance." Press release, May 10, 2013. http://summits.au.int/50th/21stsummit/news/celebrating-pan-africanism-and-african-renaissance.

———. "Charter for African Cultural Renaissance," adopted January 26, 2006. http://www.au.int/en/sites/default/files/CHARTER_FOR_AFRICAN_CULTURAL_RENAISSANCE.pdf.

Ajulu, Rok. "Thabo Mbeki's African Renaissance in a Globalising World Economy: The Struggle for the Soul of a Continent." *Review of African Political Economy* 87 (2001): 27–42.

Alexander, Neville. *An Ordinary Country: Issues in the Transition from Apartheid to Democracy in South Africa.* Pietermaritzburg: University of Natal Press, 2002.

Araoye, Ademola. "The African Peer Review Mechanism in the Context of the African Renaissance." *The Thinker* 55 (2013): 26–30.

Benjamin, Walter. "On the Concept of History." In *Walter Benjamin: Selected Writings, Volume 4,* edited by Howard Eiland and translated by Edmund Jephcott, 389–400. Cambridge, MA: Harvard University Press, 2003.

———. *The Origin of German Tragic Drama.* Translated by John Osborne. London: Verso, 1977.

Biko, Steve. *I Write What I Like.* London: Bowerdean, 1996.

Bongmba, Elias. "Reflections on Thabo Mbeki's African Renaissance." *Journal of Southern African Studies* 3, no. 2 (2004): 291–316.

Cheru, Fantu. *African Renaissance: Roadmaps to the Challenge of Globalization.* London: Zed, 2002.

Conley, Thomas. *Rhetoric in the European Tradition.* Chicago: University of Chicago Press, 1990.

Derrida, Jacques. *Dissemination.* Translated by Barbara Johnson. Chicago: University of Chicago Press, 1983.

———. *Voice and Phenomenon: Introduction to the Problem of the Sign in Husserl's Phenomenology.* Translated by Leonard Lawlor. Evanston, IL: Northwestern University Press, 2011.

Diop, Cheikh Anta. "Alarm in the Tropics." In *Towards an African Renaissance: Essays in African Culture and Development, 1946–1960.* Translated by Egbuna Modum. London: Karnak House, 1996.

———. "Cultural Contributions and Perspectives for Africa." In *Towards an African Renaissance: Essays in African Culture and Development, 1946–1960.* Translated by Egbuna Modum. London: Karnak House, 1996.

———. "When Can We Talk of an African Renaissance?" In *Towards an African Renaissance: Essays in African Culture and Development, 1946–1960.* Translated by Egbuna Modum. London: Karnak House, 1996.

Doxtader, Erik. *With Faith in the Works of Words: The Beginnings of Reconciliation in South Africa.* Cape Town: David Philip, 2008.

Dunton, Chris. "Pixley Kaisaka Seme and the African Renaissance Debate." *African Affairs* 102 (2003): 555–73.

Habermas, Jurgen. "Constitutional Democracy: A Paradoxical Combination of Contradictory Principles." Paper presented at the Northwestern School of Law, Chicago, Illinois, October 12, 2000.

Johnson, Paul. *The Renaissance.* London: Weidenfeld and Nicolson, 2000.

Jonas, Obonye. "The Quest to Achieve African Renaissance: Reflections on NEPAD." *Journal of Pan African Studies* 5, no. 3 (2012): 83–105.

Landsberg, Chris, and Francis Kornegay. "The African Renaissance: A Quest for Pax Africana and Pan Africanism." In *South Africa and Africa: Reflections on the African Renaissance*, 16–28. FGD Occasional Paper, no. 17. Braamfontein, South Africa: Foundation for Global Dialogue, 1998.

Makgoba, Malegapuru William, ed. *African Renaissance: The New Struggle*. Cape Town: Mafube, 1999.

Maloka, Eddy. "The South African 'African Renaissance' Debate: A Critique." Africa Institute of South Africa, 2001. www.polis.sciencespobordeaux.fr/vol8ns/maloka.pdf.

Mamdani, Mahmood. "There Can Be No African Renaissance without an Africa-Focused Intelligentsia." In *African Renaissance: The New Struggle*, edited by Malegapuru William Makgoba, 125–34. Cape Town: Mafube, 1999.

Mandela, Nelson. "Statement by President Nelson Mandela at the OAU Meeting of Heads of State and Government." Tunis, June 13, 1994. www.anc.org.za/show.php?id=4888.

Mavimbela, Vusi. "The African Renaissance: A Workable Dream." In *South Africa and Africa: Reflections on the African Renaissance*, 29–34. FGD Occasional Paper, no. 17, 1998. Braamfontein, South Africa: Foundation for Global Dialogue, 1998.

Mbeki, Thabo. "Address by Executive President Thabo Mbeki to Corporate Council of Africa's 'Attracting Capital to Africa' Summit.'" Chantilly, Virginia, April 19, 1997. www.sahistory .org.za/archive/address-executive-deputy-president-thabo-mbeki-corporate-council-africas -attracting-capital-.

———. "Address of the President of South Africa, Thabo Mbeki at the European Parliament." Strasbourg, November 17, 2004. www.dfa.gov.za/docs/speeches/2004/mbek1118.htm.

———. *Africa: The Time Has Come*. Cape Town: Tafelberg, 1998.

———. "I Am an African—Thabo Mbeki's Speech at the Adoption of the Republic of South Africa Constitution Bill." Cape Town, May 8, 1996. www.anc.org.za/show.php?id=4322.

Mbembe, Achille. "African Modes of Self-Writing." *Public Culture* 14 (2002): 239–73.

Nabudere, Dani. "The African Renaissance in the Age of Globalization." *African Journal of Political Science* 6, no. 2 (2001): 11–27.

———. "Toward an Afrokology of Knowledge Production and African Regeneration." *International Journal of African Renaissance Studies* 1, no. 1 (2006): 7–32.

Nauert, Charles. *Humanism and the Cultural Renaissance of Europe*. Cambridge: Cambridge University Press, 1995.

Prah, Kwesi Kwaa. "African Renaissance or Warlordism?" In *African Renaissance: The New Struggle*, edited by Malegapuru William Makgoba, 37–61. Cape Town: Mafube, 1999.

Ronca, Italo. "*Ex Africa semper aliquid novi*: The Ever Surprising Vicissitudes of a Pre-Aristotelian Proverb." *Latomus* 53, no. 3 (1994): 577.

Thiong'o, Ngũgĩ wa. *Something Torn and New: An African Renaissance*. New York: Basic Civitas, 2009.

Udogu, E. Ike. *African Renaissance in the Millennium: The Political, Social and Economic Discourses on the Way Forward*. New York: Lexington, 2007.

Vale, Peter, and Sipho Maseko. "South Africa and the African Renaissance." *International Affairs* 74, no. 2 (1998): 271–87.

Appendix A

Colonization and Independence of African Countries

Country	Beginning of Colonization	Date of Independence	Colonizer
Algeria	1830	1962	France
Angola	1575	1975	Portugal
Benin	1900	1960	France
Botswana	1885	1966	Britain
Burkina Faso	1896	1960	France
Burundi	1899	1962	Germany and Belgium
Cameroon	1884	1960	Germany, France, and Britain
Cape Verde	1462	1975	Portugal
Central African Republic	1889	1960	France
Chad	1900	1960	France
Comoros	1886	1975	France
Côte d'Ivoire (Ivory Coast)	1844	1960	France
Democratic Republic of Congo	1870s	1960	Belgium
Djibouti	1894	1977	France
Egypt	1875	1922	Britain
Equatorial Guinea	1844	1968	Spain
Eritrea	1890 (Italy) 1941 (Britain)	1941/1951	Italy and Britain

Ethiopia	Only country in Africa to defeat a European colonial power and retain its sovereignty as an independent country.		
Gabon	1885	1960	France
The Gambia	1889	1965	Britain
Ghana	1874	1957	Britain
Guinea	1890	1958	France
Guinea-Bissau	1880s	1973	Portugal
Kenya	1895	1963	Britain
Lesotho	1868	1966	Cape Colony and Britain
Liberia	1820	1847	American Colonization Society (US)
Libya	1912	1947/1951	Italy
Madagascar	1883	1960	France
Malawi	1889	1964	Britain
Mali	1905	1960	France
Mauritania	1903	1960	France
Mauritius	1810	1968	Britain
Morocco	1884 (Spanish) 1904 (French)	1956	France and Spain
Mozambique	1505	1975	Portugal
Namibia	1884	1990	Germany and South Africa
Niger	1922	1960	France
Nigeria	1900	1960	Britain
Republic of Congo	1880	1960	France
Rwanda	1884	1962	Germany and Belgium
São Tomé and Príncipe	1472	1975	Portugal
Senegal	1850s	1960	France
Seychelles	1810	1976	Britain
Sierra Leone	1880s	1961	Britain

Somalia	1920s	1960	Britain and Italy
South Africa	1806	1961	Britain
South Sudan	1890s	2011 (from Sudan)	Britain
Sudan	1890s	1956	Britain
Swaziland	1903	1968	Britain
Tanzania	1914	1961	Germany and Britain
Togo	1884	1960	Germany and France
Tunisia	1881	1956	France
Uganda	1888	1962	Britain
Zambia	1888	1964	British South Africa Company and Britain
Zimbabwe	1888	1980	British South Africa Company and Britain

Appendix B

Select Chronology of Afro-Arab Spring

This select chronology focuses on events in Tunisia, Egypt, and Libya. It is inter-spersed with abbreviated entries that reflect the regional character of the broader Arab Spring. The chronology draws from and gathers a number of sources, including histories and timelines generated by the media and nongovernmental organizations.

2010

Tunisia: December 17. In the wake of harassment and extortion by state officials, Mohamed Bouazizi, a street vendor, is provoked to undertake self-immolation. The act provokes significant outcry and mass protest.

2011

January–March

Tunisia: January 14. The scope and tenor of protests intensify; government forces kill several protestors; President Zine al-Abidine Ben Ali flees to Saudi Arabia.
Algeria: January 14. The self-immolation of Mohsen Bouterfif is held up as a reason to undertake country-wide protests.
Yemen: January 23. Arrest of Tawakul Karman, a prominent activist, sparks pro-test across the country.
Egypt: January 25. The "Day of Rage"; antigovernment protestors rally across the country, with many calling for the resignation of President Hosni Mubarak.
Egypt: January 28. Government mobilizes its response to protests; troops sup-ported by tanks are ordered to contain the demonstrations; telecommunications and internet service are blocked.
Egypt: February 2. Violence between protestors and government forces escalates. President Mubarak declares that he will not run for reelection, as protestors continue to call for his immediate escalation. There are indications that the Egyptian military's allegiances are shifting toward the interests of protestors.
Yemen: February 3. Some twenty thousand people demonstrate in the capital, Sana'a. The president, Ali Abdullah Saleh, indicates that he will not seek to serve beyond 2013.

Egypt: February 11. Mubarak relinquishes the presidency; a military council is created and charged with the task of planning for an election.

Algeria: February 12. Several thousand protesters clash with security forces.

Bahrain: February 14. Two individuals are killed at a protest in support of demonstrations in Egypt and Tunisia.

Libya: February 15. In Benghazi, protests are sparked by the arrest of Fathi Terbil, a lawyer who represented the families of victims of a 1996 massacre at the Abu Salim prison.

Bahrain: February 15. An army attack on the funeral of a prodemocracy activist leads to the resignation of the country's primary opposition party.

Libya: February 17. The intensification of protest provokes the use of live ammunition by security forces, a response that spurs additional demonstrations, many of which are dedicated to demanding the resignation of President Muammar Qaddafi.

Bahrain: February 17. Four demonstrators are killed in Pearl Square.

Libya: February 24. So-called revolutionary brigades enter the city of Mistrata, a move that provokes the Qaddafi government to deploy forces and undertake the defense of several cities.

Middle East: February 25. Protests are seen across the Middle East. **Yemen** sees its largest prodemocracy rally to date; **Egyptian** activists call for accelerated reforms. In **Bahrain,** tens of thousands of protestors gather in opposition to the government's unwillingness to undertake democratic reforms.

Libya: March 5. From Benghazi and led by rebels, the National Transitional Council (NTC) declares that it is the legitimate representative of the Libyan people.

Morocco: March 9. King Mohammed VI endeavors to preempt widespread protest with a speech in which he promises to undertake reforms.

Saudi Arabia: March 11. Government bans public protests and sends security forces to quell popular uprisings.

Bahrain: March 15. Martial law is declared; Saudi Arabia deploys some one thousand troops to the country.

Syria: March 15. Significant protests in Damascus, with protestors calling for democratic elections and the release of political prisoners.

Bahrain: March 16. Government forces respond to protestors, a crackdown in which they attempt to clear Pearl Square.

Libya: March 17. UN Security Council authorizes a no-fly zone over the country and the use of military force against Qaddafi's army.

Yemen: March 18. Forces allied with the government kill some fifty protesters at Sana'a University; a state of emergency is declared by President Ali Abdullah Saleh.

Bahrain: March 18. Pearl Square occupied by government forces.

Saudi Arabia: In response to protests, King Abdullah announces a set of reforms.

Libya: March 19. Outside of Benghazi, NATO air strikes stop the advance of government forces and target Libyan air defense systems.

Syria: March 19. Protests continue, with security forces deployed in response. Five demonstrators are killed.

Syria: March 28. Protesters are fired on by security forces, with reports suggesting that some 150 people have been killed in eleven days.

April–May

Egypt: Widespread gatherings and protests; many citizens call for Mubarak's prosecution and an end to military rule.

Bahrain: Antigovernment protesters are met with force by the government; four protestors receive the death penalty.

Syria: Volatility becomes the norm, despite the government's promise to lift the state of emergency; security forces carry on with attacks on demonstrators, including children.

Yemen: Protests against the government continue and clashes between government forces and protestors grow increasingly violent. President Saleh indicates that he has no intention of resigning his office.

June–September

Yemen: June 3. At Saleh's palace, a bomb explosion wounds the president, prime minister, and speaker of parliament. Saleh's wounds are treated in Riyadh.

Syria: June 4. As tens of thousands march against the government, at least one hundred people are killed in two days.

Kuwait: June 6. Hundreds march against the government, with many demanding that the president resign his office.

Tunisia: June 18. In absentia, Ben Ali is sentenced to thirty-five years in jail.

Morocco: July 1. Referendum results show substantial if not vast support for the reform proposal offered by the king.

Libya: July 15. The NTC is recognized by the International Contact Group as the legitimate government of Libya.

Syria: July 31. Some one hundred are killed as the government uses tanks against the resistance in Hama.

Egypt: August 3. As his trial opens, Mubarak denies killing opponents or abusing his power. The army takes control of Tahrir Square.

Libya: August 21. Rebels confront little resistance as they enter Tripoli; widespread reports indicate that Qaddafi has gone into hiding.

Libya: August 26. The rebel-led interim government is relocated to Tripoli.

Egypt: September 16. Demonstrators reoccupy Tahrir Square, in part in response to the interim government's decision to impose a state of emergency.

Libya: September 20. The NTC is recognized as the legitimate governing authority by the African Union (AU).

Yemen: September 23. In the wake of confrontations between demonstrators and government forces, Saleh returns to Yemen.

October–December

Egypt: October 10. The destruction of a church provokes demonstrations by Coptic Christians; reprisals by security forces lead to twenty-four deaths and hundreds of injuries.

Libya: October 20. Qaddafi is captured and killed.

Libya: October 23. The NTC announces the end of the war and that the liberation of Libya has been achieved.

Tunisia: October 23. First democratic election; a majority of the seats in the constituent assembly are won by the Islamist Ennahda party.

Syria: November 12. Reports that the government has killed more than thirty-five hundred people provokes the Arab League to suspend Syria's membership.

Kuwait: November 17. Widespread protests; demonstrators attempt to occupy parliament.

Egypt: November 18. Tahrir Square is the site of renewed protests and violent clashes between government forces and demonstrators.

Egypt: November 22. Hussein Tantawi, a leader in the military, declares that the election of a civilian president will occur by June 2012.

Yemen: November 23. At the urging of several states in the Gulf, Saleh agrees to give over his power to Abd-Rabbu Mansour Hadi.

Morocco: November 26. Elections are won by a moderate Islamist group, the Justice and Development Party.

Tunisia: December 12. Widely known for his human rights activism, Moncef Marzouki, is elected to lead the country. The leader of Ennahda, Hamadi Jebali, assumes the office of prime minister.

Syria: December 13. The UN reports that some five thousand people have been killed over the course of nine months of unrest and conflict.

2012

January–March

Egypt: January 24. First postrevolution election; 70 percent of the seats in parliament are won by Islamist parties.

Yemen: February 27. Following elections, Saleh resigns as president.

Libya: March 1. Deadly conflict between Arab Zawi and African Tebu groups.

Bahrain: March 9. On the anniversary of the initial uprising, some one hundred thousand people demonstrate, with many demanding the king's removal from office.

Libya: March 20. In the eastern part of the country, tribal leaders spark tensions with the NTC as they call for regional autonomy.

April–June

Syria: April 14. Siege of Homs ends with a UN-supported cease-fire; the fatalities of the siege are reported to include some two hundred rebels and thirty-eight members of the security forces.

Egypt: April 20. Protests in Tahrir Square continue. Demonstrators are provoked by the decision of the Electoral Commission to disqualify a number of candidates for president, including three individuals thought to be front-runners.

Egypt: May 23–24. Presidential election. Mohamed Morsi, the former prime minister and candidate for the Muslim Brotherhood, wins the first round.

Egypt: June 2–13. Mubarak sentenced to life in prison.

Tunisia: June 19. Ben Ali is sentenced, in absentia, to life imprisonment for his role in deaths and injuries that occurred in the Tunisian uprising. Saudi Arabia again refuses to extradite him.

Egypt: June 24. Mohamed Morsi assumes the presidency.

July–September

Libya: July 7. The General National Congress (GNC), a constituent assembly, is formed and charged to assume the power of the NTC.

Syria: July 12. Some two hundred are killed as the army attacks Tremseh. According to the Red Cross, the country is officially a civil war zone.

Tunisia: August 20. Thousands protest in Tunis, with many opposed to the government's attempt to curtail the rights of women, an action deemed to violate the terms of the country's draft constitution.

Libya: September 11. US ambassador Christopher Stevens and three other Americans are killed in Benghazi.

October–December

Bahrain: October 30. Government bans protests.

Egypt: November 22. Renewed protest in Tahrir Square, this time provoked by Morsi's decision to relieve the attorney general of his power and his contention that the Constituent Assembly cannot be dissolved.

Egypt: December 22. In a national referendum, 64 percent of voters support the country's constitution.

Egypt: December 25. With Morsi's signature, the constitution becomes official law.

2013

January–March

Egypt: January 25. Second anniversary of the country's revolution; nationwide protests against the Morsi government; hundreds are injured.

Iraq: January 25. "No Retreat Friday." Anbar province is the sight of significant protest; demonstrators clash with government forces.

Egypt: February 1. Protests continue. Clashes between demonstrators and security forces takes place outside the president's residence.

Tunisia: February 6. Chokri Belaid, the leader of the Democratic Patriots Movement, is assassinated. Belaid's death provokes significant protests in the streets and tumult in the halls of government, with the prime minister calling for the formation of a caretaker government that could lead the country to elections.

Syria: February 12. UN reports that seventy thousand people have died over the course of the ongoing civil war.

April–June

Iraq: April–May. It is reported that at least 150 people have died in a month of increased sectarian violence.

Libya: May 14. The GNC passes the Political Isolation Law (PIL), a measure that aims to bar members of the former government from seeking or holding office for a decade. The GNC's chair, Muhammad al-Magarief, resigns, reportedly on the grounds that he will challenge the law in the courts.

Yemen: June 13. A number of protestors are killed in clashes with security forces.

Libya: June 25. Nuri Abu Sahmein, a Berber leader, is elected as GNC chair.

Egypt: June 30. Huge national protests, with tens of thousands demonstrating against the president; pro-Morsi groups counter with their own demonsrations.

July–September

Egypt: July 1. Military delivers ultimatum to Morsi: resolve the current crisis in forty-eight hours or resign.

Egypt: July 2. Morsi responds to the military in a speech that refuses the military's ultimatum and touts his popular support.

Egypt: July 3. Morsi deposed by the military; domestic and international debate over whether his removal constitutes a coup d'etat.

Egypt: July 4. With the support of the military, Adly Mansour takes office as interim president. Morsi detained by military forces.

Egypt: July 8. Pro-Morsi demonstrations; some fifty protestors are killed and over four hundred are injured.

Egypt: July 24. General Abdel Fattah el-Sisi appears on national television and calls for citizens to gather in public and show their support for the military's temporary rule and its opposition to the Muslim Brotherhood.

Tunisia: July 25. Mohammed Brahimi, the founder of the People's Movement, is assassinated; thousands protest in opposition to Islamist rule.

Egypt: July 26–27. Large demonstrations across the country. Security forces open fire on pro-Morsi demonstrations; over one hundred protestors are killed and several thousand are injured.

Tunisia: August 6. Tens of thousands of protesters rally against the government in Tunis.

Egypt: August 14. Police and security forces systematically clamp down on pro-Morsi groups and demonstrators; over six hundred are killed and thousands are injured. In the aftermath of the violence, Mansour reinstates martial law.

Egypt: August 16. Violent clashes continue across the country between security forces and pro-Morsi demonstrators.

Egypt: August 20: Mohamed Badie, leader of the Muslim Brotherhood, arrested as part of military's campaign against the organization.

Syria: August 21. Ghouta chemical weapons attack.

Libya: September 22. Transitional justice bill becomes law.

Egypt: September 23. A court ruling outlaws the Muslim Brotherhood and orders its assets seized.

Tunisia: September 28. Government agrees to resign in favor of an interim government charged to lead the country in the run-up to elections.

October–December

Sudan: October 1. Protesters demand the resignation of President Omar al-Bashir.

Egypt: October 6. On the fortieth anniversary of the Middle East War, clashes between security forces and anticoup protestors kill some fifty people and injure nearly four hundred.

Sudan: October 10. Antigovernment protests continue and grow more violent, with reports indicating over two hundred deaths.

Libya: October 11. Prime Minister Ali Zeidan abducted and released on the same day.

Egypt: November 4: At a preliminary court hearing regarding charges of incitement to murder, Morsi appears in public for the first time since his detainment in July. Morsi refuses to recognize the court, a gesture that sparks protests.

Libya: November 15. In Garghour, Tripoli, militia turn antiaircraft cannons and other arms against civilian protesters; nearly fifty protestors are killed and some five hundred are wounded.

Egypt: November 17. Lieutenant Colonel Mohamed Mabrouk is assassinated.

Egypt: November 21–22. Islamist students from al-Azhar University clash with security forces; sporadic protests occur across the country, with demonstrators decrying the coup and the suppression of political speech.

Tunisia: December 14. Mehdi Jomaa named as the head of interim government.

Tunisia: December 15. The National Constituent Assembly ratifies a transitional justice law, which includes a provision for the creation of a Truth and Dignity Commission.

Egypt: December 24. The government declares the Muslim Brotherhood to be a terror group, following the explosion of a deadly car bomb at a police building in Mansoura.

Egypt: December 27. The government's condemnation of the Muslim Brotherhood sparks protests that result in a significant number of arrests.

2014

January–March

Libya: January 12. Hassan al-Drouri, the deputy minister of industry, is assassinated.

Egypt: January 14–16. Referendum on the new constitution; sporadic violence erupts across the country, with clashes between security forces and pro-Morsi forces. In the referendum, with 39 percent voter turnout, 98 percent approve the new constitution.

Egypt: January 24. A bomb explodes outside the police headquarters in Cairo; three more explosions follow in different parts of the city; several people are killed and over eighty people are injured.

Egypt: January 25. A variety of protests and demonstrations take place on the third anniversary of the revolution. In Cairo, thousands march in support of the military government as others show their support for Morsi and still others denounce both the military and the Muslim Brotherhood. Overall, some fifty people are killed.

Tunisia: January 27. New constitution approved by the national assembly—by a wide majority—and signed by President Moncef Marzouki; the constitution is held up as one of the most progressive in the Arab world.

Tunisia: January 28. Ennahda follows through on October agreement and hands over power to an interim government.

Egypt: January 29. Twenty Al Jazeera journalists are charged with various crimes, including impugning the country's reputation and supporting the banned Muslim Brotherhood.

Egypt: February 6. General Abdel Fattah el-Sisi sends informal signals that he will stand for president in upcoming elections.

Syria: February 7. The UN convenes and mediates peace negotiations between opposition forces and the Assad government.

Libya: February 7–9. In Tripoli, thousands protest the extension of the GNC's mandate beyond February 7.

Syria: February 16. Peace negotiations break down.

Egypt: February 20. Trial of Al Jazeera journalists begins.

Libya: February 23. Election for the sixty-member Constitutional Committee charged to draft the new constitution.

Egypt: March 4. The trial of Al Jazeera journalists continues; some government officials suggest that their arrest was an error.

Egypt: March 7. Three days of antigovernment protests leave eight dead.

Saudi Arabia: March 7. Saudi Arabia declares that Egypt's Muslim Brotherhood and Al-Qaeda are terrorist organizations.

Libya: March 9. Libyan prime minister Ali Zeidan threatens to bomb a North Korean tanker if it ships oil originating from rebel-held refineries.

Libya: March 11. Tanker sails with oil. It is reported that Zeidan has fled the country after having been removed from power by a vote of parliament. Defense Minister Abdullah al-Thinni is named as interim prime minister.

Egypt: March 14. Protests in Cairo, with demonstrators voicing support for Morsi and opposition to el-Sisi's likely bid for the presidency.

Egypt: March 22. Rallies in Cairo as part of an eleven-day anticoup campaign.

Egypt: March 24. Court sentences to death 529 people convicted of supporting the Muslim Brotherhood.

Egypt: March 26. El-Sisi resigns his military post.

Egypt: March 27: El-Sisi officially announces his candidacy for president.

Libya: April 13. Abdullah al-Thinni, the interim prime minister, resigns pending the naming of his replacement. War crimes trial of Qaddafi's sons begins.

Libya: April 15. The Jordanian ambassador is kidnapped.

Egypt: April 20. Nominations for the presidency close. El-Sisi is widely held to be the front-runner as various factions express doubts about the possibility of a fair election on May 26 and 27.

Egypt: April 28. Court sentences to death 683 people after they are convicted of supporting the Muslim Brotherhood and other crimes. Among those sentenced is Mohamed Badie.

Algeria: April 28. After an election process condemned by opponents, Abdelaziz Bouteflika sworn in for his fourth term as prime minister.

Libya: May 5. After a chaotic and disputed vote in parliament, Ahmed Maiteeq is appointed prime minister.

Egypt: May 6. Egyptian court bans Mubarak party leaders from running in the election; el-Sisi voices his complete opposition to the existence of the Muslim Brotherhood.

Libya: May 13. UN observer Ahmed Ghanem is detained in Tripoli; Jordanian ambassador freed.

Egypt: May 13. Abdullah el-Shamy, one of the imprisoned Al Jazeera journalists, is reported to be near death after a hunger strike lasting over one hundred days.

Libya: May 16. Heavy fighting; as part of operation Libya's Dignity, government forces attack militias in Benghazi.

Libya: May 18. Fighting in Tripoli and Benghazi; multiple armed units join a combat effort led by retired Benghazi-based army general Khalifa Haftar and dedicated to countering militant Islamist factions. Forces loyal to Haftar storm parliament. At least seventy people died in three days.

Egypt: May 21. Mubarak sentenced to three years in prison for corruption.

Libya: May 21. Haftar advocates for a crisis government, one that can lead the country to elections; the government characterizes the call as an attempted coup.

Egypt: May 26. Egyptian presidential elections begin.

Egypt: May 29. El-Sisi wins the presidential election with 90 percent of the ballots cast by 46 percent of the voters. Domestic and international observers raise questions about the integrity of the election.

Libya: June 10. Ahmed Maiteeq steps down as prime minister after a court ruling that his appointment was unconstitutional. Abdullah al-Thinni remains prime minister until August 29, 2014.

Iraq: June 29. A radical insurgency group born out of the embers of the Syrian civil war and supported by disenfranchised Iraqi Sunnis announces itself as the Islamic State of Iraq and Syria (ISIS). This group is also called the Islamic State of Iraq and the Levant (ISIL) and at times only known as the Islamic State (IS), an entity no other state has recognized. ISIS declared as its leader or caliph the person known by the nom de guerre Abu Bakr al-Baghdadi, but his proper name is Ibrahim ibn Awwad ibn Ibrahim ibn Ali ibn Muhammad al-Badri al-Samarrai.

Appendix C

Pan-Africanism

Select Initiatives, Organizations, and Conventions

	Location/Headquarters	Date
Pan African Congress	London, UK	1900
	Paris, France	1919
	London, UK	1921
	London, UK	1923
	New York, US	1927
	Manchester, UK	1945
	Dar es Salaam, Tanzania	1974
	Kampala, Uganda	1994
Inaugural meeting of the Congress of Negro Writers and Artists Name later changed to Congress of Black Writers and Artists	Paris, France	1956
Society for African Culture (SAC)	Paris, France	1956
United Nations Economic Commission for Africa (UNECA)		1958
Non-Aligned Movement (NAM)	Bandung, Indonesia	1955
	Cairo, Egypt	1961
	Colombo, Sri Lanka	1976
Organization of African Unity (OAU)	Addis Ababa, Ethiopia	1963
Union of Central African States (UEAC)	Bangui, CAR	1968
Economic Community of West African States (ECOWAS)	Lagos, Nigeria	1975
Economic Community of the Great Lakes Countries (ECGLC)	Gisenyi, Rwanda	1976

Economic Community of Central African States (ECCAS)	Libreville, Gabon	Signed 1983 Entered into force 1984
Africa's Priority Programme for Economic Recovery (APPER)	Addis Ababa, Ethiopia	1985
African Charter on Human and Peoples' Rights (Banjul Charter)	Banjul, Gambia	Adopted 1981 Entered into force 1986
African Commission on Human and Peoples' Rights	Addis Ababa, Ethiopia	1987
Arab Magreb Union (UMA)	Marrakech, Morocco	1989
Cairo Declaration on Human Rights in Islam (CDHRI)	Cairo, Egypt	1990
African Economic Community (AEC)	Abuja, Nigeria	Treaty signed 1991 Entered into force 1994
Southern African Development Community (SADC)	Windhoek, Namibia	1992
Common Market for Eastern and Southern Africa (COMESA)	Kampala, Uganda Lilongwe, Malawi	Treaty signed 1993 Ratified 1994
Intergovernmental Authority on Development (IGAD)	Nairobi, Kenya	1996
Community of Sahel-Saharan States (CEN-SAD)	Tripoli, Libya	1998
OAU Extraordinary Session in which the decision was taken to establish an African Union	Sirte, Libya	1999
East African Community (EAC)	Arusha, Tanzania	2000
The Asmara Declaration on African Languages and Literatures	Asmara, Eritrea	2000
Solemn Declaration of the Conference on Security, Stability, Development and Cooperation in Africa		2000
Millennium Partnership for African Recovery Program (MAP), commonly called the Millennium African Recovery Plan	Pretoria, South Africa	2001

Omega Plan	Yaoundé, Cameroon	2001
New Partnership for Africa's Development (NEPAD)	Lusaka, Zambia	Adopted 2001
	Durban, South Africa	Ratified 2002
New Africa Initiative	Lusaka, Zambia	2001
Launch of the African Union (AU) and First Assembly of the Heads of State of the African Union	Durban, South Africa	2002
Southern African Customs Union (SACU)	Gaborone, Botswana	2002
African Peer Review Mechanism (APRM)	Abuja, Nigeria	Memorandum of understanding signed 2003
International Conference on the Great Lakes Region (ICGLR)		2003
African Court of Human and People's Rights (ACHPR)	Arusha, Tanzania	Protocol signed 1998 Entered into force 2004
Economic, Social and Cultural Council (ECOSOCC)		2004
Pan-African Parliament, created under the auspices of the AU's Constitutive Act		2004
AU Protocol to the African Charter on Human and Peoples' Rights on the Rights of Women in Africa		Protocol signed 2003 Entered into force 2005
AU Committee of Intelligence and Security Services of Africa (CISSA)	Abuja, Nigeria	Established 2004 Endorsed 2005
AU Charter for African Cultural Renaissance		2006
AU Convention on Preventing and Combating Corruption		Protocol signed 2003 Entered into force 2006
African Free Trade Zone (AFTZ)	Kampala, Uganda	2008
African Youth Charter		Adopted 2006 Entered into force 2009

AU Non-Aggression and Common Defence Pact		Adopted 2005 Entered into force 2009
African Court of Justice		Protocol signed 2003 Entered into force 2009
AU Convention for the Protection and Assistance of Internally Displaced Persons in Africa		Adopted 2009 Entered into force 2012
African Court of Human Rights and Justice. Intended to merge the African Court of Justice and the African Court on People's Rights		Protocol signed 2008 Not yet in force
African Monetary Fund (AMF)		Memorandum of understanding signed 2008 Not yet in operation

Also see *African Union, African Union Handbook, 2014* (Addis Ababa: African Union, 2014). Available at www.au.int/en/sites/default/files/MFA%20AU%20Handbook%20-%20Text%20v10b%20interactive.pdf.

Acknowledgments

This book took form through conversations with a number of colleagues, students, and friends. We are grateful to all of those who took the time to offer their insights on the legacy of the South African transition, the possibility of an African Renaissance, and the meaning of the Afro-Arab Spring. It has been a singular pleasure to work with each of the authors who chose to contribute a chapter to this volume. Bob Edgar, the director of graduate studies and professor of Africa studies at Howard University in Washington, DC, has commented on aspects of the manuscript, which we gratefully acknowledge.

We sincerely appreciate the dedicated efforts and spirit of engagement by all concerned. Indeed, the pages that follow are underwritten by an increasingly rare spirit of collegiality. We are honored to acknowledge the formative contribution of former President Thabo Mbeki to the promotion of the African Renaissance and the foreword he has provided for this book.

The volume took form only with the assistance of several individuals, all of whom have our whole-hearted thanks. Margaret Rundle provided tremendous assistance with the editorial process. Allan Wright's computer skills were invaluable in bringing together the manuscript's discrete parts. Matt Boedy, Leen Boughouti, and Ian Smith each contributed important research. The contribution of Asif Majid went well beyond the contribution of his chapter on Libya, and Tyrone Savage helped to interpret developments in Libya from an in situ location at the height on several conflicts.

Richard Brown, the director of Georgetown University Press, has been a source of encouragement from the start. We greatly appreciate his support, along with the efforts of the entire editorial team at Georgetown.

This book has benefited from the resources provided by several academic institutions, including Duke University, Georgetown University, the University of Notre Dame, the University of South Carolina, and the University of Cape Town. It has also benefited from the interest, support, and ongoing work of the Institute for Justice and Reconciliation, a Cape Town–based nongovernmental organization whose efforts did more than a little to clarify the questions that opened the door to this project.

Abbreviations

ANC	African National Congress
APRM	African Peer Review Mechanism
AU	African Union
AWB	Afrikaner Weerstandsbeweging
AZAPO	Azanian People's Organisation
BBBEE	Broad-Based Black Economic Empowerment
BEE	Black Economic Empowerment
CCR	Center for Conflict Resolution
CCSDCA	Conference on Security, Stability, Development and Cooperation in Africa
CDA	Constitutional Drafting Assembly (Libya)
CEDAW	Convention on the Elimination of All Forms of Discrimination against Women
CIA	Central Intelligence Agency
CODESA	Convention for a Democratic South Africa
COSAS	Congress of South African Students
COSATU	Congress of South African Trade Unions
CSWUN	Commission on the Status of Women
DRC	Dutch Reformed Church
EFF	Economic Freedom Fighters
EU	European Union
FIS	Islamic Salvation Front
FJP	Freedom and Justice Party
FNLA	Frente Nacional de Libertação de Angola
FRELIMO	Frente de Libertação de Moçambique
GDP	Gross Domestic Product
GEAR	Growth, Employment and Redistribution
GIA	Armed Islamic Group
GNC	General National Congress (Libya)
GNU	Government of National Unity
ICC	International Criminal Court

ICTR	International Criminal Tribunal for Rwanda
ICTY	International Criminal Tribunal for the former Yugoslavia
ISIS	Islamic State of Iraq and Syria
IFP	Inkatha Freedom Party
MAP	Millennium Africa Recovery Plan
MDGs	Millennium Development Goals
MDM	Mass Democratic Movement
MENA	Middle East and North Africa
MK	Umkhonto we Sizwe (Spear of the Nation)
MPL	Muslim Personal Law
MPLA	Movimento Popular de Libertação de Angola
MRC	Medical Research Council
NATO	North Atlantic Treaty Organization
NDP	National Democratic Party
NEPAD	New Partnership for Africa's Development
NTC	National Transitional Council (Libya)
NUM	National Union of Mineworkers
NUMSA	National Union of Metalworkers of South Africa
OAU	Organization of African Unity
OIC	Organisation of Islamic Conference
PAC	Pan Africanist Congress
PAGAD	People against Gangsterism and Drugs
PIL	Political Isolation Law (Libya)
PRCs	Protection of the Revolution Committees (Tunisia)
PSC	Peace and Security Council (AU)
RDP	Reconstruction and Development Programme
REC	Regional Executive Committee
RENAMO	Resistencia Nacional Mocambicana
SACP	South African Communist Party
SADF	South African Defense Force
SAPS	South African Police Service
SCAF	Supreme Council of the Armed Forces
SWA	South West Africa
SWAPO	South West African People's Organization
TRC	Truth and Reconciliation Commission
UDF	United Democratic Front
UGTT	Tunisian General Labor Union
UN	United Nations
UNDP	United Nations Development Programme
UNECA	United Nations Economic Commission for Africa
UNITA	União Nacional pela Independência Total de Angola
US	United States

Contributors

Erik Doxtader: Professor of rhetoric at the University of South Carolina and senior research fellow at the Institute for Justice and Reconciliation in Cape Town.

Don Foster: Professor of psychology at the University of Cape Town and deputy dean, Faculty of Humanities.

Shamil Jeppie: Director of the Institute for Humanities in Africa (HUMA) and the Tombouctou Manuscripts Project, both at the University of Cape Town.

Chris Landsberg: National Research Foundation Chair of African Diplomacy and Foreign Policy, senior associate in the School of Leadership at the University of Johannesburg, and professor of African international relations and former chair of politics at the University of Johannesburg.

Asif Majid: Researcher and graduate student in the Conflict Resolution Program, Georgetown University.

Katherine Marshall: Senior fellow at the Berkley Center for Religion, Peace, and World Affairs, Georgetown University.

Thabo Mbeki: Former President of the Republic of South Africa.

Ebrahim Moosa: Professor of Islamic studies with appointments in the Department of History and the Kroc Institute for International Peace Studies at the University of Notre Dame.

Ebrahim Rasool: South African ambassador to the United States and founder of World for All Foundation.

Helen Scanlon: Senior lecturer and head of the Gender Studies Department, University of Cape Town.

Ibrahim Sharqieh: Fellow in foreign policy at the Brookings Doha Center and adjunct professor at Georgetown University in Qatar.

Abdulkader Tayob: Professor of religious studies at the University of Cape Town.

Charles Villa-Vicencio: Visiting professor in the Conflict Resolution Program at Georgetown University and senior research fellow at the Institute for Justice and Reconciliation in Cape Town.

Index

217